Firewalls Jumpstart for Network and Systems Administrators

Firewalls Jumpstart for Network and Systems Administrators

John R. Vacca
Scott R. Ellis

ELSEVIER
DIGITAL
PRESS

AMSTERDAM • BOSTON • HEIDELBERG • LONDON
NEW YORK • OXFORD • PARIS • SAN DIEGO
SAN FRANCISCO • SINGAPORE • SYDNEY • TOKYO

Elsevier Digital Press
200 Wheeler Road, 6th Floor, Burlington, MA 01803, USA
525 B Street, Suite 1900, San Diego, California 92101-4495, USA
84 Theobald's Road, London WC1X 8RR, UK

Permissions may be sought directly from Elsevier's Science & Technology Rights Department in Oxford, UK: phone: (44) 1865 843830, fax: (44) 1865 853333, e-mail: permissions@elsevier.com.uk. You may also complete your request on-line via the Elsevier homepage (http://elsevier.com), by selecting "Customer Support" and then "Obtaining Permissions."

Library of Congress Cataloging-in-Publication Data
Application submitted

British Library Cataloguing in Publication Data
A catalogue record for this book is available from the British Library

ISBN: 1-55558-297-4

For all information on all Digital Press publications
visit our Web site at www.digitalpress.com

Printed in the United States of America
04 05 06 07 08 09 9 8 7 6 5 4 3 2 1

*To my beloved wife Bee, without whose support
and encouragement this book would not have been possible.*

—John R. Vacca

*For Elaine. Her patience, her enduring love,
her sacrifice, and her quiet determination
have rendered the man I am today.
I am forever in her debt.
Without her, this and so much more would not have been possible.*

—Scott Ellis

Contents

3 Firewall Types   49

12   Architecture Selection   203

13   External Servers Protection   217

Section VI—Internal IP Services Protection   229

14   Internal IP Security Threats: Beyond the Firewall   231

20 Summary, Conclusions, and Recommendations   329

Section IX—Appendixes   341

Glossary   397

Index   407

Foreword

There are three basic rules about firewalls.

Firewalls are essential. Computer security professionals, governments around the world, Internet service providers, information technology associations, and computer sellers and manufacturers recommend that you install firewalls if your computers are going to be connected to the Internet.

Firewalls need to be properly installed and configured. Experience shows that if you do not properly install and configure a firewall, you might as well not install it at all.

Firewalls need to be properly maintained. Experience shows that even if you properly install a firewall, you need to update it, maintain it, and test it in order to maximize its effectiveness.

Even though the three basic rules of firewalls are rather widely known, many organizations are still not getting the best protection they can achieve by deploying firewalls. Far too often firewalls are not properly installed or configured. Far too often firewalls are not properly updated and maintained. As a result, malicious attackers still manage to penetrate weak defenses and disrupt systems and business operations.

This book will keep you from making mistakes when you select firewall products, install and configure firewalls, and maintain firewalls as a front-line defense against malicious attacks. John Vacca and Scott Ellis have covered firewall topologies, firewall installation and configuration, and firewall maintenance.

The novice as well as the seasoned security professional will benefit from this book. I highly recommend it as an essential tool to maximize the effectiveness of a critical element of network security.

Michael Erbschloe
IT Strategy Advisor
Alexandria, Virginia

Introduction

Security infrastructure technology overview

To benefit fully from the opportunities offered by intranets, extranets, or the Internet without incurring undue risk, enterprises and organizations need strong security. It is a matter of urgency to prevent internal attacks, safeguard against break-ins, protect information systems, and preserve your enterprise's confidential information.

Global protection must include solutions dedicated to protect IT systems from unwanted intruders, granting specific individuals selective access to information resources and applications. Control of transactions, filtering of malicious content, and protection of confidentiality and integrity of communications must be ensured. Powerful tools to audit and manage security are also needed.

Firewall solutions are a key component of such a security policy. Protecting the point of interconnection between several networks, they allow filtering and control of network transactions. All traffic passing through firewall points (web accesses, electronic mail, application transactions) is precisely identified, checked, and allowed through or rejected, and eventually encrypted, depending on the rules and regulations set out in the security policy. Interposing security gateways between the outside world and the organization's inner networks, or between distinct subnetworks of the same organization, meets a fundamental network security need.

Using a gateway may dictate your network architecture. If you install a single gateway at the entrance of the network, it may act as a big filtering switch, forcing all intranet traffic to pass through it. However, it is not always possible to force the flows to pass through a unique point of control. Such an architecture is especially difficult when a fully meshed IP network has been deployed for the exact opposite goal. A good solution in such a case is to use host firewalls in addition to classical firewalls. Host firewalls are installed right on servers, so there is no dependence on the network architecture. Moreover, it increases the level of protection because the traffic can be controlled from the network card of the source to the network card of the destination. It is also a solution when you want end-to-end encryption.

With the preceding in mind, there are four main Internet security and firewall technology approaches that are used to combat intrusion in a TCP/IP network:

- Static IP filtering
- Stateful IP filtering
- Application proxies
- Encryption with a VPN (Virtual Private Network).

A very brief overview is given in this introduction. A more detailed explanation is given in the rest of the book.

Static IP filtering

Internet Protocol (IP) firewalls work by filtering IP packets on the network. Each IP packet trying to cross the IP layer is compared with an Access Control List, using rules concerning the source and destination address, protocol, service or time frame, etc.

These rules are used to decide whether or not the packet is allowed to cross the firewall. Static filtering devices, such as filtering routers, provide a very simplistic filtering, with a low level of protection.

Stateful IP filtering

Advanced firewalls on the market now provide a high security level of IP filtering, called "stateful" filtering. This filtering checks major Internet protocols (TCP, UDP, etc.), services (web, mail, FTP, Telnet, etc.), and business applications (RPC, SQL*Net, etc.) by memorizing and constantly evaluating the state and progress of each connection or transaction.

Application proxies

Application firewalls implement a proxy on the gateway for each TCP/IP application supported. A proxy acts as a relay between specific applications and their users. Remote users first connect to these proxies and authenticate themselves, as required, before connecting to the target server. All traffic must pass through the proxy, which performs checks and filtering based on the commands specific to the application. For a high level of protection, both types of techniques (stateful IP filtering and proxy) are in fact complementary, and indeed must act together to attain the highest levels of security.

Encryption with virtual private networks

The full development of the web's information-sharing potential requires confidence and trust in the ability of network security measurements to safeguard the intellectual capital of an enterprise. Virtual private networks (VPNs), in assuring secret business communications, make it possible to conciliate the security and the reduction of telecommunication costs. This represents a powerful complement to the access control capabilities of firewalls.

On the other hand, Network Address Translation (NAT) is a method to connect multiple computers to the Internet or any other IP network using one IP address. It operates on the firewall, usually connecting two networks together, and translates the private addresses in the internal network into legal addresses before packets are forwarded onto another network. It can be configured in such a way that only one address for the entire network is exposed to the outside world so that the entire internal network can be hidden and provided security. The aim of NAT is to hide the inside network topology from anyone listening to the company communication flows.

Is firewall security effective?

The firewall market is considered a mature market, even though some analysts claim that, from a technical point of view, security is the least mature IT domain. In fact, the differences among the various suppliers is not only due to marketing or pricing aspects; there are very different approaches. Indeed, as the firewall is the key component controlling access, it must not be seen as a box with filtering capabilities. The firewall must provide security expertise and should not require experts to write scripts; it must use the existing user management repository and not require an additional repository; it must be managed in coherence with other firewalls and not simply be managed remotely. Not all firewall suppliers provide all of the following mandatory features: a real central and coherent security policy management, enterprise-class scalability, and a high level of control.

Firewall security policy management

The firewall security policy management must provide a solution to reduce human errors and to reduce the use of widely open configurations. Both issues result from the complexity of handling diverse security technologies. It is a difficult task to build filtering rules based on IP addresses, when the same source can be seen with a different IP address because of NAT. If the management tool does not solve such issues, the result is that the addition of two security technologies causes weaker security.

In addition, the main challenge for large enterprises lies not in the power of the technology used at each control point, but in the ability to manage the protection policy centrally and consistently across all enterprise access points. A large enterprise may often need tens or even hundreds of Internet and intranet firewalls. How does one ensure good protection and apply a genuine security policy without overwhelming security officers with repetitive, endless configuration tasks, or risk security holes due to misconfigurations? For this reason, these enterprises require powerful management capabilities that are centralized and coherent and that allow you to simply replicate configurations.

Numerous suppliers provide protection technology. Only a very few vendors, however, are able to provide both Internet security and firewall management. A good solution must let security officers define a truly business-driven policy, with the proper rules being centrally generated and automatically distributed to all firewall points.

Enterprise-class scalability

Enterprise-class scalability is not only a matter of performance and bandwidth capacity. It is also a matter of all of the following:

First, being able to manage a large quantity of users thanks to user profiling. It is the only way to efficiently use the authentication capabilities of a firewall.

Second, distributing management control. Constraining all the communication flows to pass through a unique point of control is not a scalable architecture, whatever the performances of this point of control are. The solution must impose as few network topology constraints as possible.

Third, reducing the number of rules managed. Managing thousands of rules on each firewall is not realistic. The solution is to simplify the management of security policy; an operator cannot safely manage more than 100 rules. The management tool must provide the capacity to work at a business level, because there are much fewer rules at the business level. Hence, the operator will manage 100 business rules, and the tool will transparently transform that into the necessary thousands of rules on each firewall.

Finally, being able to change the global configuration in a matter of minutes and, soon, in a matter of seconds.

Firewall protection from a high-end perspective

To ensure good protection, one has to make sure that the system is not breakable using backdoors or security weaknesses. This means that security must be ensured at all levels, using both IP checks and application proxies. The solution must provide a complete set of protection facilities in order to grant or deny access in accordance with the security policy and prevent information disclosure. This includes strong authentication capabilities to ensure that the users are whom they claim to be and the data encryption capabilities. It must also be able to operate with content security solutions (in order to filter viruses, malicious Java applets, or ActiveX controls) and complement firewall access control protection with strong encryption (to build virtual private networks) and extended audit and alert facilities. Finally, it must be able to operate with other security solutions through a set of open interfaces.

Purpose

With the preceding in mind, the purpose of this book is to show experienced (intermediate to advanced) firewall security and law enforcement professionals how to analyze and conduct firewall security and report the findings that will lead to the incarceration of the perpetrators. This book also provides the fundamental knowledge you need to analyze risks to your system and implement a workable firewall security policy that protects your information assets from potential intrusion, damage, or theft. Through extensive hands-on examples (field and trial experiments) and case studies, you will gain the knowledge and skills required to master the deployment of firewall security systems to thwart potential attacks.

Scope

Throughout the book, extensive hands-on examples provide you with practical experience in firewall security analysis and reporting as well as future directions. In addition to advanced firewall security technology considerations in commercial organizations and governments, the book addresses, but is not limited to, the following line items as part of the discovery of electronic evidence:

First, you will learn how to analyze your exposure to security threats and protect your organization's systems and data; manage risks emanating from inside the organization and from the Internet and extranets; protect network users from hostile applications and viruses; reduce your susceptibility to an attack by deploying firewalls, data encryption, decryption, and other countermeasures; and identify the security risks that need to be addressed in a security and firewall security policy.

Second, there are chapters on how to gain practical experience in analyzing the security risks and countermeasures that need to be addressed in your organization. This includes maintaining strong authentication and authenticity, preventing eavesdropping, retaining integrity of information, evaluating the strength of user passwords, selecting a firewall topology, and evaluating computer and hacker ethics.

This book leaves little doubt that the field of firewall security is about to evolve even further. This area of knowledge is now being researched, organized, and taught. No question, this book will benefit organizations and governments, as well as their firewall security professionals.

Target audience

With regard to firewall security, this book is primarily targeted at those in government and law enforcement who require the fundamental skills to develop and implement security schemes designed to protect their organizations' information from attacks, including managers, network and systems administrators, technical staff, and support personnel. This also includes those involved in securing Web sites, including Web developers; Web masters; and systems, network, and security administrators.

Organization of this book

This book is organized into nine sections, including 12 appendixes (including a glossary of firewall security terms and acronyms).

Section I: overview of firewall technology

Section I discusses firewall security fundamentals, types of firewall security policies, and firewall security types.

Chapter 1, "Firewalls: What Are They?," sets the stage for the rest of the book by showing the importance of firewalls as a method of protection for corporate networks.

Chapter 2, "Type of Firewall Security Policy," will help the responsible manager and firewall administrator create useful policy for the firewall.

Chapter 3, "Firewall Types," is intended to present a brief overview of firewall types available and the relative advantages and disadvantages of each.

Section II: firewall topologies

The second section of this book discusses how to choose the right firewall and firewall topologies themselves.

Chapter 4, "Choosing the Right Firewall," explores, in depth, the aspects of security and exemplifies several existing solutions.

Chapter 5, "Defense in Depth: Firewall Topologies," focuses on independent utilities that may be assembled to provide an in-depth defense against intrusion, extrusion, and collusion.

Section III: firewall installation and configuration

Section III covers firewall installation preparation and configuration.

Chapter 6, "Installation Preparation," is a discussion on how to install a firewall and the tools that are needed. This chapter also illustrates the need and the methods of hardening a firewall system in order to protect it from exploitation.

Chapter 7, "Firewall Configuration," assumes that a firewall server has been built, its Operating System (OS) has been hardened, and firewall software has been installed that will allow further flexibility and management of traffic passing through the firewall.

Section IV: supporting outgoing services through firewall configuration

Section IV discusses how to implement a simple policy, the management of complex web services, and content filtering.

Chapter 8, "Simple Policy Implementation," provides *in situ* deployment tactics.

Chapter 9, "Complex Web Services Management," specifically focuses on understanding protocol vulnerabilities, vulnerabilities of wireless access, streaming audio and video, and FTP and Telnet.

Chapter 10, "Content Filtering," explores the many types of content filtering in order to establish a trailhead, with a map of known routes and avenues.

Section V: secure external services provision

Section V discusses the implementation of publicly accessible servers, architecture selection, and protection of external servers.

Chapter 11, "Publicly Accessible Servers Implementation," introduces types of server environments, remote versus self-hosted, types of web server specific attacks, and e-mail servers.

Chapter 12, "Architecture Selection," is an in-depth examination of how to choose an effective architecture, perimeter and DMZ subnets, blended defense, and dual-homed host firewalls and understanding security risks of each architecture.

Chapter 13, "External Servers Protection," focuses on Web site strategy, secure server communications, secure application development, server performance, using SSL, and Internet server VPN.

Section VI: internal IP services protection

Chapter 14, "Internal IP Security Threats: Beyond the Firewall," recommends tools that will mitigate risks and make management of a layered security program easier and more efficient.

Chapter 15, "Network Address Translation Deployment," shows you how to set up a Linux-based personal firewall for the small office home office (SOHO), broadband-attached network. It also takes a look at several SOHO firewalls and assesses whether or not they can keep your system safe from intruders.

Section VII: firewall remote access configuration

Chapter 16, "Privacy and Authentication Technology," offers an overview of how to address firewall privacy and authentication in a comprehensive fashion, outlining the key building blocks of a privacy and authentication implementation and offering detailed guidance for each of these areas.

Chapter 17, "Tunneling: Firewall-to-Firewall," discusses how to exploit VPNs, exchange keys between firewalls, implement the IPsec tunnel mode, focus on DMZ, and keep the firewall tunneling security rules up-to-date.

Section VIII: firewall management

Chapter 18, "Auditing and Logging," makes recommendations on how to audit your firewall and set up your firewall log activities and your firewall rulebase.

Chapter 19, "Firewall Administration," looks at how to report and manage incidents for firewalls. This chapter also looks at the keys to unlocking your firewall's secrets.

Chapter 20, "Summary, Conclusions, and Recommendations," wraps things up by showing you how to design and implement future firewalls, thwart future firewall attacks, recommend future firewall technology, and evaluate firewall intrusion prevention systems

Section IX: appendixes

Eleven appendixes provide additional resources that are available for firewall security. Appendix A is a list of contributors of firewall software. Appendix B is a worldwide survey of firewall products. Appendix C is a list of firewall companies. Appendix D lists commercial products or consultants who sell or service firewalls. Appendix E discusses how to establish your organization's security. Appendix F discusses how network interconnections are a major point of vulnerability. Appendix G discusses how to deter masqueraders and ensure authenticity. Appendix H discusses how to prevent eavesdropping to protect your privacy. Appendix I discusses how to thwart counterfeiters and forgery to retain integrity. Appendix J discusses how to avoid disruption of service to maintain availability. Appendix K discusses how to develop your security policy. The book ends with a glossary of firewall-security related terms and acronyms.

Conventions

This book uses several conventions to help you find your way around and to help you find important sidebars, facts, tips, notes, cautions, and warnings.

John R. Vacca

jvacca@hti.net

Acknowledgments

There are many people whose efforts on this book have contributed to its successful completion. I owe each a debt of gratitude and want to take this opportunity to offer my sincere thanks.

A very special thanks to my editor and publisher Theron Shreve, without whose continued interest and support this book would not have been possible. Thanks to my production editor, Keith Roberts; Senior Project Manager, George Morrison; and copyeditor, Rachel D. Henriquez, whose fine editorial work has been invaluable. Thanks also to my marketing manager, Georgina Edwards, whose efforts on this book have been greatly appreciated. Finally, thanks to all of the other people at Elsevier Digital Press whose many talents and skills are essential to a finished book.

Thanks to my wife, Bee Vacca, for her love, her help, and her understanding of my long work hours. Finally, a very, very special thanks to Michael Erbschloe for writing the foreword.

—John R. Vacca

I would like to extend thanks to the many people who have asked me to support their technology over the years. I enjoy working with each and every one of them, learning about them, exploring new possibilities, and helping them create new opportunities. Without them, my contributions would not have been possible; this is a book about them.

I would like to thank my wife, Elaine Ellis, for her love and patience and for making sure I ate properly and always had enough coffee. I would like to thank my son, Ethan Ellis, for the calm and quiet nights and for his laughter and his smiles, which are worth a dozen pots of coffee. Additional thanks to Keith Roberts and his team for his hard work and for being such a great listener. And of course, I would like to thank my coauthor, John Vacca, and publisher, Theron Shreve, for the opportunity to write and to work with them on this project over the past three years.

—Scott Ellis

Section I

Overview of Firewall Technology

Firewalls: What Are They?

1.1 Chapter objectives

- Showing the components of a firewall
- Showing what firewalls can and cannot do
- Comparing firewall types
- Using application proxies
- Showing the four-way security model

Today, when an organization connects its private network to the Internet, security has to be a primary concern. In the past, before the widespread interest in the Internet, most network administrators were concerned about attacks on their networks from within, perhaps from disgruntled workers. But for most organizations now connecting to the Internet and big business and big money moving toward electronic commerce at warp speed, the motive for mischief from outside is growing rapidly and creating a major security risk to enterprise networks.

Reacting to this threat, an increasing number of network administrators are installing the latest firewall technology as a *first line of defense* in the form of a barrier against outside attacks. These firewall gateways provide a choke point at which security and auditing can be imposed. They allow access to resources on the Internet from within the organization while providing controlled access from the Internet to hosts inside the virtual private network (VPN).

A virtual private network (VPN) is a network that is constructed using public wires to connect nodes. It comes bundled with many of today's firewall devices. In other words, a VPN is ideal for businesses with multiple offices or remote workers who need access to resources within the corporate network. Rather than maintaining separate and expensive private network and remote access servers to provide access to remote workers and offices, a VPN allows a company to leverage the Internet to provide secure access to employees anywhere and anytime while protecting corporate data from unauthorized access via firewall devices. For example, a number of systems enable you to create networks using the Internet as the medium for transporting data. These systems use encryption and other security mechanisms to ensure that only authorized users can access the network and that the data cannot be intercepted. (See Chapter 5 and Chapter 17 for detailed information on VPNs.)

With that in mind, this chapter sets the stage for the rest of the book by showing the importance of firewalls as a method of protection for corporate networks. With the continued exponential growth of the Internet, the threat of attack on your network increases proportionally. If it is necessary for you to connect your network to the Internet, an appropriate security protocol should be chosen and implemented. This book illustrates many reasons why this is necessary, as well as a large number of different techniques to consider for your firewall solution. The bottom line is that you do not connect your network to the Internet without some sort of protection. Also, do not put sensitive information in a place where it can be accessed over the Internet. The firewall you decide to use will prevent most of the attacks on your network; however, firewalls will not protect against dial-in modem attacks, virus attacks, or attacks from within your company.

Nevertheless, a number of the security problems with the Internet can be remedied or made less serious through the use of existing and well-known techniques and controls for host security. For example, say you've ordered a new firewall, and you want to get it running on your network ASAP. Your first reaction is probably to put every client and server behind it. That's fine for a small company, but a larger company should consider creating a perimeter security network called a *demilitarized zone* (DMZ) that separates the internal network from the outside world.

DMZs are the best place for your public information. That way customers, potential customers, and outsiders can obtain the information they need about your company without accessing the internal network. Your confidential and proprietary company information should be stored behind your DMZ on your internal network. Servers on the DMZ shouldn't contain sensitive trade secrets, source code, or proprietary information. A breach of your DMZ servers should at worst create an annoyance in the form of downtime while you recover from the security breach. Here are examples of systems to put on your DMZ:

- A web server that holds public information.
- The front end to an e-commerce transaction server through which orders are placed.
- Keep the back end, where you store client information, behind the firewall.
- A mail server that relays outside mail to the inside.
- Authentication services and servers that let you in to the internal network.
- VPN endpoints.
- Application gateways.
- Test and staging servers.[1]

Typically services like HyperText Transfer Protocol (HTTP) for general public usage, secure Simple Mail Transfer Protocol (SMTP), secure File Transport Protocol (FTP), and secure Telnet are deployed on the DMZ. If you use your firewall to block all incoming HTTP connections headed for your internal network, people from the outside can't surf your internal network. Once outside, HTTP is blocked, and departments within your organization can then safely deploy web servers solely for internal use.

So, if you want to deploy secure FTP and secure Telnet bastion hosts that have built-in authentication mechanisms such as S/Key or time-based token IDs, your DMZ is the place to put them. Because e-mail starts out by traversing public networks, it is inherently insecure. By having an SMTP gateway on your DMZ that transfers e-mail to an internal mail hub, you can place potentially infected public e-mail on the SMTP gateway, inoculate it with antivirus software, and then securely deposit it on an internal mail hub that is configured to receive "cleaned" mail from your secure SMTP gateway.

To build a DMZ, your firewall has to have three network interfaces, as most nowadays do. One interface goes to the inside of your network, one goes to the untrusted Internet, and the third goes to the DMZ. The DMZ consists of those servers you need to connect outside of the firewall. Servers containing your mission-critical data are protected behind the firewall.

Also, when you configure your firewall rule set, you want to put tight restrictions on the traffic you let through to your internal network and use different and perhaps less restrictive rules for your DMZ. For example, you can allow HTTP to the web server on your DMZ, but not allow HTTP to your internal network. Systems in the DMZ should be as securely locked down as you can make them. You might use application-locking devices to prevent unauthorized behavior on your DMZ, and you might have an intrusion detection system in place on your DMZ. You can monitor machines on the DMZ fairly simply, because you know what ports need to be used and how the general public or your internal employees need to use the DMZ servers.

By contrast, you need highly restrictive firewall rules for traffic heading to your internal network for a variety of reasons. First, because security is typically an afterthought, the security of your internal network is typically in some sort of nebulous or unknown state, so you need to create a penetration barrier. Second, users inside your network will want maximum flexibility and, therefore, will reject internal security mechanisms as much as they can. You basically need to protect these users and their systems from their own naiveté.

In other words, you might not be able to secure all the systems on your network, but you can secure a small handful of systems—those on your DMZ. Therefore, it only takes securing a few systems to create a security perimeter around your internal network. If your internal network has grown to an ocean-sized state, putting a DMZ in place is a security project that has a defined scope—and that's something you can turn into a security success story.

With the preceding in mind, a firewall can significantly improve the level of site security while permitting access to vital Internet services. This chapter, as well as those in Section I, provide an overview of firewall technology, including how firewalls protect against the vulnerabilities, what firewalls don't protect against, and the components that make up a firewall. This part of the book gives special emphasis to the use of advanced authentication (see Chapter 3) and the importance of policy (see Chapter 2 for determining how a firewall will implement a protection scheme).

However, the burning question that needs to be answered before we go any further is what really is a network firewall?

1.2 Firewall defined

A firewall is a system or group of systems that enforces an access control policy between two networks, as shown in Figure 1.1. The actual means by which this is accomplished varies widely, but in principle, the firewall can be thought of as a pair of mechanisms: one that exists to block traffic and the other to permit traffic. Some firewalls place greater emphasis on blocking traffic, while others emphasize permitting traffic. Probably the most important thing to recognize about a firewall is that it implements an access control policy. If you don't have a good idea of what kind of access you want to permit or deny, or if you simply permit someone or some product to configure a firewall based on what they or it thinks it should do, then they are making policy for your organization as a whole.

In other words, a firewall is a network security product that acts as a barrier between two or more network segments. The firewall is a system (which consists of one or more components) that provides an access control mechanism between your network and the network(s) on the other side(s) of it. A firewall can also provide audit and alarm mechanisms that will allow you to keep a record of all access attempts to and from your network, as well as a real-time notification of things that you determine to be important.

Nevertheless, perhaps it is best to describe first what a firewall is not: A firewall is not simply a router, host system, or collection of systems that provides security to a network. Rather, a firewall is an

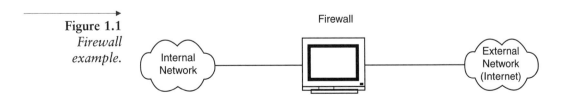

Figure 1.1
Firewall
example.

approach to security; it helps implement a larger security policy that defines the services and access to be permitted, and it is an implementation of that policy in terms of a network configuration, one or more host systems and routers, and other security measures such as advanced authentication in place of static passwords. The main purpose of a firewall system is to control access to or from a protected network (a site). It implements a network access policy by forcing connections to pass through the firewall, where they can be examined and evaluated.

Furthermore, a firewall system can be a router, a personal computer, a host, or a collection of hosts, set up specifically to shield a site, subnet, or even a single computer or web server from protocols and services that can be abused from external hosts. A firewall system is usually located at a higher level gateway, such as a site's connection to the Internet, as shown in Figure 1.2. However, firewall systems can be located at lower level gateways to provide protection for some smaller collection of hosts or subnets.

So, why do we need firewalls? What can a firewall do for you? Why would you want a firewall? What can a firewall not do for you? All of these burning questions are answered next for those inquiring security minds that want to know.

1.3 Why firewalls?

The general reasoning behind firewall usage is that without a firewall, a subnet's systems expose themselves to inherently insecure services such as Network File System (NFS) or Network Information

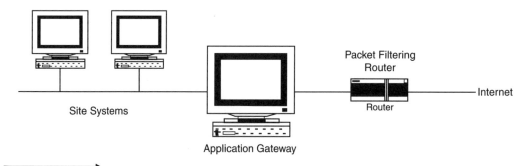

Figure 1.2   *Router and application gateway firewall example.*

Service (NIS) and to probes and attacks from hosts elsewhere on the network (see FYI 1.1).

In a firewall-less environment, network security relies totally on host security, and all hosts must, in a sense, cooperate to achieve a uniformly high level of security. The larger the subnet, the less manageable it is to maintain all hosts at the same level of security. As mistakes and lapses in security become more common, break-ins occur not as the result of complex attacks, but because of simple errors in configuration and inadequate passwords.

1.3.1 The need for firewalls

As technology has advanced to greatly expand the information technology (IT) systems capabilities of corporations, the threats to these systems have become numerous and complex. In today's world, corporations face a variety of information system attacks against their local area networks (LANs) and wide area networks (WANs). Many of these attacks are directed through the Internet. These attacks come from three basic groups:

- Persons who see attacking a corporation's information system as a technological challenge

FYI 1.1 *Why Would You Want a Firewall?*

The Internet, like any other society, is plagued with the kind of jerks who enjoy the electronic equivalent of writing on other people's walls with spray paint, tearing their mailboxes off, or just sitting in the street blowing their car horns. Some people try to get real work done over the Internet, and others have sensitive or proprietary data they must protect. Usually, a firewall's purpose is to keep the jerks out of your network while still letting you get your job done.

Many traditional-style corporations and data centers have computing security policies and practices that must be adhered to. In a case where a company's policies dictate how data must be protected, a firewall is very important, because it is the embodiment of the corporate policy. Frequently, the hardest part of hooking to the Internet, if you have a large company, is not justifying the expense or effort, but convincing management that it's safe to do so. A firewall provides not only real security, but it often plays an important role as a security blanket for management.

Lastly, a firewall can act as your corporate "ambassador" to the Internet. Many corporations use their firewall systems as a place to store public information about corporate products and services, files to download, bug fixes, and so forth. Several of these systems have become important parts of the Internet service structure (UUnet.uu.net, whitehouse.gov, gatekeeper.dec.com) and have reflected well on their organizational sponsors.

- Persons with no identified political or social agenda who see attacking a corporation's information system as an opportunity for high-tech vandalism

- Persons associated with a corporate competitor or political adversary who see the corporation's information system as a legitimate strategic target[2]

To combat this growing and complex threat to a corporation's LAN and/or Internet site, a series of protective countermeasures needs to be developed, continually updated, and improved. Security services that are important to protecting a corporation's strategic information include the following:

- *Data integrity:* Absolute verification that data have not been modified

- *Confidentiality:* Privacy with encryption, scrambled text

- *Authentication:* Verification of originator on contract

- *Nonrepudiation:* Undeniable proof of participation

- *Availability:* Assurance of service demand[2]

Note: It's really the endpoints, like the servers, on your network you need to secure, right? After all, that's where the sensitive data live. You've got password protection on your servers, and you've implemented other security measures on your servers. You may even have an administrator for your servers who is security savvy; however, are you willing to bet your company's private information in this way?

The building and implementation of firewalls is an effective security countermeasure used to implement these security services. An external firewall is used to counter threats from the Internet. An internal firewall is used to primarily defend a corporation's LAN or WAN. The internal firewall is used to separate and protect corporate databases (e.g., financial databases can be separated from personnel-databases). In addition, internal firewalls can be used to separate different levels of information being sent over a corporate LAN or

WAN (e.g., corporate proprietary information dealing with research projects, financial data, or personnel records).

Firewalls, however, are just one element in an array of possible IT systems countermeasures. The most effective security countermeasure is a good corporate security strategy. The effectiveness of this strategy will have a direct bearing on the success of any firewall that a corporation builds or purchases. For example, the two critical elements that form the basis of an effective corporate security strategy are *least privilege* and *defense in depth*.

Least privilege

The principle of least privilege means that only those privileges that the object needs to perform are assigned tasks. Least privilege is an important principle in countering attacks and limiting damage.

Defense in depth

Don't depend on one security solution. Good security is usually found in layers. These layers should consist of a variety of security products and services.

Note:

> Not enough can be said regarding the importance of installing the latest security update patches and staying abreast of which ones are needed. All the firewalls in all the world might not help you if someone discovers you have not patched an exploit that they can breach your system through! This is especially true for firewalls that are not configured as tightly for the more publicly used servers that are running FTP, RDS, and web servers.

The solutions could be network security products (firewalls that could be both internal and external) and information systems security (INFOSEC) training (employee education through classes and threat/vulnerability briefings).

Note:

> Do you want to let *them* even begin to work against your server's security? Isn't it possible that your administrator might go home at night and miss the attack? Can't human errors in password security be made now and then? Firewalls are designed to allow you a very important second layer of protection. Detection of security problems can be made at this layer before any security breach can begin on any of your data-sensitive servers.

A firewall approach provides numerous advantages to sites by helping increase overall host security. The following section provides an overview of the primary benefits of using a firewall.

1.4 Benefits of firewalls

A firewall provides a leveraged choke point for network security. It allows the corporation to focus on a critically vulnerable point: where the corporation's information system connects to the Internet.

The firewall can control and prevent attacks from insecure network services. A firewall can effectively monitor all traffic passing through the system. In this manner, the firewall serves as an *auditor* for the system and can alert the corporation to anomalies in the system. The firewall can also log access and compile statistics, which can be used to create a profile of the system.

Some firewalls, on the other hand, permit only e-mail traffic through, thereby protecting the network against any attacks other than attacks against the e-mail service. Other firewalls provide less strict protection and block services that are known to be problems.

Generally, firewalls are configured to protect against unauthenticated interactive logins from the *outside* world. This, more than anything, helps prevent vandals from logging into machines on your network. More elaborate firewalls block traffic from the outside to the inside but permit users on the inside to communicate freely with the outside. The firewall can protect against any type of network-borne attack if you unplug it.

Firewalls are also important because they can provide a single *choke point (bottleneck)* where security and audit can be imposed. Unlike in a situation where a computer system is being attacked by someone dialing in with a modem, the firewall can act as an effective *phone tap* and tracing tool. Firewalls provide an important logging and auditing function. Often, they provide summaries to the administrator about what kinds and amount of traffic has passed through it, how many attempts there were to break into it, etc. The following are the primary benefits of using a firewall:

- Protection from vulnerable services that are running on the server that may increase its vulnerability to attack

- Controlled access to site systems
- Concentrated security
- Enhanced privacy
- Logging and statistics on network use, misuse
- Policy enforcement
- VPN
- DMZ[2]

1.4.1   Protection from vulnerable services

A firewall can greatly improve network security and reduce risks to hosts on the subnet by filtering inherently nonsecure services. As a result, the subnet network environment is exposed to fewer risks, because only selected protocols will be able to pass through the firewall.

For example, a firewall could prohibit certain vulnerable services such as NFS from entering or leaving a protected subnet. This provides the benefit of preventing the services from being exploited by outside attackers while permitting the use of these services with greatly reduced risk to exploitation. Services such as NIS or NFS that are particularly useful on a LAN basis can thus be enjoyed and used to reduce the host management burden.

Firewalls can also provide protection from routing-based attacks, such as source routing and attempts to redirect routing paths to compromised sites via Internet Control Message Protocol (ICMP) redirects. A firewall could reject all source-routed packets and ICMP redirects and then inform administrators of the incidents.

1.4.2   Controlled access to site systems

A firewall also provides the ability to control access to site systems. For example, some hosts can be made reachable from outside networks, whereas others can be effectively sealed off from unwanted access. A site could prevent outside access to its hosts except for special cases such as mail servers or information servers.

This brings to the fore an access policy that firewalls are particularly adept at enforcing: Do not provide access to hosts or services that do not require access. Put differently, why provide access to hosts and services that could be exploited by attackers when the access is not used or required? If, for example, a user requires little or no network access to his or her desktop workstation, then a firewall can enforce this policy.

Note:

ICMP is an extension to the Internet Protocol (IP) defined by RFC 792. ICMP supports packets containing error, control, and informational messages. The *ping* command, for example, uses ICMP to test an Internet connection.

1.4.3 Concentrated security

A firewall can actually be less expensive for an organization in that all or most modified software and additional security software could be located on the firewall systems as opposed to being distributed on many hosts. In particular, one-time password systems and other add-on authentication software could be located at the firewall as opposed to each system that needed to be accessed from the Internet.

Other solutions to network security such as Kerberos involve modifications at each host system. Although Kerberos and other techniques should be considered for their advantages and may be more appropriate than firewalls in certain situations, firewalls tend to be simpler to implement because only the firewall need run specialized software.

Note:

Kerberos is an authentication system developed at the Massachusetts Institute of Technology (MIT). Kerberos is designed to enable two parties to exchange private information across an otherwise open network. It works by assigning a unique key, called a ticket, to each user who logs on to the network. The ticket is then embedded in messages to identify the sender of the message.

1.5 Enhanced privacy

Privacy is of great concern to certain sites, because what would normally be considered innocuous information might actually contain clues that would be useful to an attacker. Using a firewall, some sites want to block services such as finger and Domain Name Service (DNS). Finger displays information about users such as their last login time and whether they've read mail and other items. However, finger could leak information to attackers about how often a system is used, whether the system has active users connected, and whether the system could be attacked without drawing attention.

Firewalls can also be used to block DNS information about site systems, making the names and IP addresses of site systems unavailable to Internet hosts. Some site administrators feel that by blocking this information, they are hiding information that would otherwise be useful to attackers.

1.5.1 Logging and statistics on network use and misuse

If all access to and from the Internet passes through a firewall, the firewall can log accesses and provide valuable statistics about network usage. A firewall, with appropriate alarms that sound when suspicious activity occurs, can also provide details on whether the firewall and network are being probed or attacked.

It is important to collect network usage statistics and evidence of probing for a number of reasons. Of primary importance is knowing whether the firewall is withstanding probes and attacks and determining whether the controls on the firewall are adequate. Network usage statistics are also important as input into network requirements studies and risk analysis activities.

1.5.2 Policy enforcement

Lastly, but perhaps most importantly, a firewall provides the means for implementing and enforcing a network access policy. In effect, a firewall provides access control to users and services. Thus, a network access policy can be enforced by a firewall, whereas without a firewall, such a policy depends entirely on the cooperation of users. A site may be able to depend on its own users for their cooperation, but it cannot and it should not depend on Internet users in general.

Given these benefits to the firewall approach, there are also a number of disadvantages and a number of things that firewalls cannot protect against. A firewall is not by any means a panacea for Internet security problems.

1.6 Limitations of firewalls

Firewalls can't protect against attacks that don't go through the firewall. Many corporations that connect to the Internet are very concerned about proprietary data leaking out of the company through that route. Unfortunately for those concerned, a magnetic tape can just as effectively be used to export data. Many organizations that are terrified (at a management level) of Internet connections have no coherent policy about how dial-in access via modems should be protected. It's silly to build an 8-foot-thick steel door when you live in a wooden house. But, there are a lot of organizations out there buying expensive firewalls and neglecting the numerous other back-doors into their network. For a firewall to work, it must be part of a consistent overall organizational security architecture. Firewall policies must be realistic and reflect the level of security in the entire network. For example, a site with top secret or classified data doesn't need a firewall at all; it shouldn't be hooking up to the Internet in the first place; or the systems with the truly secret data should be isolated from the rest of the corporate network.

Another thing a firewall can't really protect you against is traitors or idiots/morons inside your network. While an industrial spy might export information through your firewall, he or she is just as likely to export it through a telephone, fax machine, or floppy disk. Floppy disks are a far more likely means for information to leak from your organization than a firewall! Firewalls also cannot protect against stupidity. Users who reveal sensitive information over the telephone are good targets for social engineering. An attacker may be able to break into your network by completely bypassing your firewall, if he or she can find a *helpful* employee inside who can be fooled into giving access to a modem pool (see FYI 1.2).

A firewall opens communications channels between two networks and has no control over what users choose to transmit using these

FYI 1.2 *Failsafe*

Who's responsible for your data security? You are, right? You and the other people in your IT shop.

Ever since databases began to be stored in computer-readable form, it's been IT's job to protect them. That doesn't just mean managing the technology to protect the data. It means protecting the data. And that, in turn, means that news reports coming out of hacker conferences (consisting of self-professed hackers, crackers, and phreakers) should have you grinding your teeth, tearing out your hair, and reaching for the TUMS.

The big news is that these days you don't have to be a technology Dark Force to breach firewalls, crash servers, and otherwise wreak havoc on corporate IT systems. In other words, "social engineering" is back with a vengeance.

Social engineering is hacker speak for using nontechnological ways of getting access to your systems—dumpster diving for passwords, say, or making friends with your company's employees just so they can be pumped for useful information, or using the phone and a few glib lies to collect the keys to your kingdom.

Maybe the most chilling presentation from the hacker conferences was an account of how one hacker cracked a bank's security using only a phone. First, he called an executive's secretary, posing as a human resources (HR) staffer, and pumped her for information on the executive. Then he called HR, posing as the executive whose identity he had just stolen, and talked a gullible staffer out of a list of new employees and their ID numbers over the phone. Finally, he called the employees, posing as an information systems staffer, and talked dozens of them into divulging their logins and passwords.

Yes, he's an expert, and yes, he lied a lot. But that's all it took to render the bank's three firewalls completely useless.

Social engineering isn't new. Spies, hackers, and unscrupulous competitors have used these techniques for decades. But now it's more popular than ever. So if you're going to protect that data, you'll have to start doing some social engineering of your own. You'll have to drill this into the brain of every new hire and longtime executive and everyone in between: They must not divulge key information to anyone they don't know, with certainty, is inside the company. Not by e-mail. Not over the phone. Not in person. No logins. No passwords. No employee ID numbers. Not even information about what software they use.

You've got to get to new employees first and renew the message often. You've got to hammer it home every time an IT staffer makes contact with any other employee.

Call it a campaign of paranoia. You've got to make them understand that loose lips really can sink your corporate ship. It won't make you popular. It may put you at odds with HR or departmental managers who think you're worrying their people needlessly. But let's face it; they're not responsible for the security of your data. And if you don't take every step necessary to protect that data, who will?

channels. It has no concept of the value or sensitivity of the data it is transferring between networks, and therefore, it cannot protect information on that basis. A firewall cannot control what users choose to do with the data once they have received it. If a user chooses to modify or propagate that information, the firewall has no effect.

A firewall can protect the integrity of information from the time that it receives the information until it releases it on the other network. It cannot, however, test or ensure information integrity before it receives it or after it releases it. It also cannot prevent trusted users from disclosing (either accidentally or deliberately) information if they choose to do so.

However, a firewall cannot provide access control on any of your inside systems from someone already inside the firewall. If someone has already bypassed your firewall or is physically located on your inside network, then access attempts to your inside systems no longer need to go through the firewall, and the firewall will provide no protection.

Furthermore, a firewall cannot protect you from war driving or wireless hacking. War driving involves roaming around a neighborhood looking for the increasingly numerous "hot spots" where high-speed Internet access is beamed to a small area by a low-power radio signal—thanks to a scheme called *Wireless Fidelity*. In other words, it's where hackers drive around with a wireless network PC, looking for unsecure wireless networks—networks that may very well have a firewall to protect them from the Internet but do nothing to protect the wireless internal network (often in peoples' homes). Furthermore, war driving is also using wireless computers to find and "plug into" wireless networks, often without the owner's permission or knowledge. For example, imagine your computer as a walkie-talkie, but instead of talking, you're getting high-speed Internet access. Wi-Fi, as it's generally called ("propeller heads" call it *802.11b*), has unexpectedly emerged as the wireless world's Maltese falcon, something truly lustworthy and, once possessed, impossible to let go of.

Finally, a firewall cannot completely protect your systems from any data-driven attack such as viruses.

1.6.1 What about viruses?

Firewalls can't protect very well against things like viruses. There are too many ways of encoding binary files for transfer over networks and too many architectures and viruses to try to search for them all. In other words, a firewall cannot replace security consciousness on the part of your users. In general, a firewall cannot protect against a data-driven attack—attacks in which something is mailed or copied to an internal host, where it is then executed. This form of attack has occurred in the past against various versions of Sendmail (Unix e-mail server) and GhostScript, a freely-available PostScript viewer.

Note:

> Data-driven attacks are those that are transferred as data to the target system by user applications such as FTP, WWW, and e-mail. This type of attack includes malicious programs, viruses, and web applets. A firewall cannot completely eliminate the threat of this type of attack. Some restrictions may be able to be put in place to limit the types of data that are received; however, they cannot be completely eliminated by a firewall, and user awareness and host-based virus scanning is important.

Finally, organizations that are deeply concerned about viruses should implement organization-wide virus control measures. Rather than trying to screen viruses out at the firewall, make sure that every vulnerable desktop has virus scanning software that runs when the machine is rebooted. Blanketing your network with virus scanning software will protect against viruses that come in via floppy disks, modems, and the Internet. Trying to block viruses at the firewall will only protect against viruses from the Internet, and the vast majority of viruses are caught via floppy disks.

Tip:

> Running server-level anti-spam software, scanning the Outlook Exchange e-mail folders continuously, and educating users about not giving out their e-mail address on web sites, etc., are helpful ways to reduce e-mail virus threats. Also, that preview pane in Outlook is like a window to your universe!

1.7 Summary

As previously discussed, a firewall is a system or group of systems that enforces an access control policy between two networks. There are many ways to implement firewalls on today's corporate networks. Usually they can be thought of as two mechanisms: one that permits traffic and one that exists to block traffic. Whether a company wishes to place more emphasis on permitting or blocking traffic is up to the individuals who set the security policies for that company. A company should not leave this to the discretion of the service or product that will supply the security because only the company knows what kind of protection it needs. If a company is unsure about what kind of protection is necessary, there are numerous vendors that will help set up a secure network (see Chapter 4).

Firewalls are designed to protect your network from attacks originating from another network. An effective firewall will allow authorized access only to the protected network and deny access to those who don't have it. Some firewalls permit only e-mail traffic through them, thereby protecting the network against any attacks other than those against the e-mail service. Other firewalls provide less strict protections and block services that are known to be problems. A more effective firewall will allow users on the protected network to communicate freely with the outside world, as this is the reason a company connects its LAN to the Internet. If a company wants to monitor the types and amounts of traffic that are directed at its network, a firewall can effectively supply this information to the system administrator.

A firewall will not block attempts to break into a network that come from external modems or from internal attacks. In other words, a firewall will not protect against any other attacks except for those originating on external networks. If a company has top secret information that it wants to keep that way, it should not connect any machines with this information to the Internet. It is important to note that this is probably the most effective firewall to implement. Most companies would like to have some kind of Internet access available to their employees. If this is the case, then a firewall implemented at the application level will be able to supply the amount of security necessary to meet the company's needs. Finally, another important point to note is that leaks of information are far more likely to walk out the front door of the office on a floppy disk, rather than over the Internet through your firewall.

This chapter provided an overview of the importance of a firewall as a method of protection for corporate networks. Firewalls were defined to give the reader some understanding of what they are and can accomplish. Some reasons for the need of firewalls were illustrated to provide some motivation for the use of firewalls. Several firewall techniques were presented. What a firewall can do for you and what it cannot do were also presented.

Finally, the next chapter provides guidance on designing a network security service policy and choosing a firewall design policy. It then discusses the next steps in obtaining a firewall, choosing a generic stance and specific policy, and where firewalls fit in. The discussion also serves to raise issues concerning the selection and implementation of the right type of security policy for your organization.

1.8 References

1. Lee Joyner (USN), "Development of a Load-Balancing Mechanism for Parallel Firewalls," Masters Thesis, Naval Postgraduate School, Monterey, California, March 1999, 2004.

2. John Wack, Ken Cutler, and Jamie Pole, "Guidelines on Firewalls and Firewall Policy: Recommendations of the National Institute of Standards and Technology," National Institute of Standards and Technology, U.S. Department of Commerce, Gaithersburg, Maryland, January 2002.

2

Type of Firewall Security Policy

2.1 Chapter objectives

- Understanding different types of security policies
- Choosing a generic stance
- Setting up a specific policy
- Showing where firewalls fit in

Network administrators have increasing concerns about the security of their networks when they expose their organization's private data and networking infrastructure to Internet crackers. To provide the required level of protection, an organization needs a security policy to prevent unauthorized users from accessing resources on the private network and to protect against the unauthorized export of private information. Even if an organization is not connected to the Internet, it may still want to establish an internal security policy to manage user access to portions of the network and protect sensitive or secret information.

With regards to the Internet, many organizations have connected or want to connect their private LANs to the Internet so their users can have convenient access to Internet services. Because the Internet as a whole is not trustworthy, their private systems are vulnerable to misuse and attack. A *firewall* is a safeguard one can use to control access between a trusted network and a less trusted one. A firewall is not a single component, but a strategy for protecting an organization's Internet-reachable resources. Firewalls can also be used to secure segments of an organization's *intranet*, but this chapter will concentrate on the Internet aspects of firewall policy.

A firewall enforces a security policy, so without a policy, a firewall is useless. This chapter will help the responsible manager and firewall administrator create a useful policy for the firewall. Throughout this chapter, the term *firewall* refers to the sum of the hardware, software, policy, and procedures used to implement the firewall policy. A firewall is not necessarily a single piece of software sitting on a single computer system.

2.2 Firewall protection

The main function of a firewall is to centralize access control. A firewall serves as the gatekeeper between the untrusted Internet and the more trusted internal networks. If outsiders or remote users can access the internal networks without going through the firewall, its effectiveness is diluted. For example, if a traveling manager has a modem connected to his or her office PC that he or she can dial into while traveling (war driving), and that PC is also on the protected internal network, an attacker who can dial into that PC has circumvented the firewall. Similarly, if a user has a dial-up Internet account with a commercial Internet Service Provider (ISP) and sometimes connects to the Internet from his or her office PC via modem, he or she is opening an unsecured connection to the Internet that circumvents the firewall. Firewalls provide several types of protection, including the following:

- They can block unwanted traffic.

- They can direct incoming traffic to more trustworthy internal systems.

- They hide vulnerable systems that can't easily be secured from the Internet.

- They can log traffic to and from the private network.

- They can hide information like system names, network topology, network device types, and internal user IDs from the Internet.

- They can provide more robust authentication than standard applications might be able to do.[1]

Each of the preceding functions is described in greater detail next.

As with any safeguard, there are trade-offs between convenience and security. Transparency is the visibility of the firewall to both inside users and outsiders going through a firewall. A firewall is transparent to users if they do not notice or stop at the firewall in order to access a network. Firewalls are typically configured to be transparent to internal network users (while going outside the firewall); on the other hand, firewalls are configured to be non-transparent for outside network users coming through the firewall. This generally provides the highest level of security without placing an undue burden on internal users.

2.3 Firewall architectures

Firewalls can be configured in a number of different architectures, providing various levels of security at different costs of installation and operation. Organizations should match their risk profile to the type of firewall architecture selected. This part of the chapter describes the following typical firewall architectures and sample policy statements:

- Multi-homed host
- Screened host
- Screened subnet[2]

2.3.1 Multi-homed host

A multi-homed host is a host (a firewall in this case) that has more than one network interface, with each interface connected to logically and physically separate network segments. A dual-homed host (host with two interfaces) is the most common instance of a multi-homed host.

A dual-homed firewall is a firewall with two network interfaces cards (NICs), with each interface connected to a different network. For instance, one network interface is typically connected to the external or untrusted network, whereas the other interface is connected to the internal or trusted network. In this configuration, a key security tenet does not allow traffic coming in from the untrusted network to be directly routed to the trusted network, and the firewall must always act as an intermediary.

Tip: | Routing by the firewall is usually disabled for a dual-homed firewall so that Internet Protocol (IP) packets from one network are not directly routed from one network to the other.

2.3.2 Screened host

A screened host firewall architecture uses a host (called a *bastion host*) to which all outside hosts connect, rather than allowing direct connection to other, less secure, internal hosts. To achieve this, a filtering router is configured so that all connections to the internal network from the outside network are directed toward the bastion host.

Tip: | If a packet-filtering gateway is to be deployed, then a bastion host should be set up so that all connections from the outside network go through the bastion host to prevent a direct Internet connection between the organization's network and the outside world.

2.3.3 Screened subnet

The screened subnet architecture is essentially the same as the screened host architecture, but the screened subnet architecture adds an extra stratum of security by creating a network in which the bastion host resides (often called a *perimeter network*), which is separated from the internal network.

Tip: | A screened subnet should be deployed by adding a perimeter network to separate the internal network from the external. This ensures that if there is a successful attack on the bastion host, the attacker is restricted to the perimeter network by the screening router that is connected between the internal and the perimeter network.

2.4 Types of firewalls

There are different implementations of firewalls that can be arranged in different ways. The various firewall implementations are discussed next and example policies are presented. Table 2.1 depicts several firewall architectures and their ratings, as they would apply to low, medium-risk, and high-risk processing environments.

Table 2.1 *Firewall Security Risk*

Firewall Architecture (If any one of these is being implemented)	High Risk Environment (Hospital)	Medium Risk Environment (University)	Low Risk Environment (Florist shop)
Packet filtering	0	1	4
Application Gateways	3	4	2
Hybrid Gateways	4	3	2

Note: The rating numbers for various firewall types are as follows: 4, recommended choice; 3, effective option; 2, acceptable; 1, minimal security; 0, unacceptable.

Caution: Actually, universities are very often the targets of attacks and should be considered high risk. They have extremely large conduits to the Internet that, if accessed, can be very desirable and advantageous to pirates for the purpose of launching effective, large scale attacks against industrial/commercial locations such as banks and e-commerce operations.[1]

- Packet filtering
- Application gateways
- Hybrid gateways[1]

2.4.1 Packet-filtering gateways

Packet-filtering firewalls use routers with packet-filtering rules to grant or deny access based on source address, destination address, and port. They offer minimum security, but at a very low cost, and can be an appropriate choice for a low-risk environment. They are fast, flexible, and transparent. Filtering rules are not often easily maintained on a router, but there are tools to simplify the tasks of creating and maintaining the rules. Filtering gateways do have inherent risks, including the following:

- The source and destination addresses and ports contained in the IP packet header are the only information that is available to the router when deciding on whether to permit traffic access to an internal network.
- They don't protect against IP or Domain Name Server/Service (DNS) address spoofing.
- An attacker will have direct access to any host on the internal network once access has been granted by the firewall.
- Strong user authentication isn't supported with some packet-filtering gateways.
- They provide little or no useful logging.[1]

2.4.2 **Application gateways**

An application gateway uses server programs (called *proxies*) that run on the firewall. These proxies take external requests, examine them, and forward legitimate requests to the internal host, which provides the appropriate service. Application gateways can support functions such as user authentication and logging. Because an application gateway is considered the most secure type of firewall, this configuration provides a number of advantages to the medium- to high-risk site:

- The firewall can be configured as the only host address that is visible to the outside network, requiring all connections to and from the internal network to go through the firewall.

- The use of proxies for different services prevents direct access to services on the internal network, protecting the enterprise against unsecured or misconfigured internal hosts.

- Strong user authentication can be enforced with application gateways.

- Proxies can provide detailed logging at the application level.[1]

Application-level firewalls should be configured so that outbound network traffic appears as if the traffic had originated from the firewall (i.e., only the firewall is visible to outside networks). In this manner, direct access to network services on the internal network is not allowed. All incoming requests for different network services such as Telnet, File Transport Protocol (FTP), HyperText Transfer Protocol (HTTP), Remote Login (rlogin), etc., regardless of which host on the internal network will be the final destination, must go through the appropriate proxy on the firewall.

Applications gateways require a proxy for each service, such as FTP, HTTP, etc., to be supported through the firewall. When a service is required that is not supported by a proxy, an organization has three choices:

- Deny the service until the firewall vendor has developed a secure proxy: This is the preferred approach, as many newly introduced Internet services have unacceptable vulnerabilities.

- Develop a custom proxy: This is a fairly difficult task and should be undertaken only by very sophisticated technical organizations.

- Pass the service through the firewall: Using what are typically called *"plugs,"* most application gateway firewalls allow services to be passed directly through the firewall with only minimal packet filtering. This can limit some of the vulnerability but can result in compromising the security of systems behind the firewall.[2]

Low risk

When an inbound Internet service not supported by a proxy is required to pass through the firewall, the firewall administrator should define the configuration or plug that will allow the required service. When a proxy is available from the firewall vendor, the plug must be disabled and the proxy made operative.

Medium to high risk

All inbound Internet services must be processed by proxy software on the firewall. If a new service is requested, that service will not be made available until a proxy is available from the firewall vendor and tested by the firewall administrator. A custom proxy can be developed in-house or by other vendors only when approved by the CIO.

2.4.3 Hybrid or complex gateways

Hybrid gateways combine two or more of the previously mentioned firewall types and implement them in series rather than in parallel. If they are connected in series, then overall security is enhanced. On the other hand, if they are connected in parallel, then the network security perimeter will be only as secure as the least secure of all methods used. In medium- to high-risk environments, a hybrid gateway may be the ideal firewall implementation.

2.5 Issues

Now, let's look at some firewall policy issues. These issues include the following:

- Authentication
- Routing versus forwarding

- Source routing
- IP spoofing
- DNS and mail resolution[1]

2.5.1 Authentication

Router-based firewalls don't provide user authentication. Host-based firewalls can provide these kinds of authentication:

- *Username/password*: This provides the lowest level of protection, because the information can be sniffed off the network or "shoulder surfed."

- *One-time passwords*: One-time passwords using software or hardware tokens generate a new password for each session. This means that old passwords cannot be reused if they are sniffed or otherwise borrowed or stolen.

- *Digital certificates*: Digital certificates use a certificate generated using public key encryption.[1]

2.5.2 Routing versus forwarding

A clearly defined policy has to be written as to whether the firewall will act as a router or a forwarder of Internet packets. This is trivial in the case of a router that acts as a packet-filtering gateway: The firewall (router in this case) has no option but to route packets. Applications gateway firewalls should generally not be configured to route any traffic between the external interface and the internal network interface, because this could bypass security controls. All external-to-internal connections should go through the application proxies.

2.5.3 Source routing

Source routing is a routing mechanism whereby the path to a target machine is determined by the source, rather than by intermediate routers. Source routing is mostly used for debugging network problems but could also be used to attack a host. If an attacker has knowledge of some trust relationship between your hosts, source routing can be used to make it appear that the malicious packets are coming from a trusted host. Therefore, because of this security threat, a packet-filtering router can easily be configured to reject packets containing a source route option. Thus, a site administrator who wants to avoid the problem of source routing entirely would write a policy.

2.5.4 IP spoofing

IP spoofing is when an attacker masquerades his or her machine as a host on the target's network (fooling a target machine that packets are coming from a trusted machine on the target's internal network). Policy regarding packet routing has to be clearly written so that they will be handled accordingly if there is a security problem. It is necessary that authentication based on source address be combined with other security schemes to protect against IP spoofing attacks.

Tip:

> For example, if you have a Netopia router (and have five static IP addresses assigned to your account) and you have it set up with an IP range (no machine on the internal network has an IP address in your block), the Netopia router should be able to discern whether an IP address is being spoofed simply by blocking anything that comes in with a static IP address in its range. This isn't very useful if you need your static IP addresses, but it is, in a sense, spoofing prevention. Earlier I said that routers can't do this, but in this case, they can.

2.5.5 DNS and mail resolution

On the Internet, the DNS provides the mapping and translation of domain names to IP addresses, such as mapping server1.acme.com to 123.45.67.8. Some firewalls can be configured to run as a primary, a secondary, or a caching DNS server.

Deciding how to manage DNS services is generally not a security decision. Many organizations use a third party, such as an ISP, to manage their DNS. In this case, the firewall can be used as a DNS caching server, improving performance but not requiring your organization to maintain its own DNS database.

If the organization decides to manage its own DNS database, the firewall can (but doesn't have to) act as the DNS server. If the firewall is to be configured as a DNS server (primary, secondary, or caching), other security precautions must be in place. One advantage of implementing the firewall as a DNS server is that it can be configured to hide the internal host information of a site. In other words, with the firewall acting as a DNS server, internal hosts get an unrestricted view of both internal and external DNS data. External hosts, on the other hand, do not have access to information about internal host machines. To the outside world, all connections to any host in the internal network will appear to have originated from the firewall. With the host information hidden from the outside, an attacker will not know the host names and addresses of internal hosts that offer service to the Internet.

Tip: | A security policy for DNS hiding might state the following: If the firewall is to run as a DNS server, then the firewall must be configured to hide information about the network, so that internal host data are not advertised to the outside world.

2.6 Intranet

Although firewalls are usually placed between a network and the outside, untrusted network, large companies or organizations often use firewalls to create different subnets of the network, often called an *intranet*. Intranet firewalls are intended to isolate a particular subnet from the overall corporate network. The reason for the isolation of a network segment might be that certain employees can only access subnets guarded by these firewalls on a need-to-know basis. An example could be a firewall for the payroll or accounting department of an organization. The decision to use an intranet firewall is generally based on the need to make certain information available to some, but not all, internal users, or to provide a high degree of accountability for the access and use of confidential or sensitive information.

Tip: | For any systems hosting organization critical applications or providing access to sensitive or confidential information, internal firewalls or filtering routers should be used to provide strong access control and support for auditing and logging. These controls should be used to segment the internal organization network to support the access policies developed by the designated owners of information.

2.7 Network trust relationships

Business networks frequently require connections to other business networks. Such connections can occur over leased lines, proprietary wide area networks (WANs), value-added networks (VANs), or public networks such as the Internet. For instance, many local governments use leased lines or dedicated circuits to connect regional offices across the state. Many businesses use commercial VANs to connect business units across the country or the world.

The various network segments involved may be under control of different organizations and may operate under various security policies. By their very nature, when networks are connected, the security of the resulting overall network drops to the level of the weakest network. When decisions are made for connecting networks, trust relationships must be defined to avoid reducing the effective security of all networks involved.

Trusted networks are defined as networks that share the same security policy or implement security controls and procedures that provide an agreed upon set of common security services. Untrusted networks are those that do not implement such a common set of security controls or where the level of security is unknown or unpredictable. The most secure policy is to only allow connection to trusted networks, as defined by an appropriate level of management. However, business needs may force temporary connections with business partners or remote sites that involve the use of untrusted networks.

2.7.1 High

All connections from the organization network to external networks must be approved by and managed by a network services manager. Connections should be allowed only with external networks that have been reviewed and found to have acceptable security controls and procedures. All connections to approved external networks should pass through organization-approved firewalls.

2.7.2 Low to medium

All connections from the organization network to external networks should be approved by a network services manager. All connections to approved external networks should pass through organization-approved firewalls. To eliminate a major vulnerability, all connections and accounts related to external network connections should be periodically reviewed and deleted as soon as they are no longer required.

Tip:

> Audit trails and system logs for external network connections should be reviewed weekly. Any accounts related to these connections that are not used on a monthly basis should be deactivated. A network services manager should ask functional managers to validate the need for all such connections on a quarterly basis. When notified by the network system manager that the need for connection to a particular network is no longer valid, all accounts and parameters related to the connection should be deleted within one working day.

2.8 Virtual private networks

Virtual private networks (VPNs) allow a trusted network to communicate with another trusted network over untrusted networks such as the Internet. Because some firewalls provide VPN capability, it is necessary to define policy for establishing VPNs. Firewall-based VPNs can be established in a number of configurations.

Tip:

> Any connection between firewalls over public networks should use encrypted VPNs to ensure the privacy and integrity of the data passing over the public network. All VPN connections should be approved and managed by a network services manager. Appropriate means for distributing and maintaining encryption keys must be established before operational use of VPNs.

2.9 Firewall administration

A firewall, like any other network device, has to be managed by someone. Security policy should state who is responsible for managing the firewall.

Tip:

> Two firewall administrators (one primary and secondary) should be designated by a chief information security officer (or other manager) and should be responsible for the upkeep of the firewall. The primary administrator should make changes to the firewall, and the secondary administrator should only do so in the absence of the former so there is no simultaneous or contradictory access to the firewall.

Tip: | Each firewall administrator should provide his or her home phone number, pager number, cellular phone number, and other numbers or modes by which they can be contacted when support is required.

2.9.1 Qualification of the firewall administrator

Two experienced people are generally recommended for the day-to-day administration of the firewall. In this manner, availability of the firewall administrative function is largely ensured. Security of a site is crucial to the day-to-day business activity of an organization. It is, therefore, required that the administrator of the firewall have a sound understanding of network concepts and implementation. For instance, because most firewalls are TCP/IP based, a thorough understanding of this protocol is mandatory. An individual who is assigned the task of firewall administration must have good hands-on experience with networking concepts, design, and implementation, so the firewall is configured correctly and administered properly. Firewall administrators should receive periodic training on the firewalls in use, as well as in network security principles and practices.

2.9.2 Remote firewall administration

Firewalls are the first line of defense visible to an attacker. By design, firewalls are generally difficult to attack directly, causing attackers to often target the administrative accounts on a firewall. The username/password of administrative accounts must be strongly protected.

The most secure method of protecting against this form of attack is to have strong physical security around the firewall host and to allow firewall administration only from an attached terminal. However, operational concerns often dictate that some form of remote access for firewall administration be supported. In no case should remote access to the firewall be supported over untrusted networks without some form of strong authentication. In addition, to prevent eavesdropping, session encryption should be used for remote firewall connections.

Low

Any remote access over untrusted networks to the firewall for administration should use strong authentication. This would consist of one-time passwords and/or hardware tokens.

Medium

The preferred method for firewall administration is directly from the attached terminal. Physical access to the firewall terminal is limited to the firewall administrator and backup administrator.

Tip:

> When remote access for firewall administration must be allowed, it should be limited to access from other hosts on the organization's internal network. Such internal remote access requires the use of strong authentication, such as one-time passwords and/or hardware tokens. Remote access over untrusted networks such as the Internet requires end-to-end encryption, such as VPN tunneling, as well as strong authentication.

High

All firewall administration must be performed from the local terminal. No access to the firewall operating software should be permitted via remote access. Physical access to the firewall terminal should be limited to the firewall and backup administrators.

2.9.3 User accounts

Firewalls should never be used as general-purpose servers. The only user accounts on the firewall should be those of the firewall administrator and any backup administrators. In addition, only these administrators should have privileges for updating system executables or other system software.

Tip:

> Only the firewall and backup administrators should be given user accounts on the organization firewall. Any modification of the firewall system software must be done by the firewall administrator or backup administrator and requires approval of the network services manager.

2.9.4 **Firewall backup**

To support recovery after failure or natural disaster, a firewall, like any other network host, has to have some policy-defining system backup. Data files and system configuration files need to have some backup plan in case of firewall failure.

Tip:

> The firewall (system software, configuration data, database files, etc.) should be backed up daily, weekly, and monthly so that in case of system failure, data and configuration files can be recovered. Backup files should be stored securely on a read-only media so data in storage are not overwritten inadvertently, and they should be locked up so that the media is only accessible to the appropriate personnel.

Another backup alternative is to have another firewall configured as the one already deployed. This firewall would be kept safe so that if there is a failure of the current one, this backup firewall would simply be turned on and used as the firewall while the previous one is undergoing a repair.

Tip:

> At least one firewall should be configured and reserved (not in use) so that in case of a firewall failure, this backup firewall can be switched on to protect the network.

2.9.5 **System integrity**

To prevent unauthorized modifications of the firewall configuration, some form of integrity assurance process should be used. Typically, checksums, cyclic redundancy checks, or cryptographic hashes are made from the runtime image and saved on protected media. Each time the firewall configuration has been modified by an authorized individual (usually the firewall administrator), the system integrity online database must be updated and saved onto a file system on the network or removable media. If the system integrity check shows that the firewall configuration files have been modified, it should be known that the system has been compromised.

Tip: The firewall's system integrity database should be updated each time the firewall configura-
      tion is modified. System integrity files must be stored on read-only media or offline storage.
      System integrity should be checked on a regular basis on the firewall, so the administrator
      can generate a listing of all files that may have been modified, replaced, or deleted.

2.9.6 Documentation

It is important that the operational procedures for a firewall and its
configurable parameters are well documented, updated, and kept in
a safe and secure place. This ensures that if a firewall administrator
resigns or is otherwise unavailable, an experienced individual can
read the documentation and rapidly pick up the administration of
the firewall. In the event of a break-in, such documentation also supports trying to recreate the events that caused the security incident.

2.9.7 Physical firewall security

Physical access to the firewall must be tightly controlled to preclude any
authorized changes to the firewall configuration or operational status
and to eliminate any potential for monitoring firewall activity. In addition, precautions should be taken to ensure that proper environment
alarms and backup systems are available so the firewall remains online.

Tip: The organization firewall should be located in a controlled environment, with access
      limited to a network services manager, the firewall administrator, and the backup firewall
      administrator.

Tip: The room in which the firewall is to be physically located must be equipped with heat, air
      conditioner, and smoke alarms to ensure the proper working order of the room. The
      placement and recharge status of the fire extinguishers should be checked regularly.
      If uninterruptible power service is available to any Internet-connected systems, such service
      should be provided to the firewall as well.

2.9.8 **Firewall incident handling**

Incident reporting is the process whereby certain anomalies are reported or logged on the firewall. A policy is required to determine what type of report to log and what to do with the generated log report. This should be consistent with incident-handling policies discussed earlier in this chapter. The following policies are appropriate to all risky environments:

- The firewall should be configured to log all reports daily, weekly, and monthly so that the network activity can be analyzed when needed.

- Firewall logs should be examined on a weekly basis to determine whether attacks have been detected.

- The firewall administrator should be notified at any time of any security alarm by e-mail, pager, or other means so that he or she may immediately respond to such alarm.

- The firewall should reject any kind of probing or scanning tool that is directed to it so that information being protected is not leaked out by the firewall. In a similar fashion, the firewall should block all software types that are known to present security threats to a network (such as ActiveX, Java, etc.) to better tighten the security of the network.[1]

2.9.9 **Restoration of services**

Once an incident has been detected, the firewall may need to be brought down and reconfigured. If it is necessary to bring down the firewall, Internet service should be disabled or a secondary firewall should be made operational; internal systems should not be connected to the Internet without a firewall. After being reconfigured, the firewall must be brought back into an operational and reliable state. Policies for restoring the firewall to a working state when a break-in occurs are needed.

Tip:

In case of a firewall break-in, the firewall administrators are responsible for reconfiguring the firewall to address any vulnerabilities that were exploited. The firewall should be restored to the state in which it was before the break-in, so the network is not left wide open. While the restoration is going on, the backup firewall should be deployed.

2.9.10 Upgrading the firewall

It is often necessary that the firewall software and hardware components be upgraded with the necessary modules to ensure optimal firewall performance. The firewall administrator should be aware of any hardware and software bugs, as well as firewall software upgrades that may be issued by the vendor. If an upgrade of any sort is necessary, certain precautions must be taken to continue to maintain a high level of operational security. Sample policies that should be written for upgrades may include the following:

- To optimize the performance of the firewall, all vendor recommendations for processor and memory capacities should be followed.

- The firewall administrator must evaluate each new release of the firewall software to determine whether an upgrade is required. All security patches recommended by the firewall vendor should be implemented in a timely manner.

- Hardware and software components should be obtained from a list of vendor-recommended sources. Any firewall-specific upgrades should also be obtained from the vendor. In addition, Network File System (NFS) should not be used as a means of obtaining hardware and software components. The use of virus-checked CDROM or FTP to a vendor's site is an appropriate method.

- The firewall administrators should monitor the vendor's firewall mailing list or maintain some other form of contact with the vendor to be aware of all required upgrades. Before an upgrade of any of the firewall component, the firewall administrator must verify with the vendor that an upgrade is required. After any upgrade, the firewall should be tested to verify proper operation before going operational.[1]

2.9.11 Logs and audit trails: audit/event reporting and summaries

Most firewalls provide a wide range of capabilities for logging traffic and network events. Some security-relevant events that should be recorded on the firewall's audit trail logs are: hardware and disk media errors; login/logout activity; connect time; use of system administrator privileges; inbound and outbound e-mail traffic; TCP network connect attempts; and inbound and outbound proxy traffic type.

2.10 Revision/update of firewall policy

Given the rapid introduction of new technologies and the tendency for organizations to continually introduce new services, firewall security policies should be reviewed on a regular basis (see FYI 2.1). As network requirements change, so should security policy.

FYI 2.1 *Example of General Policies*

The following policy statements are only examples. They do not constitute a complete firewall policy, and even if they did, they would not necessarily apply to your organization's environment. The statements are grouped into those applicable to low-, medium-, and high-risk environments. Within each category, they are divided into statements targeted toward users, managers, and technicians. In general, all organizations would employ at least the low-risk policies.

Low-Risk Environment Policies: User

- All users who require access to Internet services must do so using organization-approved software and Internet gateways.

- A firewall has been placed between your private networks and the Internet to protect your systems. Employees must not circumvent the firewall by using modems or network tunneling software to connect to the Internet.

- Some protocols have been blocked or redirected. If you have a business need for a particular protocol, you must raise the issue with your manager and the Internet security officer.[1]

Low-Risk Environment Policies: Manager

- A firewall should be placed between the organization's network and the Internet to prevent untrusted networks from accessing the organization network. The firewall should be selected and maintained by a network services manager.

- All other forms of Internet access (such as via dial-out modems) from sites connected to the organization's wide area network are prohibited.

- All users who require access to Internet services must do so using organization-approved software and Internet gateways.

FYI 2.1 *Example of General Policies (Continued)*

Low-Risk Environment Policies: Technician

- All firewalls should fail to a configuration that denies all services and requires a firewall administrator to re-enable services after a failure.

- Source routing should be disabled on all firewalls and external routers (discussed earlier in this chapter).

- The firewall should not accept traffic on its external interfaces that appear to be coming from internal network addresses (discussed earlier in this chapter).

- The firewall should provide detailed audit logs of all sessions so that these logs can be reviewed for any anomalies.

- Secure media should be used to store log reports so that access to this media is restricted to only authorized personnel.

- Firewalls should be tested offline and the proper configuration verified.

- The firewall should be configured to implement transparency for all outbound services. Unless approved by a network services manager, all inbound services should be intercepted and processed by the firewall.

- Appropriate firewall documentation should be maintained on offline storage devices at all times. Such information should include but not be limited to the network diagram, including all IP addresses of all network devices, the IP addresses of relevant hosts of the Internet service provider (ISP) such as external news server, router, DNS server, etc., and all other configuration parameters such as packet filter rules, etc. Such documentation should be updated any time the firewall configuration is changed.[1]

Medium-Risk Environment Policies: User

When you are off-site, you may only access internal systems by using organization-approved one-time passwords and hardware tokens to authenticate yourself to the firewall. Any other means of accessing internal systems is prohibited.

Medium-Risk Environment Policies: Manager

- Strong authentication using organization-approved one-time passwords and hardware tokens is required for all remote access to internal systems through the firewall.

- The network security policy should be reviewed on a regular basis (every 3 months minimum) by the firewall administrators and other top information (security) managers. When requirements for network connections and services have changed, the security policy should be updated and approved. If a change is to be made, the firewall administrator should ensure that the change is implemented and the policy modified.

- The details of the organization internal trusted network should not be visible from outside the firewall.

FYI 2.1 *Example of General Policies (Continued)*

Medium-Risk Environment Policies: Technician

■ The firewall should be configured to deny all services not expressly permitted and should be regularly audited and monitored to detect intrusions or misuse.

■ The firewall should notify the system administrator in near–real time of any item that may need immediate attention such as a break into the network, little disk space available, or other related messages so that an immediate action could be taken.

■ The firewall software should run on a dedicated computer; all non–firewall-related software, such as compilers, editors, communications software, etc., should be deleted or disabled.

■ The firewall should be configured to deny all services not expressly permitted and should be regularly audited and monitored to detect intrusions or misuse.

High-Risk Environment Policies: User

■ All nonbusiness use of the Internet from organization systems should be forbidden. All access to Internet services should be logged. Employees who violate this policy should be subject to disciplinary action.

■ Your browser has been configured with a list of forbidden sites. Any attempts to access those sites should be reported to your manager.[1]

High-Risk Environment Policies: Manager

All nonbusiness use of the Internet from organization systems is forbidden. All access to Internet services should be logged. Employees who violate this policy should be subject to disciplinary action.

High-Risk Environment Policies: Technician

All access to Internet services should be logged. Summary and exception reports should be prepared for the network and security managers.

2.11 Examples of service-specific policies

Connecting to the Internet makes a wide range of services available to internal users and a wide range of system accesses available to external users. Driven by the needs of the business or mission side of the organization, policy has to be clearly written to state which services to allow or disallow to both inside and outside networks.

A wide range of Internet services are available. The most popular services, such as FTP, Telnet, HTTP, etc., were discussed earlier in this chapter. Other common services include the following:

- Berkeley Software Distribution (BSD) UNIX "r" commands, such as rsh, rlogin, rcp, etc., are designed to allow UNIX system users to execute commands on remote systems. Most implementations do not support authentication or encryption and are very dangerous to use over the Internet.

- Post Office Protocol (POP) is a client–server protocol for retrieving electronic mail from a server. POP is a TCP-based service that supports the use of non-reusable passwords for authentication, known as APOP. POP does not support encryption, so retrieved e-mail is vulnerable to eavesdropping.

- Network News Transfer Protocol (NNTP) is used to support Usenet newsgroups. NNTP is a TCP-based service that implements a store-and-forward protocol. Although NNTP is a relatively simple protocol, there have been attacks against common NNTP server software. NNTP servers should not be run on the firewall, but standard proxy services are available to pass NNTP.

- Finger and whois are similar functions. Finger is used to retrieve information about system users. Finger often gives out more information than is necessary; for most organizations, finger should be disabled or limited at the firewall. Whois is very similar and should also be disabled or limited at the firewall.

- The UNIX remote printing protocols lp and lpr allow remote hosts to print using printers attached to other hosts. Lpr is a store-and-forward protocol, whereas lp uses the rsh function to provide remote printing capabilities. In general, lp and lpr should be disabled at the firewall unless vendor-supplied proxies are available.

- NFS allows disk drives to be made accessible to users and systems across the network. NFS uses a very weak form of authentication and is not considered safe to use across untrusted networks. NFS should not be allowed through a firewall.

- Real Audio provides for the delivery of digitized audio over TCP/IP networks; to take advantage of the multimedia capabilities of the World Wide Web, a number of new services have been developed.[1]

Which Internet services to allow or deny must be driven by the needs of the organization. A sample security policy for some of these Internet services that might be required by a typical organization is illustrated in Table 2.2. Table 2.3 shows the managerial-level concerns.

Table 2.2 *Service-Specific Policies*

	Policy				
	Inside to Outside		Outside to Inside		
Service	Status	Auth	Status	Auth	Sample Policy
FTP	Yes	No	Yes	Yes	FTP access should be allowed from the internal network to the external. Strong authentication should be required for FTP access from the outside to the inside.
Telnet	Yes	No	Yes	Yes	Telnet access should be allowed from the inside network to the outside network. For the Telnet from the outside to the inside network, authentication should be required.
Rlogin	Yes	No	Yes	Yes	Rlogin to organization hosts from external networks requires written approval from the Network Services Manager and the use of strong authentication.
HTTP	Yes	No	No	No	All WWW servers intended for access by external users should be hosted outside the organization firewall. No inbound HTTP should be allowed through the organization firewall.
SSL	Yes	No	Yes	Yes	Secure Sockets Layer sessions using client-side certificates is required when SSL sessions are to be passed through the organization firewall.
POP3	No	No	Yes	No	The organization Post Office Protocol server is to be hosted inside the organization firewall. The firewall should pass POP traffic only to the POP server. The use of APOP is required.
NNTP	Yes	No	No	No	No external access should be allowed to the NNTP server.

Auth, whether any form of authentication (strong or otherwise) is performed before the service can be used; Status, whether users can use the service.

Table 2.2 *Service-Specific Policies (Continued)*

| Service | Policy | | | | Sample Policy |
| | Inside to Outside | | Outside to Inside | | |
	Status	Auth	Status	Auth	
Real Audio	No	No	No	No	There is currently no business requirement for supporting streaming audio sessions through the organization firewall. Any business units requiring such support should contact a network services manager. *Warning:* Real or not, this can be a problem. There are many headaches caused by various spywares that people install from web sites. It's a constant battle, letting users have a high level of control over their PC, and keeping them from installing every cute little widget they run into on the Internet. It's better to do high-security work and button everything down! Low-security workplaces are a nightmare. Also, tools like QuickTime and Windows Media Player are also doing stuff with streaming audio and video.
Lp	Yes	No	No	No	Inbound lp services are to be disabled at the organization firewall.
finger	Yes	No	No	No	Inbound finger services are to be disabled at the organization firewall.
gopher	Yes	No	No	No	Inbound gopher services are to be disabled at the organization firewall.
whois	Yes	No	No	No	Inbound whois services are to be disabled at the organization firewall.

Auth, whether any form of authentication (strong or otherwise) is performed before the service can be used; Status, whether users can use the service.

Table 2.2 *Service-Specific Policies (Continued)*

Service	Policy				Sample Policy
	Inside to Outside		Outside to Inside		
	Status	Auth	Status	Auth	
SQL	Yes	No	No	No	Connections from external hosts to internal databases must be approved by the network services manager and use approved SQL proxy services.
Rsh	Yes	No	No	No	Inbound rsh services are to be disabled at the organization firewall.
Other, such as NFS	No	No	No	No	Access to any other service not mentioned above should be denied in both directions so that only Internet services we have the need for and we know about are allowed and all others are denied.

Auth, whether any form of authentication (strong or otherwise) is performed before the service can be used; Status, whether users can use the service.

Table 2.3 *Managerial Concerns*

Purpose	Protocols	What	Why
E-mail		Users have a single external e-mail address.	Does not reveal business information.
	SMTP	A single server or cluster of servers provides e-mail service for organization.	Centralized e-mail is easier to maintain. SMTP servers are difficult to configure securely.
	POP3	POP users must use AUTH identification.	Prevents password sniffing
	IMAP	Groups are encouraged to transition to IMAP.	Better support for travel, encryption
Usenet news	NTTP	Blocked at firewall	No business need
WWW	HTTP	Directed to www.my.org	Centralized WWW is easier to maintain. WWW servers are difficult to configure securely.
*	All others	Routed	

Table 2.4 *Summarized Security Policy*

Policy	Non-anonymous FTP Service	Anonymous FTP Service
Put server machine outside the firewall	No	Yes
Put server machine on the service network	No	Yes
Put server machine on protected network	Yes	No
Put server machine on the firewall itself	No	No
Server should be accessed by everyone on the Internet	No	Yes

2.12 Summary

An organization may want to support some services without using strong authentication. For example, an anonymous FTP server may be used to allow all external users to download open information. In this case, such services should be hosted outside the firewall or on a service network not connected to corporate networks that contain sensitive data. Table 2.4 summarizes a method of describing such a policy for a service such as FTP.

2.13 References

1.   Barbara Guttman and Robert Bagwill, "Implementing Internet Firewall Security Policy," National Institute of Standards and Technology, U.S. Department of Commerce, Gaithersburg, Maryland, April, 2001.

2.   John Wack and Lisa Carnahan, "Keeping Your Site Comfortably Secure: An Introduction to Internet Firewalls," National Institute of Standards and Technology, U.S. Department of Commerce, Gaithersburg, Maryland, April, 2000.

Firewall Types

3.1 Chapter objectives

- Identifying the advantages and disadvantages of stateless and stateful packet filters
- Implementing circuit-level gateways
- Certifying application proxies
- Selecting criteria

As previously explained, a firewall puts up a barrier that controls the flow of traffic among domains, hosts, and networks. The safest firewall blocks all traffic, but that defeats the purpose of making the connection. According to a logical security policy, you need strict control over selected traffic. Organizations typically put a firewall between the public Internet and a private and trusted network. A firewall can also conceal the topology of your inside networks and network addresses from public view, here, as well as elsewhere. But, that's only the beginning.

This chapter is intended to present a brief overview of firewall types available, as well as the relative advantages and disadvantages of each. It is intended to lay out a general roadmap for administrators who want to publish information for public consumption while preventing unauthorized access to their private or confidential network.

The information presented in this chapter is intended to simplify what can sometimes be intimidating or complex security and network setups. This chapter is not intended to be a complete manual on firewall types. Unfortunately, the nature of firewall technology does not allow for a uniform "drop-in" installation setup, so every private network administrator should research the topic of firewalls and network security to find a personalized solution or type that best fits their needs. This chapter should not be used as a replacement for knowledgeable network or security administrators.

3.2 Types of firewalls

Conceptually, there are three types of firewalls. Now, let's start off with a brief review of all three of the basic firewall types:

- *Simple packet filtering:* IP or filtering firewalls—block all but selected network traffic

- *Application-layer firewalls:* Proxy servers—act as intermediary to make requested network connections for the user

- Stateful multilayer-inspection firewalls[1]

The preceding firewall types are not as different as you might think, and the latest technologies are blurring the distinction to the point where it's no longer clear whether any one is "better" or "worse." As always, you need to be careful to choose the type that meets your needs. (For further information, see Chapter 4.)

Which is which depends on what mechanisms the firewall uses to pass traffic from one security zone to another. The International Standards Organization (ISO) Open Systems Interconnect (OSI) model for networking defines seven layers, where each layer provides services that "higher level" layers depend on. In order from the bottom, these layers are physical, data link, network, transport, session, presentation, and application.

The important thing to recognize is that the lower level the forwarding mechanism, the less examination the firewall can perform. Generally speaking, lower level firewalls are faster but are easier to fool into doing the wrong thing.[2]

3.2.1 Simple packet filtering: IP or filtering firewalls

An IP filtering firewall works at the simple IP packet level. It is designed to control the flow of data packets based on their header information (source, destination, port, and packet type).

In other words, these types of firewalls generally make their decisions based on the source, destination addresses, and ports in individual IP packets. A simple router is the "traditional" packet-filtering firewall because it cannot make particularly sophisticated decisions about what a packet is actually talking to or where it actually came from. Modern simple packet-filtering firewalls have become increasingly sophisticated and now maintain internal information about the state of connections passing through them, the contents of some of the data streams, and so on. One thing that's an important distinction about many simple packet-filtering firewalls is that they route traffic directly though them, so to use one, you either need to have a validly assigned IP address or need to use a "private Internet" address. Simple packet-filtering firewalls tend to be very fast and tend to be very transparent to users.

In Figure 3.1, a simple packet-filtering firewall, called a *screened host firewall,* is represented. In a screened host firewall, access to and from a single host is controlled by means of a router operating at a network layer. The single host is a bastion host; a highly defended and secured strong point that (hopefully) can resist attack.

Note: | Most commercially available routers come with some form of integrated firewall security. Chapter 4 discusses what types they come with.

Figure 3.1
Screened host firewall

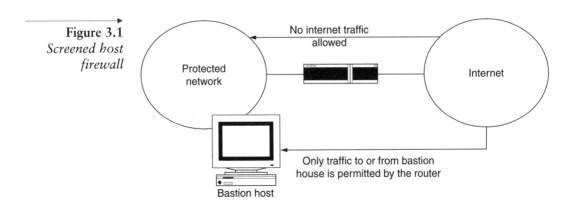

Example of simple packet-filtering firewall

In Figure 3.2, a simple packet-filtering firewall called a *screened subnet firewall* is represented. In a screened subnet firewall, access to and from a whole network is controlled by means of a router operating at a network layer. It is similar to a screened host, except that it is, effectively, a network of screened hosts.

A filtering firewall is more secure, but lacks any sort of useful logging. It can block the public from accessing a private system, but it will not indicate what connections have been made to the Internet from the inside.

Filtering firewalls are absolute filters. They do not support individual access control. So a private server cannot be made accessible to a particular outside user without opening it up to the entire public.

Now packet filters work by distinguishing packets based on IP addresses or specific bit patterns. Packet filters are unable to protect against application-level attacks and may be susceptible to sophisticated IP fragmentation and IP source routing attacks because of the limited information accessed. This kind of firewall is typically found in routers, so they're economical and fast. There usually is no extra charge, because you probably need a router to connect to the Internet in the first place. You'll probably find that it will install any filter you want, even if the router belongs to your network service provider. Or your router can simply be a computer that runs an operating system

Figure 3.2
Screened subnet firewall

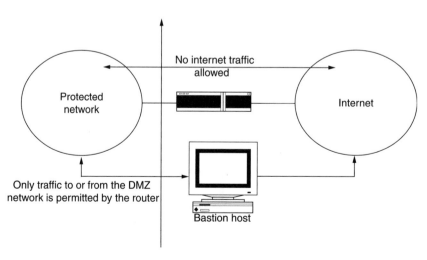

like Windows NT or Novell NetWare and contains two network interface cards (a dual-homed system).[3]

Note: | Most security policies require finer control than this. |

3.2.2 Application-layer firewalls: Proxy servers

Application-layer firewalls generally are hosts running proxy servers, which permit no traffic directly between networks, and which perform elaborate logging and auditing of traffic passing through them. Because the proxy applications are software components running on the firewall, it is a good place to do lots of logging and access control. Application-layer firewalls can be used as network address translators (NATs), because traffic goes in one "side" and out the other, after having passed through an application that effectively masks the origin of the initiating connection. Having an application in the way in some cases may affect performance and may make the firewall less transparent. Early application-layer firewalls such as those built using the Trusted Information Systems (TIS) firewall toolkit (www.tis.com/) are not particularly transparent to endusers and may require some training. Modern application-layer firewalls are often fully transparent. Application-layer firewalls tend to provide more detailed audit reports and tend to enforce more conservative security models than simple packet-filtering firewalls.

Example: Application-layer firewall

In Figure 3.3, an application-layer firewall called a *dual-homed gateway* is represented. A dual-homed gateway is a highly secured host that runs proxy software. It has two network interfaces, one on each network, and blocks all traffic passing through it.

By acting as an intermediary between the private network and the outside, proxy servers allow indirect Internet access. All network requests made by an internal computer to an outside source are intercepted by the proxy server, which logs the request and then passes it along to the outside. Similarly, data passed back to an internal

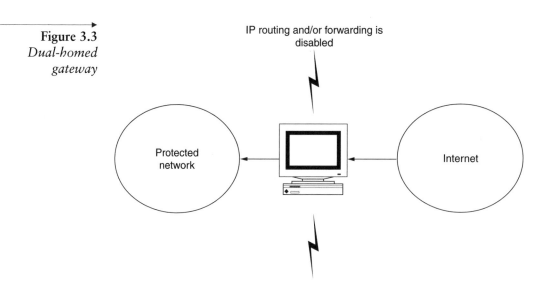

Figure 3.3
*Dual-homed
gateway*

IP routing and/or forwarding is
disabled

Protected
network

Internet

user from the outside is received by the proxy server, logged, and
then passed along.

Furthermore, application-layer firewalls, or gateways, focus on the
application layer of the OSI reference model of network architecture.
Working at this level allows them to use dedicated security proxies
to examine the entire data stream for every connection attempt.
A virtual "air gap" exists in the firewall between the inside and the
outside networks, and proxies bridge this gap by working as agents
for internal or external users. The proxies are specific for applications
such as FTP or Telnet or protocols such as Internet Inter-ORB
Protocol (IIOP) and Oracle's SQL*Net. In the application approach,
information flows through the firewall, but no outside packets do,
thus providing a virtually "fail-safe" architecture. Typically, they
support security policies that require fine-grain control.

3.2.3 Stateful multilayer-inspection firewalls

Stateful multilayer-inspection firewalls extract the relevant communication and application state information and analyze all packet
communication layers. They keep state information about connections
in the operating system kernel and parse IP packets. The firewalls
compare the bit patterns to packets that are already known to be

trusted instead of examining the contents of each packet. Stateful multilayer-inspection firewalls can be faster than application-layer firewalls (the proxy mechanism is at a lower level), but they are more complex. They also have some of the advantages and shortcomings of each of the previous two firewall types.

3.3 Understanding firewall types

Now you are probably asking yourself, of the preceding three different types of firewalls, which is most secure and delivers the best performance? As is so often the case, this question can only be answered on a case-by-case basis after you consider the topology of your network, the services you plan to use, and the services you plan to offer. In limited circumstances, a simple packet-filtering router can be just as secure as a firewall costing 10 or 20 times as much. The reverse is also true: Buying an expensive firewall will give little security if it is not properly configured.

3.4 Firewall types drawbacks

The problem with filtering firewalls is that they inhibit access to the private network from the Internet. Only services on systems that have pass filters can be accessed. With a proxy server, users can login to the firewall and then access the private network. Also, the rapid growth of network client–server technology makes supporting and controlling developing network services a constant challenge.

Finally, the future of firewalls lies someplace between simple packet-filtering firewalls and application-layer firewalls. It is likely that simple packet-filtering firewalls will become increasingly "aware" of the information going through them, and application-layer firewalls will become increasingly "low level" and transparent. The result will be a fast packet-screening system that logs and audits data as they pass through. Increasingly, firewalls (simple packet filtering and application layer) incorporate encryption so that they may protect traffic passing between them over the Internet. Firewalls with end-to-end encryption can be used by organizations with multiple points of Internet connectivity to use the Internet as a "private backbone" without worrying about their data or passwords being sniffed.

3.5 Summary

As explained in earlier chapters, a firewall on a computer network is a device that protects a private local network from the rest of the world (public parts of the same network or the Internet at large). The role of a firewall is typically filled by a computer (or computers) that can reach both the private network and the Internet, thereby allowing it to restrict the flow of data between the two. The protected network, therefore, cannot reach the Internet, and the Internet cannot reach the protected network unless the firewall computer allows it. For someone to reach the Internet from inside the protected network, they must login to the firewall (via Telnet, rlogin, etc.) and use the Internet from there.

With the preceding in mind, a dual-homed system (i.e., a system with two network connections) is the simplest form of a firewall. A firewall can be set up with IP forwarding or "gatewaying" turned off, and accounts can be given to everyone on the network—that is, if system users can be trusted. The users can then login to the firewall and run their network services (FTP, Telnet, mail, etc.) from there. Thus, the only computer on the private network that knows anything about the outside world is the firewall with this setup. Therefore, a default route is not needed by the other systems on the protected network.

Such a system relies entirely on all users being trusted, and that's its greatest weakness. It is, therefore, not recommended.

Nevertheless, firewalls are indispensable assets in most organizations today. However, like all technologies, firewalls can create problems of their own. Imagine the case where your organization's Web server publishes a Java applet that makes calls to a Java Database Connectivity (JDBC) client. It then sends messages to a JDBC server (a Transmission Control Protocol [TCP] service) running on a particular port of a host at your site. As the administrator of your site, you configure your firewall (see Chapter 7 for detailed information) to allow this traffic in either direction. But, you may have neither knowledge nor control of the remote site whose browser downloaded your applet. If a firewall at that site is configured to deny traffic destined for this same port, you have a problem. This is an instance where an intranet over which you have control can provide a more certain solution than the Internet, over which you have relatively little control.

Finally, implicit in this discussion has been the notion that the firewall is positioned to protect internal hosts (like DataBase Management Systems [DBMS]) from outsiders. However, an Internet firewall is only a controlled gateway. It cannot stop attacks from malicious insiders, nor can it take the place of education and security policies and procedures. An Internet firewall is part of an overall security plan. Because the majority of network and system attacks occur from inside of the corporate networks and are launched by "inside" or trusted people, you may also want to consider additional firewalls behind the perimeter ("bastion") firewall defense. Chapter 4 will show you how to choose the right firewall to do this.

3.6 **References**

1. John Wack, Ken Cutler, and Jamie Pole, "Guidelines on Firewalls and Firewall Policy: Recommendations of the National Institute of Standards and Technology," National Institute of Standards and Technology, U.S. Department of Commerce, Gaithersburg, Maryland, January, 2002.

2. "Information Security: Mechanisms and Techniques," National Institute of Standards and Technology, U.S. Department of Commerce, Gaithersburg, Maryland, January, 2002.

3. Shirley Radack (Ed.), "Selecting Information Technology Security Products," National Institute of Standards and Technology, U.S. Department of Commerce, Gaithersburg, Maryland, 2004.

Section II

Firewall Topologies

4

Choosing the Right Firewall

4.1 Chapter objectives

- Methods of hacking
- Secure content management
- Understanding the avenues of attack
- Adapting to change
- Firewall product reviews

As the topology and "threatscape" of modern networks becomes increasingly complex, enterprise and administrative resources have become stretched ever thinner. Corporations and businesses are increasingly reliant on both the internal resources of the network as well as on external communications for day-to-day business functions. More and more of these functions are relegated to automation, with things like faxing, scanning, and document management integrating with network resources. Networks have truly emerged in this century as the cornerstone, if not the foundation, of critical business operations.

When the Internet is down, when the server is down, if faxing is offline, or if the network copier is on the blink, business literally grinds to a halt. And, typically, the reason that these things happen is because malicious software has wormed its way into the network, somewhere, somehow. There are many avenues of intrusion, and there are many things that can ostensibly be implemented to fortify against such occurrences. But implementing all of them, and then maintaining patches, product updates, definitions, etc., for a slew of devices and products is not at the top of any network administrator's list of favorite things to be doing. The most rewarding and creative part of a network administrator's job is to introduce and manage change in ways that are beneficial to business, that improve the ability to do business, and that streamline business functions.

Playing babysitter to a bunch of equipment and software programs and subsequently playing checkpoint police plus border guard doesn't fit into a philosophy of network change designed to improve competitiveness. As a result of the overwhelming market demand, most security firms that create firewall and other security products have moved toward a secure content management (SCM) approach.

In these times, everyone—from the local florist to small law firms to multinational corporations—is prey to harvesters seeking to build their own personal empires of subjugated computers around the world. With cracker-hackers-jackers running Internet Protocol (IP) address scanners and automated cracking software, and with so many Digital Subscriber Line (DSL) install techs leaving the default username and password for router access, it is actually a rather simple matter to crack into small networks. This chapter explores, in depth, the aspects of security and exemplifies several existing solutions.

Firewalls, from policy development to deployment, have a wide variety of incarnations. Interestingly enough, physical firewalls—those things that are used to actually stop the spread of fire in the firefighting and fire prevention professions—are closely analogous to information security firewalls. Just as fire needs fuel, heat, and oxygen, security attacks are also dependent on several factors, each of which can be addressed by a single unit or by a more elaborate, specialized system. Such a system brings together best-of-breed products in a serialized approach to examining network activity, traffic, habits, and characteristics to determine if, in fact, an attack is in progress. It will also prevent known types of attacks, viruses, worms, e-mail, spam, etc., from ever entering the network.

Such systems are discussed in this chapter; systems that through a single appliance or several appliances are capable of noticing and controlling an intrusion, regardless of its methods. This chapter also highlights single products that are part of a larger whole, or collective, of products that is marketed within a firewall context. This context is referred to by some as an SCM offering. Central management of a host of firewall duties is the goal, something intended to de-stress the life of the network administrator and simplify security controls.

Some sources (Task Force on Information Warfare and Information Assurance) estimate that over 20 million people on this planet are equipped with and are knowledgeable in the use of cracking tools. It's no surprise, then, that in the last few years, permutations in methods of attack have telescoped like a power function while the solutions and varieties of methods to repulse them have experienced little growth. They have, in fact, experienced a contraction, or convergence, of sorts.

4.2 Convergence

As attack methods grow in complexity and sophistication, it is almost beyond the ability, if not the scope, of one manufacturer to present a solution that can effectively strip the ground, evacuate the villages, provide aerial extinguishment, patrol surrounding areas for additional threats, and provide crowd control, perimeter security, and damage control. Such an operation invariably requires the efforts and cooperation of multiple platforms of proficiency: spam, viruses, Trojans, spyware, adware, malware, critical updates, patches, and packet filtering. Forces beyond anyone's ability to control are creating virtual conflagrations on a historic scale; they have free reign and are here to stay for as long as there is an Internet.

4.2.1 The criminal meagermind

Cyber crime is the highway robbery of the next-generation criminal, and with its high cash payoffs, light sentencing (if caught), and book and movie consultation deals, it doesn't take a mastermind to figure out how to run a scam that will lift session cookies and steal credit card data from unsuspecting users. Many, many of these criminal sites set up their own shopping cart systems. Most of them play the numbers and hope for a break; after all, it is the credit card companies that will be left holding the bag. Consumers pay for it with higher interest rates and higher prices; it's rare these days that a credit card company will actually be able to pinpoint where the theft originated. Attackers are diverse and wily in their approaches; getting greedy will surely kill the goose. Why steal a thousand credit card numbers from one database when you can steal a hundred thousand numbers from a hundred thousand databases? Theirs is an economy of scale; 100,000 credit card numbers charged varying amounts, diverted to hundreds of different accounts, can yield a multimillion dollar payoff. And insecure, open systems, with no true firewall policy, are the key to many of these schemes. Harvesting information, hijacking, creating identities, stealing identities, and assembling a powerful, ensnared network with the sole purpose of cracking open a secure location is the strategic objective. Creating a base of operations, a safe harbor with the computing power, the anonymity, and the available bandwidth necessary to engage in a broad spectrum of illicit activities, from wandering nomad warez and codez sites, to way stations for pornographic sneakware installing pop-up generators, to spam servers, to DoS slaves, to personal file servers, etc., is the immediate, tactical objective. There is a war raging on the Internet, and these systems are the pawns.

The firewall technologies of today and tomorrow are best-of-breed solutions that manage a pool of resources and allow for simplified grouping of such things as desktop antivirus definition updates, e-mail virus attachment filtering, web site filtering, spam detection, and intrusion prevention. Some of these systems consolidate functions to one appliance, whereas others provide distributed management tools. Consolidation of these resources onto one appliance provides convenient and low-cost manageability but may not consider scalability or planned redundancy. Placing an e-mail server, a web server, a file server, virus protection, packet filtering, and intrusion detection into one appliance may seem like a great idea, and it is a great idea for a small law firm or a small consulting practice sitting on one or two DSL lines, but it can have consequences that need to be considered:

- Loss of connectivity means no services—contingency planning is a must.

- Bandwidth usage is only going to go up.

- Backups and restorations of complex and proprietary appliances can be difficult to perform. Fail-over alternatives will double the cost.

4.2.2 Considerations

Some things to be sure to consider when building out a firewall policy framework include explanations that require a broad range of historical and explanatory background. Terminology and nomenclature are often intermingled. Protocol names are bandied about with little or no explanation, and the avenues of attack, while clear and understood by the attack originator, are frequently misused and underexplained by firewall and security marketing concerns. This section clearly explains the terminology and the concepts that are needed to establish a firm grasp of security requirements.

Zero-day attacks

The sheer percentage of attacks and outages that are a result of zero-day attacks both frightens and amazes. Typically, for the most widespread of attacks that are virus based, the antivirus companies create and release countermeasures within hours. However, the period during that free-reign period, before countermeasures are released, is known as a *zero-day attack*. It is a period that may span hours, days, or even months for tortoise-like logic bomb attacks that move at slow speeds with little or no observed impact. These "zero-day attacks" can compromise resources and inflict extensive damage.

Tip: Intrusion
Detection and
Prevention is
the Key

> During these times in which we live, it is critical that the product protecting your network be capable of intrusion detection and prevention; this will be the only defense, the only way that the firewall will be able to discern between legitimate and intruder activity. Intrusion prevention *and* detection is the top priority. Don't get caught without it.

Intrusion detection and prevention (IDP)

The best intrusion detection software provides monitoring of network traffic on all TCP/IP ports and can match these activities to known threats. It won't just log the event, or send an e-mail, or show a pretty graph—it will actually halt the intrusion. Some firewalls can not only prevent it but can go so far as to provide forensic evidence that can hold its weight in a court of law. IDP can also provide a toolset that will allow administrators to tune sensitivity to reduce false positives or to merely focus the tool on a particular area. Triggers can be established for any number of unusual activities:

- Excessive login attempts
- Bandwidth spiking
- Stateful signature
- Denial of service
- Protocol anomaly
- Traffic anomaly

Password cracking

Dictionary attack: software that will automatically attempt thousands (if not millions) of passwords to gain access. Available for order online and delivered by UPS is a CD with 20+ human language dictionaries, including mangled words and common passwords, lists of common passwords, and unique words for all the languages. A software called *John the Ripper* is included. Technically, this software falls into the category of a security tool, used for detecting and strengthening weak passwords. John the Ripper is a part of Owl, Debian GNU/Linux (GNU, a recursive acronym for "GNUs Not UNIX," is pronounced "guh-noo"), Linux, EnGarde Linux, Gentoo Linux, Mandrake Linux, and SuSE (Gesellschaft für Software und Systementwicklung mbH, rhymes with "moose"). It is in the ports/packages collections of FreeBSD (Berkeley Software Development), NetBSD, and OpenBSD.

Keyboard loggers (physical and software)

Keyboard loggers are devices and software programs that are used for the sole purpose of capturing keystrokes. A physical device will be readily visible as a small unit that attaches between the keyboard and the PC. Software will run in the background and do everything from harvesting specific passwords to actually gathering and transmitting them to locations unknown.

Viruses

Viruses can be used to install, and spread throughout the internal network, "sneaks" that will send outgoing traffic disguised as e-mails containing passwords, login names, and information about internal IP addresses. Mail is picked up at a prearranged drop that may or may not change according to an algorithm. Some will attempt to disable antivirus, antispam, or antispyware software. For example, the Cool Web Search virus is known to disable Spybot (v1.2) once it is removed.

Worms

Worms are self-replicating, malicious pieces of code that leverage weaknesses in either firewalls or operating systems. Upon the discovery of an exploit, someone releases a piece of code that then propagates throughout the Internet. The "Code Red" worm, for example, would randomly locate port 80 on a server and attempt to exploit a known vulnerability in IIS servers. Once an exploitable machine was located, the Code Red worm would then execute, deface web page requests, disable certain types of routers, and continue its search for more machines to infect. As a result, many machines were infected multiple times. Some machines on the Internet are still infected, and the Code Red worm has been around for over three years. New worms and new exploits seem to appear and be discovered daily; many of them don't make it very far since they are poorly written or are merely experimental.

Packet attacks

On April 2, 2004, iDEFENSE issued a warning related to a newly discovered remote exploitation that leverages systems' memory allocations when a particular combination of fragmented TCP, UDP, ICMP, etc., packets with specific offsets are sent to a host. This combination of packets causes the system to allocate memory, and if enough packets are sent, the system under attack may allocate large portions of memory and can result in system failures. Many operating systems are capable of handling fragmented packets; these systems are vulnerable and include Windows 2000 and XP, Windows Server 2000 and 2003, Unix, Linux, BSD, and Mac OS.

Logic bombs

A logic bomb is a piece of software that is triggered by an event, such as a date or a particular event. Typically, when triggered, a logic bomb executes malicious code, such as the deletion of critical system files, the reformatting of a hard drive, or simply doing something annoying, such as resetting the system clock on a continuous and random basis. Once installed, these buggers can be very difficult (some claim impossible) to detect and de-vein. Software such as Tripwire is excellent for prevention of this sort of attack but comes with a sacrifice of system resources and at the price of intensive configuration; Tripwire is not for the faint of heart.

Session hijacking

Session hijacking is a form of "sniffing" previously visited sites session IDs and hijacking user accounts in this manner. It is not particularly relevant to this discussion; however, certain industries will encapsulate web security within their firewall policy, and certainly the development or installation of software that can detect these sorts of attacks is meaningful.

(Remote access) trapdoor

(Remote access) trapdoor, or RAT, is a very common and recent method of exploitation that leverages social engineering to trick users into installing software on their computers that will allow remote access of the PCAnywhere or Terminal Services variety. In these cases, the hacker can actually watch desktop activity, load and upload files, copy files, run software, and do anything else a computer can do. Home and small network users not adequately protected by a firewall policy, such as a small firm that may only be protected by a NAT router, are particularly and almost exclusively susceptible to these types of attacks. Larger corporations with comprehensive firewalls are not usually vulnerable to this sort of activity. There is no way through the firewall for this particular type of activity without first establishing a virtual private network (VPN). RAT crawlers are known to search dial-up, cable, and DSL IP address pools, searching for either security flaws or existing trapdoors, such as BackOrifice or NetBus. With the explosion in the past three years of "always-on" Internet connections, of MS Windows exploits, and of millions of users who don't even take the most basic of security precautions, small offices, networks, and homes are being constantly probed. Being online without a firewall setup on a bastion server is peril incarnate.

Phantoms and honey pots

Phantoms and honey pots include all methods that various firewalls and security products use to distract or decoy attackers. A phantom is a cache of fake information about a user that actually replaces existing information in software systems for the sole purpose of allowing it to be taken. A honey pot is similar but is more likely to exist as a false service that tricks the hacker into thinking he has accessed a system when, in fact, he hasn't. This allows the firewall to detect the origination of an attacker and prevent further attempts.

Terminology in the world of computer security can be obfuscating, however. Some viruses make use of a "phantom," in which case the phantom results from the virus actually partitioning and reformatting a portion of a hard drive.

Blended threats

Last, and in no way least, are blended threats. As illustrated in Figure 4.1, a typical (successful) attack is a blended threat—one that is multifaceted and may even be tailored for a particular type of network system or firewall, a specific IP address, or a specific range of IP addresses. A single attack may or may not be limited to any (or all) of the previously described methods.

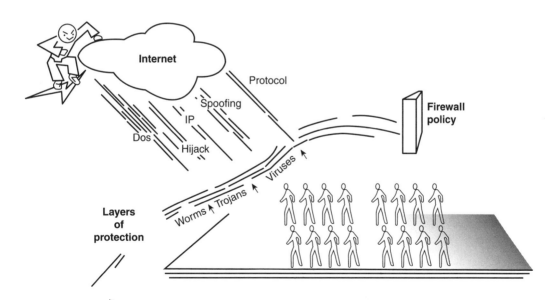

Figure 4.1 *An attacker literally generates a storm of malicious activity on the Internet raining down bogus requests, port scans, and crack attempts upon a broad spectrum of IP addresses.*

4.2.3 **Products**

There are many, many products available, and more seem to emerge every day. In fact, or in odd coincidence, solutions seem to emerge with almost the same frequency as new threats; you draw your own conclusions, but don't let the paranoia of this author sway you. Each product has a primary focus, an area where the product is truly strong, as well as subsidiary foci that work to shore up the defenses of the primary focus, making the product more attractive and increasing market traction. They all claim to be the answer, but each truly has its own strengths and weaknesses; an efficient firewall policy will usually incorporate multiple solutions leveraged to protect and harden vital areas with respect to security and will address multiple venues of the threatscape that may be transports for the multiple prongs of a well-engineered, blended threat.

The challenge

There are currently on the market, or on their way to market, many applications for business productivity that are purposed for real-time use, and as a result of being on the bleeding edge of technology, many of them implement protocols that today's firewalls and security systems are either not aware of or simply do not support. This is for a plethora of reasons, many of them good. Many times, these productivity enhancing applications utilize parallel channels of UDP or TCP communications, and as a result, they require the use of the opening and closing of a broad spectrum of logical ports. This is the crux of the matter: Some protocols, by virtue of whom they are, wish to have multiple unsecured doors opened for them. Just like any software, they are designed by people and, as a result, act just like them.

With this in mind, then, it may be desirable to purchase a firewall that can manage the introduction of new and complex software programs that are used for real-time business communication. This may be especially useful to some administrators where there is high volatility in the application base.

Intrusion prevention

True intrusion prevention is in the eye of the beholder, so where is the common ground? How do today's IT generalists know where product creators have actually developed true intrusion prevention or have merely relabeled their intrusion detection wares "intrusion prevention" to align themselves with a shifting market paradigm? True intrusion prevention can be determined with a simple series of litmus tests:

- Can it block known attacks without disruption in service?
- Can it respond to attacks within milliseconds?
- What is its system resource load? You will know if it is too much for your environment.
- A network-based system should not introduce excessive drag on the network, and a host-based system should not overwhelm local resources. Business as usual should continue.
- False positives: 5% is an acceptable number.

Every network is unique: Each has its own set of quirks and foibles, and each seems to have its own set of special little friends who are trying, daily, to hack access. It follows, then, that every firewall will perform differently, and it can be expected that even a top-of-the-line product may have issues under extreme and constant duress.

Host or network based?

Host-based systems are typically installed on servers and are designed only to protect a particular machine. A true network system must embrace the following aspects:

- Perform packet inspection with no loss of performance (speed).
- Include stateful packet inspection, protocol anomaly analysis, protocol awareness, signature analysis, and behavior analysis as methodologies of packet inspection. To be generic, they should provide anomaly detection in each of the following three areas:
  - Behavioral
  - Traffic
  - Protocol

Drop malicious sessions; don't simply reset connections.

4.3 About packet inspection

Before investing in a firewall appliance or software that claims to provide packet-level intrusion prevention, it is important that certain nuances of terminology be clarified (so you know what you're getting). Trying to pass a set of "words" to a vendor is useless without clarity of definitions. What do all these terms mean (see FYI 4.1)?

4.3.1 Selecting a firewall

A clear threatscape defense architecture begins to emerge, one that portrays a firewall collective as an array of security tools—one that is manageable under one roof with software and servers working in concert to provide a secure computing environment. The following sections aptly examine the strengths and weaknesses of several of the market's best solutions. Ultimately, the pass/fail indicators of any firewall system are the following questions: How well does it handle attacks unknown? How well can it defend, can it recognize, and can it respond? Any system connected to the Internet is subjected to daily attempts to access; its ports are scanned, probed, and checked perhaps hundreds of times per day, even per hour.

What to expect

What can a firewall do against all this? Many routers provide basic packet filtering, but as I have mentioned to many clients, this is only the foundation of a good system. A router's packet filtering is usually quite simple, and it is expected that it will only act as a subsidiary firewall device. As has been mentioned before in this book, a firewall is a policy that encapsulates the entire security philosophy. A "Firewall" may also be marketed by marketers (who else?) as a single device, usually a computer, that straddles a network connection and prevents all that is "bad" on one side—the outside—from getting through to the inside. How does it do this?

CONTROLLING PROTOCOLS

Most firewalls will allow the administrator to configure the most common protocols that are known by the administrator to be used in the firewall environment. If there are DNS, FTP, web, file, e-mail,

------------------------------→

FYI 4.1 *Terminology Introspective*

Packet-level intrusion-prevention terms are defined as follows:

Packets: Packets are the little bundles of information that, when pieced together at the end of a transfer, compromise a file, a request, a validation, a confirmation, etc., that other packets were received or transmitted successfully.

Stateful packet inspection: Most modem/routers provide some level of stateful packet inspection. Packets come in through the modem from the Internet and are passed outward through internal switches and routers, and the firewall device "inspects" each one. Simply put, packets that don't match known protocols are discarded and "good" packets are passed. Unfortunately, the constraints for determining what is a "good packet" have very little to do with the overall purpose of what will be assembled at the application level; stateful inspection is merely the inspection of packets with the knowledge of the protocol and the ability to categorize the packets' current states.

Deep packet inspection: Deep packet inspection may involve a certain level of modeling and may be connected with larger resources that require continuous threat updates.

Protocol: A protocol of the transport layer of a network is the predefined means whereby packets are organized, sequenced, received, and interpreted. A protocol is, essentially, a regulatory method for information packets to be received and interpreted, and it ensures that each packet reaches its intended destination intact. Most simply put, it is the agreed on format for the transmission of data from one device to another. It dictates the type of error checking (such as handshake or checksum).

Protocol analysis: A generic term that can be grouped with protocol analyzer, packet sniffing, and network analysis. Protocol analysis is the process of collecting packets and differentiating the type of packet stream protocol, such as UDP, TCP, FTP, SPP, or HTTP.

Protocol anomaly analysis/detection: A piece of software through which a packet stream passes, is inspected, and is compared to existing packets; packets that do not match known protocols are identified. This can be as specific as determining if a particular packet stream is unusual in a certain environment. This is accomplished by knowing what is "good," because knowing what is "bad" would require a definition set that would require updating almost daily. Protocol anomaly analysis is to packet streams as white-listing is to e-mail. Because it does not require updates but is based on existing standards, packet analysis is one of the first tiers of defense and is often the only defense against zero-day attacks.

Application protocol modeling: This uses a dictionary of protocol specifications and variations for the purpose of comparing a flow and locating anomalous behavior based on delta deviation that is outside an acceptable width.

Protocol decoding: When a network analyzer gathers and reads data from the network, it needs to interpret the information and provide an understandable interface to the user about the data. Protocol decoding is the human act of studying and interpreting results from packet analysis.

Signature analysis: Not dissimilar to virus signature analysis, protocol signature analysis attempts to match protocols to known malicious protocols.

Behavior analysis: Capturing and analyzing packets is almost an art form. Some software will capture and log packets, other software will analyze them, and some will do both. Typically, one or the other can be obtained as freeware, but when software offers both tasks, it is not free. Ethereal is a great packet analysis software, it is free, and it is open source.

and other servers behind the firewall, it is possible to use the firewall as a sort of traffic cop; it will map the correct traffic to the IP address that it is intended to reach. Likewise, it will allow the target IP address to respond in like. Should a hacker manage to access the web server, through its protections, the firewall would prevent enslavement of the web server for other types of attacks, merely by limiting the type of traffic to HTTP. Furthermore, the firewall could be configured with a quota so that if it is hijacked and abnormal amounts of traffic begin to issue forth, the quota would be reached and service terminated.

PACKET INSPECTION

Much has already been said about packet inspection in this chapter. In most networks, packet inspection and protocol control should typically be conducted on separate machines, with the packet inspection coming first. It's probably a bad idea for bad packets to even reach the back end of an Internet router. Most firewall products, however, do boast of some "stateful" packet inspection. And packet states are well known—it is uncommon that a stateful packet inspection tool would need to be updated with "definitions"—and even should it need it, because it is such a rare thing, these engines are rarely updatable. Since this is something that occurs in the transport layer, a firmware or hardware update would likely be needed to accomplish significant reform to the processing rules.

ATTACK RESPONSE

"In the event of an emergency, please break glass." It's not quite like that, but close. In the event of an attack, a system needs to know what to do. The more elaborate the system and the more expensive the system, the more appropriate and effective shall be the response. And this response varies from complete system shutdown to selective restriction to IP address blocking, IP block blocking, forensics, tracing, reporting, and actually going to the house of the hacker and arresting him. Well, that's not available yet, but we can all dream. Modern firewalls can (and should) tell the difference between a legitimate connection and one that is specifically designed to arm wrestle a server into the dirt. Nobody, except the attacker (and sometimes not even then), wants an operating system to be overwhelmed by invalid requests, as is the case in the infamous DoS attacks of the early part of this century.

FILE EXAMINATION

File examination is, perhaps, one of the single greatest performance and latency-introducing aspects of traffic monitoring. File examination is the process of reviewing each and every file that passes through, whether on FTP, HTTP, or VPN, and attempting to detect nasty executables, disallowed file types, known viruses, worms, logic bombs, or otherwise embedded and malicious scripts. Hughes Systems Satellite firewall, at least the portion that it cordons off for home users, introduces approximately 10 to 60 seconds of latency to traffic transfer and requests and diminishes the performance and ability of any user of its satellite network to the point that the system is, effectively, useless. Companies such as Earthlink and DirecWay are resellers of the Hughes Satellite services, and while highly secure, the system is under such continuous threat that it is constantly changing and its service is completely unpredictable. Such latency can be a scourge, is avoidable, and in the process of building out a secure firewall policy that spans several networks—internal, external, corporate, and so on—latency will be the primary consideration. VPNs are highly sensitive to latency, which is good because if a VPN connection begins to lag, it simply assumes that it is being hijacked and disconnects. This can be highly annoying to your superintendent when he is trying to download his favorite videos of his toy poodle from his home network and can't maintain a VPN connection for more than 30 seconds because he is going through six stages of firewall just to reach the gateway.

4.3.2 Firewall solutions

The following firewall solutions have been selected for review because of their best-of-breed approach, their scalability, and their approach to central management. Each solution boasts weaknesses and strengths and may or may not be suitable to some environments. When selecting a firewall solution, be sure to evaluate all of the variables that are unique to the network being protected.

eSoft

eSoft is an emerging market leader in the area of firewall appliances and managed solutions. Setting up an eSoft InstaGate Appliance or SCM solution can solve many of the security concerns of any small to medium-sized business that has a budget of less than $5K to spend on security policy. The HIPAA-certified eSoft product line is also a wise choice for many types of medical professional services (see FYI 4.2 for details on an InstaGate implementation). In particular, this author finds that the EX2 line is ideal for very small businesses that simply want to protect their server from what is, essentially, an open door if all that is sitting on their pipe to the Internet is a modem. It is a step above the competition with enhanced scalability and SoftPak portability options. The EX2 provides protocol filtering and stateful packet inspection while offering a full range of product consolidation.

FYI 4.2 *eSoft Case Study*

This was an interesting case because it started with a request by the clients for a backup DSL line; they had just been without service for 4 days across a weekend, and that was far too long (and this was the third time in 3 months an outage had occurred). I told them that there were no guarantees, even with a second line from a different provider, and that if there was an area-wide outage, no amount of redundancy (except maybe a satellite dish, with its own set of problems) would help them. After noticing that the client had no firewall setup, one thing that I could guarantee was that their intrusion risk on the Internet would double with the addition of another gateway. A firewall had been something they had not wanted to purchase, but with the increased risk and the additional bonus of VPN technology that would enable work-at-home, they agreed (see firewalls and load balancing dual DSLs for shared offices in Figure 4.2).

We chose eSoft's InstaGate Pro appliance for a number of reasons. Primarily, it offers the easiest access to product updates, definitions, configurations, and rules management. The web interface is very easy to use and offers an entire suite of tools that allow you to configure the device remotely. Secondly, the price was right. Even with licensing for up to 100 users, the price was perfect and beat the competition.

After getting the local phone company to come out and install the additional line and DSL modem, the most difficult part of this project was getting the addressing scheme set up in such a way as to not conflict with the DHCP server sitting behind the firewall. Originally, one of the DSL routers had a configuration in the 10.xx.xx.xx range. One phone call to XO and they were happy to change it to the 192.xx.xx.xx range so that it wouldn't conflict with the internal network.

To ensure full firewall protection of the network, we interfaced the firewall behind the load balancer; it provides bottleneck security on both lines. The load balancer is the lynch pin to this setup because without it we would have needed two firewall appliances. Since the load balancer is relatively transparent, we are able to "see through" it to the InstaGate; this allows VPN functionality as well as remote updates of the device. Furthermore, we got the additional bonus of a honey-pot–like subnet sitting between the load balancer and the routers. If someone does get through, they won't see anything but a single piece of hardware—the load balancer, which is password protected and adds another layer of security in that it hides the internal LAN addressing scheme. Remarkably, since the installation of the firewall, the internal network is running more smoothly, they have not experienced a single outage, and the rate of virus infections is down.

FYI 4.2 *eSoft Case Study (Continued)*

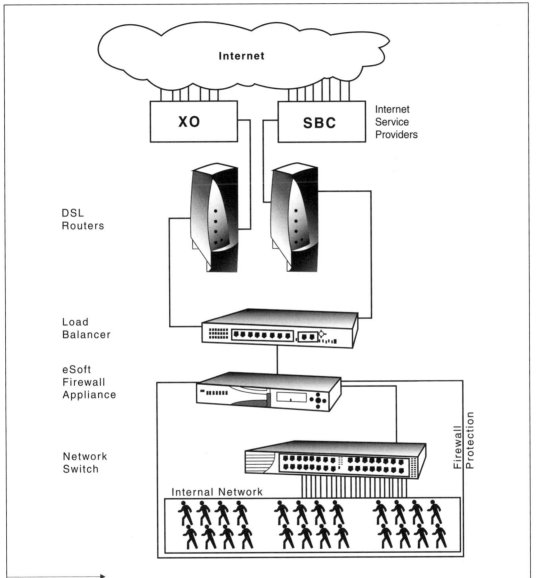

Figure 4.2 *Dual DSL routers, a load balancer, and a firewall bring durable, high-speed, and secure WAN access and capabilities to a small (30 employees) office.*

A multilayer defense against the complexity of today's threatscape requires the development of an additional security application environment. The key to an integrated and effective security environment is no longer contingent on a single appliance or piece of software such as a firewall, but in a secure applications management approach that brings together the multifaceted points of a distributed firewall policy. It depends on the layering of defenses.

InstaGate's approach to SCM, called *InstaGate SCM*, brings together all the points of a secure computing environment through the leverage of a single management tool/catalog that permits the implementation of various security SoftPaks.

Tip:

> The diversity and the purchase-only-what-you-need approach of SCM engenders a security environment tailored to the needs of a single organization while permitting scalability.

The most difficult aspect of security control is adapting to user habits and combating social engineering. Users will, in general, click on anything that moves. If it is a cute animation and it promises to help with something, many users will think they are being helpful to their probably overburdened IT support staff and will click on it. NetSky is possibly one of the biggest offenders (see FYI 4.3).

FYI 4.3 *Social Engineering: "These People Will Click on Anything" (Overheard Being Muttered by an Antagonized Network Administrator)*

Lazaro, an attorney for a midsize, Midwest law firm, received an e-mail from his wife. The e-mail contained an attachment. He opened it. The zip file opened, and in it was yet another attachment. He clicked on it, too, and a window opened on his screen and it told him that he could protect his computer against viruses by clicking a button. Now, Laz is not entirely to blame. A consultant working on the site was in the process of upgrading all the users to a SCM-style desktop antivirus solution, but a number of other issues had delayed the implementation by several days. Meanwhile, Laz's existing virus protection had expired. The consultant was aware that several of the users' virus protection software were expiring and had expired, but a firewall in place had given her a false sense of security; she felt that nothing could get in and that the user base had enough training at this point, and enough experience, not to click on anything suspect. She failed to account for the combination of multiple events—daily pop-ups that told Laz his virus protection had expired, and an e-mail from Laz's wife that contained a promised solution.

And then, when you factor in that Laz and the consultant are married to each other. . . . Of course, you may realize by now that the e-mail did not come from Laz's wife, the consultant. It didn't even

FYI 4.3 *Social Engineering: "These People Will Click on Anything" (Overheard Being Muttered by an Antagonized Network Administrator) (Continued)*

come from her computer. It came from one of her client's computers, who had her e-mail address in his address book, because he had received a similar e-mail from his supervisor, who had received it from his wife, who had received it from her brother, and so on, all the way back to a newsgroup where someone clicked on a NetSky-A–infected file that promised free and unlimited virus protection. This is what "social engineering" is all about. Creating a set of social circumstances to optimize the probability that a certain event will occur.

And in a distorted way, the NetSky variants *a* through *m* delivered as promised and removed any instances of the Bagel virus. But it only did this because the author of the NetSky variants is in a distance contest with the author of the Bagel viruses to see who can infect and dominate more computers. They do, in fact, hate each other and frequently leave messages within their code that deride and insult each other.

The moral of this story is that an unforeseeable combination of events can create a situation in which even a normally smart and savvy user will click on anything. *It can happen to anyone.*

The above story is true. Here is a sample communication from the network administrator concerning the opening of socially engineered attachments, sent 2 weeks before the story transpired:

```
                  ——-Original Message——-
          From: The Client
          Sent: Wednesday, March 03, 2004 9:54 AM
          To: Network Administrator
          Subject: FW: Notify about your e-mail account
          utilization.
          I opened this by mistake. Anything you recommend?
          ——-Original Message——-
          From: noreply@.theClient.com
          [mailto:noreply@theClient.com]
          Sent: Wednesday, March 03, 2004 8:30 AM
          To: The Client
          Subject: Notify about your e-mail account
          utilization.
          Dear user of theClient.com gateway e-mail server,
          We warn you about some attacks on your e-mail
          account. Your computer may contain viruses, in order
          to keep your computer and e-mail account safe,
          please, follow the instructions. For details see the
          attached file.
          For security reasons attached file is password
          protected. The password is "54215".
          Cheers,
          The theClient.com team
          http://www.theClient.com
          Network Admin RESPONSE:
```

Social Engineering: "These People Will Click on Anything" (Overheard Being Muttered by an Antagonized Network Administrator) (Continued)

——Original Message——-
From: Network Admin
Sent: Monday, March 15, 2004 9:57 AM
To: Everyone
Subject: For the record
In light of the recent outbreak of hoax and virus emails, I have composed the following in an effort to clarify and establish policy:
I will never send you an email with an attachment asking you to configure or reconfigure anything.
If I do send you an email (such as this one), it will be purely informational and I will never ask you to reconfigure your account information.
I will never ask you for your account information via email.
You will never receive a legitimate notification regarding your account or internet connection from anyone other than "The Consultant". Should you accidentally find yourself in a situation where your computer is asking you to install software, call me before proceeding. If you can't reach me, cancel the operation.
I will not, except in very rare circumstances and on an individual basis, ask you to click on any links to visit a web site or to download anything and install it on your computer.
You will never receive any legitimate email from me from any theClient.com email address, such as admin@theClient.com or accounts@theClient.com or support@theClient.com. These email addresses do not even exist on the theClient.com email system.
In the rare case where I do send you an email with an attachment, it will be something that you are expecting because you asked me for it, or we already discussed it and determined that you needed it. And it will be from this email address.
Thank You
Network Administrator
IT Support

Stories such as that illustrated in FYI 4.3 exemplify and underscore the need—the requirement—for a more comprehensive security solution than that which can be provided by any single device. Here is a checklist of the items that are provided within an eSoft SCM deployment:

- *Mail content security* utilizes virus scanning of e-mail attachments and spam filtering to reduce the possibility of attack. Requires the installation of a mail server and a static IP address/domain name mapping in either the MX record or individual forwards.

- Servers:
    - Desktop antivirus
    - Internal file server
    - POP and SMTP
    - VPN
    - Dial-in
    - Web
    - FTP
    - DNS

- *Web content security* can provide site filtering to limit employee access to the web.

- *Integrated management* deployable to a single server, with management and automation tools that allow configuration and monitoring from any location. Supports RADIUS and LDAP authentication.

- *The SoftPak Director,* a part of the SCM, may contain the following SoftPaks, some with yearly fees, some with one-time fees:
    - Web server
    - FTP server
    - Desktop antivirus
    - Spam filter
    - E-mail antivirus
    - VPN client
    - Web mail

- Site filter

- VPN manager

- App filter

Sun iForce perimeter security solution

> The iForce Perimeter Security Solution provides multi-
> layer internet security to protect vital business
> information networks from today's threats. Combining
> seven essential components, the Perimeter Security
> Solution provides increased prevention, detection, and
> response. This is achieved by integrating applications
> from industry-leading iForce and SunTone Certified
> Partners: Check Point Software, Symantec, Trend Micro,
> Tripwire, Sanctum, and eSecurity.—www.sun.com

The keystone of Sun's IForce Perimeter Security Solution rests in what Sun describes as a "rock solid foundation" of Sun Microsystem servers. Running Sun Solaris, a flavor of UNIX, Sun provides a reliable and secure interface that can be placed between LAN and WAN environments. These servers, which are grouped in the iForce configuration, are all running Sun Microsystems' Trusted Solaris Operating System (SMTSOS), a hardened version of Sun Solaris (see FYI 4.4). This iForce configuration, a collective firewall, is a deployment of the following technologies across multiple servers:

- VPN/firewall security through CheckPoint VPN-1/FireWall-1 software.

- Virus detection and scanning with Trend Micro InterScan VirusWall.

- While, for intranet, Internet, and extranet applications, Sanctum AppShield Web application firewall provides cookie snapping/ session hijacking.

- The Sun company has developed what can only be described as a hardened kernel approach to the SMTSOS.

- Intrusion detection and forensics are handled by Symantec Corporation ManHunt and ManTrap threat management software.

- Data Integrity assurance with Tripwire software.

- Security event correlation management with e-Security, e-Sentinel, and e-Wizard products.

Sana security

Can a firewall be more than just a prophylactic barrier? The future of effective security may very well lie within the realm of application security and intrusion prevention. Host-based firewall software released by Sana Security can do the following:

- Adapt to changes in application behavior

- Detect and prevent known and unknown attacks

- Provide centralized management

- Shield custom and in-house–developed applications

- Does not require full-time or extensive management

FYI 4.4 *Key iForce Components Explained*

The iForce system, as a collective, comprises multiple components.

CheckPoint VPN-1: The foundation of the iForce collection of best-of-breed products, the CheckPoint firewall VPN, in addition to offering weak and strong encryption, embodies the crisp aromas and flavors of the most rarefied of mountain ranging blended units. Just kidding, this author has had way too much coffee.

Trend Micro InterScan VirusWall: This detects the presence of viruses and worms in e-mail, FTP, and HTTP traffic.

Sanctum AppSHield: Protects web servers.

SMTSOS: Each server in the iForce collection is loaded with the Solaris operating environment and subsequently, after all patches are installed, is hardened with the Sun Solaris Security Toolkit. This is a process of eliminating or disabling nonessential services (for example, FTP services running or even installable on a web server may not be desirable), modification of user and directory permissions, and installation of any necessary tools needed for the system of secure TCP wrappers used by the security solution to facilitate collective crosstalk.

Symantec Manhunt: Detects unusual behavior in network traffic.

Tripwire: A longtime UNIX component on many versions of UNIX, this can require excessive overhead as it uses a cryptographic checksum auditing method to determine if a file has been changed in a way that it shouldn't have. This software requires an extremely high level of expertise to set up properly. Otherwise, many false alarms will ensue as the software is indiscriminate and it logs whatever it is told to log. Sun offers the management expertise needed to configure this software properly on certain servers, but it is not recommended for deployment in areas of high customization.

Professional Guidance: Part of the iForce solution includes support from Sun security experts.

- Deploy in minutes without requiring a restart
- Protect applications that may be unable to protect themselves

"Primary Response" monitors internal systems, understands the normal behavior, and shuts down any abnormal or strange behavior. It operates on an immune system analogy. They call it an application security agent, "Primary Response."

APPLICATION SECURITY

Primary Response was developed on a signatureless approach to infiltration detection. Rather, it is dependent on intensive configuration to specific environments and is based on research into how the human immune system repels viruses. The key to Sana's success is in the software's ability to learn and relearn independently of human interaction. This software observes and learns normal behavior for software, it watches code paths, learns what is acceptable for those applications, and then continues to monitor the system for abnormal change. It is in this manner that Primary Response reduces time and effort spent on security.

It is a known and common trick of virus and stealth authors to write code that closely mimics applications, from masquerading as a notepad or IIS executable to actually replacing portions of legitimate executables with spoolers and SMTP engines; there is no known end to their chicanery. Once infiltration is successful, there are often few options to root them out, and the impact can be as random and chaotic as trying to pick up the pieces and put a house together after it is hit by a hurricane. Often, rebuilding it is the only option. Tripwire-style systems like First Response are excellent "backyard" watchdogs suitable for targeted enterprise deployment across a conglomerate of small to medium-sized networks where extremely high levels of security are *required.*

First Response, among others in this genre of firewall technology, positions itself in the marketplace as an enterprise-grade, standalone solution; with the ability to provide support for up to 7,000 agents per management server, it comes in as a close runner to the Lucent Brick-10000 solution. It provides role-based user management, agent management groups, and third-party management systems integration. These features are among those of the Sana system that put it at the forefront of host-based firewall technology:

- Prevents vulnerability exploits
- Based on a unique, viral metaphor technology
- Automated patch updates
- Protects existing and developed applications
- Requires no signature subscription
- Provides comprehensive forensics

SOCKS

Not to be confused with footwear, SOCKS (SOCKetS) is to firewalls as 802.11x is to wireless; that is, it is a standard. It is a networking proxy protocol that allows servers on each side of a network barrier to communicate with each other. It is often used as a firewall that straddles the network barrier and permits the communication. David Koblas is the author of the two major versions of SOCKS, SOCKSv4 and SOCKSv5. SOCKSv5 supports UDP, whereas SOCKSv4 does not.

Most proxy technologies such as Network Address Translation (NAT) only support unidirectional proxy; they only allow one-way communication. SOCKS delivers the proxy mechanism at the transport layer, which allows it the flexibility to manage access based on application, user, address, etc.

SOCKS is a good place to start for those who wish to gain an understanding of the core, underlying principles of a firewall, or for those interested in developing their own custom solutions.

SOCKS IMPLEMENTATIONS

It is not easy to determine exactly what the underlying principle of a firewall is. Wading through the marketing hype seldom reveals the true nature of a firewall. Permeo, for example, makes no mention of its use of SOCKSv5 as its substrate logic, but the SOCKS web site clearly (and often) points to Permeo as a prime example of a company that makes broad use of the standard. Whether a firewall maker uses SOCKS, a proprietary method, or some other standard is oftentimes a matter of conjecture. Chances are good that if the firewall under review exhibits the following aspects, it is either SOCKS or something very similar:

- Support for an unusually broad range of TCP protocols with the ability to add and manage protocols easily.

- A broad range of supported IP-based applications.

- Weighs in on the side of application security as opposed to network security.

- Controls outbound and inbound access.

- Is proxy based.

- SOCKS is UDP and TCP only—ICMP (tracert and ping) applications will not work.

- Client security driver required to intercept and route communications through a SOCKS server.

SOCKS support

As technology evolves, new products emerge, and new methods of threatening security present themselves, it's apparent that something as limited in focus as SOCKS will never penetrate a wide market application. Rather, it is more and more an item that finds specialized use as a firewall/VPN tool for application proxies.

Permeo

Permeo's ongoing support for SOCKS is questionable. On the Permeo SOCKS web site, there is a FAQ about whether the software is Y2K compliant—draw your own conclusions. The site copyright is 1998–2002.

Distinct

Distinct is a security software firm that provides a SOCKS client for Yahoo! Paging users that allows them to connect through SOCKS firewalls. Again, this site has a questionable copyright date.

SSH tectia

A managed security middleware solution, SSH is an industry leader in financial and government managed security solutions. While the white paper makes little mention of SOCKS, descriptions and naming conventions within the framework suggest a high degree of parallelism to SOCKS. This is not to say that SSH is SOCKS. It is to say, however, that there are powerful similarities, and SSH may have SOCKS at its core with additional administrative capabilities that are custom SSH value add-ons. There are also similarities between the old SOCKS NEC site and the SSH Tectia white paper that leave one with an overwhelming sense of déjà vu.

HUMMINGBIRD

Hummingbird is a classic example of a specialized use of SOCKS to coordinate application communications through firewall devices. The Hummingbird SOCKS Client, in tandem with SOCKSv4/v5 servers on gateways, authenticates users, authorizes requests, and establishes a proxy connection. This creates a conduit whereby data pass transparently between the destination and the requesting client.

SOCKS METHODOLOGY

In Figure 4.3, communication with the destination (far right) is initiated by the left-hand, client device (PC, server, or handheld). Two additional mechanisms, or components, are introduced by SOCKS for the purposes of, well, "socksifying" and enabling SOCKS. These

Figure 4.3
A gateway server provides SOCKSv4/5 support and acts as the relay mechanism for secure communication between a client and a destination.

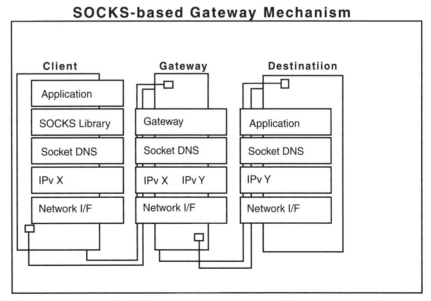

SOCKS-based Gateway Mechanism

are the SOCKS library, introduced at the client, or requesting, device, and the gateway component installed on, of all places, the gateway. . . (yes, the terminology can be a little obfuscated by indiscriminate redundancy).

The gateway is purposed with intercepting and replacing client application socket APIs and DNS name-resolving APIs (these are the components of software that are responsible for establishing and controlling communication between different software). IE Software A and Software B both have APIs that allow Software A to send and receive information from Software B, with Software B residing either locally or remotely.

"Gateway" on the gateway is an enhanced SOCKS server. As such, it provides protocol translation services in a relaying fashion, between protocol X and the destination protocol Y.

The SOCKS Library communicates with the gateway through the SOCKS protocol, SOCKSv5, is a unique connection, special to SOCKS, and therefore is called a "SOCKsified" connection and is, consequently, homogenous. This allows the limitation, in a sense, of communication to a single protocol. This connection also permits the exchange of control information, information that details location and destination information. The SOCKSv5 implementation introduced support for IPv6 as well as enhanced security to the SOCKS standard (see FYI 4.5). Once through the firewall in the LAN sphere, the connection between the gateway and the destination is a normal one.

Lucent-Enterasys secure networks solution

In the same vein as many other secure network market leaders, Lucent has entered into a partnership that integrates the Enterasys security product and network management tools with Lucent's firewall products. In this new market space for Lucent dwells a software portfolio and service offering with capabilities designed to address many of the critical security demands detailed in this chapter. Much like the Sun system, Lucent-Enterasys offers a wide variety of products grouped under a single umbrella-like management philosophy.

LUCENT VPN FIREWALL BRICK

A carrier-grade solution, Lucent VPN Firewall Brick hits hard in the arena of firewalls. Lucent claims the throughput and manageability

FYI 4.5 *SOCKS Advantages and Differences*

Internet Protocol version 6 (IPv6) offers several improvements and enhancements to IPv5 that extend the protocol's capabilities: Some of the primary and advantageous differences in IPv6 compared to v5 and v4 include the following:

- "Anycast" addressing to provide a method of sending messages to several of the nearest gateways so that, conceptually, they may manage the forwarding of packets to others, updating routing tables along the line.

- IP addresses increase in length from 32 to 128 bits.

- Tasking is relegated to the destination, thereby speeding delivery and decreasing latency.

- Identification of packets as members of a particular "stream" is possible.

- Increased security is possible with the addition of extensions to this version that allow for the indication of an authenticating or specifying authority/ mechanism to allow the verification of point of origin.

of as many as a million concurrent VPN sessions, bandwidth management tools, and mobile data service. There are, however, multiple product levels, from the entry-level Brick-80 appliance to the advanced enterprise Brick-1000 that boasts 1.5-Gbps throughput and is actually more like the size and dimension of a cinderblock than a brick. Each of the firewalls in the product line claims to "stretch your investment dollars" and provide carrier-grade IP services with 7,500 concurrent VPN tunnels. It's unclear how the "million" VPN tunnels is formulated, perhaps on a carrier-grade Internet connection in a service center equipped with 150 Brick-1000 appliances. In fact, the Brick-1000 allows for central management of up to 1,000 Brick devices and 10,000 IPSec clients. The Brick-1000 features the following:

- Nine 10/100 Ethernet ports and four fiber gigabit ports

- 4,094 VLANS

- VPN clocking in at 400 Mbps

- Content security

- DoS protection

- SYN flood protections
- Intelligent cache management
- Stateful packet inspection
- TCP and IP packet validation
- Virus scanning
- Strong authentication
- Runs on Bell Labs' Inferno operating system
- 1.5-Gbps throughput
- VitalQIP DNS/DHCP/IP management software
- Navis/Radius authentication server
- Network security assessment service
- Security policy development
- Security incident response

4.4 Summary

Simply setting up a firewall and then walking away and relying on product updates and equipment upgrades to completely manage and protect your system is not entirely wise. Users are often the first to notice attacks; while IT management and staff are busy repairing, replacing, upgrading, and planning, users are actually using the system. They will likely notice performance degradation before anyone else. In these cases, a cadre of tools in the IT manager's war chest will serve to detect and neutralize attempts. An informed complaint to a firewall manufacturer/support will enable a quick and effective response. Packet sniffers, such as TCPDUMP, can be set to watch for particular patterns.

The difficulty inherent in packet analysis is characterized by an inability to accurately gage the deleterious impact of anomalous packets. Its overwhelming failure is that any type of attack looks perfectly innocent to even the best of packet analyzers. After all, an e-mail, apparently from your best friend that contains a link to a malicious web site is, for all inspective purposes, perfectly legitimate traffic. To expect that the packet analyzer (or any firewall device) will assemble the e-mail, open it, follow the link, download and inspect all the material from the link, test it, check it against a database of known offenders, validate IP addresses, etc., anyone can see that it may be a while before the e-mail reaches its destination if it has to undergo security procedures of airport proportions.

At the end of the war that rages on the Internet, where security is the primary concern of administrators who must defend against unknown attackers who are simply attacking because they can, throughput will be king. The system that can do the most, can dig deep enough, and can do it with lightning speed will reign. The impact of the results of socially engineered attacks can be mitigated and reduced; it remains to be seen if they can ever be prevented.

Selecting the most suitable firewall for an organizational need depends, in large part, on the firewall policy. Certain organizations have needs that cannot be met by the smaller, less redundant products. Others have needs that are suited just fine by an "out-of-box" solution. The best solutions are tailored by a network administrator who understands and anticipates the needs and demands of his client. He creates a defense that includes a combination of firewall policy, effective technology, and a program of training and education.

5

Defense in Depth: Firewall Topologies

5.1 Chapter objectives

- Understanding a VPN
- Incorporating VPN into firewall policy
- Incorporating remote authentication
- Integrating a DMS with a firewall policy
- DMZ, NAT, and other security features clarified

From hardware to software, there are myriad choices in the realm of security wares that provide the cast of supporting characters on the firewall stage. A firewall is more than just a single piece of equipment; as the authors of this fine book have asserted, a firewall is a policy, often a well-documented policy, that encapsulates equipment, software, and usage policies. No one piece of equipment should or could act as your entire firewall. For example, having a policy of changing your passwords frequently would be part of your firewall. However, whereas the focus of the previous chapter centered on firewalls and the often accompanying software bundled with them, this chapter focuses on independent utilities that may be assembled to provide an in-depth defense against intrusion, extrusion, and collusion. Two major areas in this defense involve network topology, especially in terms of the wide area network (WAN). How these two areas are handled, how they are managed, and how they are secured are the measures of success of any firewall security policy. Coincidentally, the implementation and subsequent user leveraging of these security resources greatly improves workforce-life quality and productivity. It also makes managing remote networks from a central location a very real possibility.

5.2 Virtual private network

One of the first areas to cover then becomes one of intentionally opening "holes" in the firewall to allow desirable traffic through. One such hole through a firewall is the virtual private network (VPN) as shown in Figure 5.1.

Often, when presenting the concept of a VPN as a solution to clients, co-workers, and customers, there will be some resistance.

Figure 5.1
With today's high-speed connections and advanced encryption algorithms, a possibility of virtual private networking has been created that traditionally was accomplished by dial-up servers and modems.

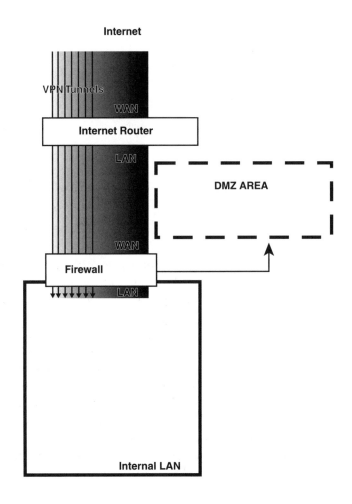

VPN technology is relatively straightforward and easy to manage. The greatest obstacles to creating a VPN are

- The technical abilities of the user, his understanding of the concept
- Sensitivity of data

Once these obstacles are conquered, and before the actual equipment purchase and integration, policy needs to be established. Questions that may arise include the following:

- How sensitive is corporate data?
- How will decisions be made regarding access?
    - At the individual server level?
    - At the PC level?
    - At the workgroup or domain level?

This is where the topology of the internal network plays a pivotal role. It can be very time consuming and difficult to arrange servers and information in ways that are particular to one user or even one group of users. Mapping drives is well and good, but can you map drives over a VPN? This is not a book about access control, however, but suffice it to say that yes, if permissions can be managed in the internal network, then the same administrative tools may be applied to the user who has connected to the LAN across a VPN.

However, opening a VPN to the network in a certain way can often open a door to the network that allows the user access to everything. If it is a concern, then the method of authentication needs to be reviewed before allowing full unrestricted access to all network resources. Most firewalls let you create and manage user accounts that can be enabled for VPN access. These are generic accounts and as such will often have the same level of access permissions to the network that the firewall enjoys. In access-controlled areas, it is preferable to pass users through the VPN to an ancillary authenticating server that has a better idea of user roles. Documents needed in one place may not be needed in another and, in fact, may even be restricted from certain users.

In any environment, it follows that decisions must be made regarding who will have access to what, how the firewall will be positioned to allow access, what type of VPN will be used, how it will be setup, and whether ancillary authentication will be necessary. Furthermore, bandwidth usage must be considered. What sort of user activity will be typical? Running thin clients? Accessing their Outlook Exchange accounts? Moving large media files? Many of the firewall appliances discussed in the previous chapter are capable of tremendous throughput as well as tremendous numbers of VPN sessions. This can be very useful in WAN implementations where public communications systems may be used to establish a large far-reaching network. Often, in large enterprise deployments, a single (or several) server farm(s) will be centrally located and VPN technology will be used to link many thousands of remote locations.

5.2.1 Remote office VPN

A VPN will allow organizations to leverage the backbone of the Internet to build their own secure WAN. For companies with many branch offices, the ability to build multiple, stable, Internet Protocol Security (IPSec) tunnels is the ideal way to stay connected. A remote office VPN differs from a remote user VPN in that there exists, on each side of the connection, a firewall that has remote office VPN capabilities. Usually, internal subnets for an enterprise may have similar subnet IP addressing schemes; where remote user VPNs fail because of this, remote office VPNs may succeed. They also provide two-way communication and visibility, whereas remote user VPNs create a single point on the network and do not allow for connectivity between any machine except the attached user device. Remote user VPNs do not broadcast on the network; they can only be seen by direct IP address scanning or through prior knowledge of the VPN configuration.

5.2.2 Remote user VPN

Remote user VPN describes a VPN circumstance where the remote PC uses client software to achieve the connection. Generally, the advantages of *remote user VPN* over *Point-to-Point Tunneling Protocol (PPTP) VPN* reside in the greater configurability and flexibility of the *remote user VPN* client to operate successfully in harsher network environments, where a great level of convolution or complexity exists.

5.2.3 Point-to-point tunneling protocol VPN

No firewall solution worth its salt comes without PPTP support and passthrough support. PPTP settings will allow VPN passthrough (in which the connection is passed to an internal VPN server for encryption and management). PPTP boasts ease of use, so it also fails the most easily and is the flakiest of the connections. Think overcooked fish. But it works, and for all intents and purposes, it works with the same level of security as other options. With PPTP VPN there is no need for additional software installation: Windows 98, Windows NT, and Windows 2000 all come with PPTP VPN clients as part of the operating system (OS). For additional security, strong encryption is available, but it must be configured when creating the connection on the user side, and Windows client connections must be set to use MS CHAP version 2.0 and 128-bit encryption.

5.2.4 Authenticating with a remote access dial-in user service server

Many firewall remote user VPN solutions offer remote access dial-in user service (RADIUS) compatibility, and an administrative screen may exist whereby the RADIUS server IP address and other configuration options may be entered. If this is the case, then the VPN users' authentication passes through to the RADIUS server for authentication. The firewall may or may not allow configuration of "password-only" or "login and password" authentication from the RADIUS server.

5.3 Firewall policies

Decide and establish policies. Cordon off the restricted areas (if they aren't already), and create a written firewall policy. Many organizations create firewalls within firewalls within firewalls. There may be information that should never leave the office. There may be information so sensitive that you don't even want you to know that you know about it. An effective network administrator has created a book to store information about the firewall (kept under lock and key in a safe location with a duplicate stored in a secure location off-site). A section of this notebook will outline VPN policy (for example, see FYI 5.1).

5.3.1 How secure is VPN technology?

If they want it bad enough, they will get it, even if your policy is to never let it leave the office. Your secrets are more likely to walk out your front door in an employee's pocket or in a USB hard drive in plain view on the employee's key chain than they are to be stolen by someone who has hacked your VPN. With 128-bit encryption on all VPN traffic, it would take millions of years for a single computer to crack the code by guessing it.

Many firewall products are RADIUS compatible and use key-chain tokens and intrusion prevention for security. David Aylesworth,

FYI 5.1 *VPN Policy Sample*

Here is a sample page from a network administrator's security policy book. The names and IP addresses have been changed, but it is an authentic representation of an actual law firm security policy. Additional pages that detail Windows authentication, RADIUS server authentication, and other user privileges or access methods may be necessary. If there are groups of users with separate privileges, this must be detailed in the firewall policy. This layer of protection will ensure a long-term continuity of security, as well as provide training and support materials for existing and future Network Administrative staff:

1. All full time attorneys of the Firm are allowed VPN access through Firewall 10.0.0.3 on IP 68.xxx.xxx.102.

2. Upon request for VPN access, Form 203-b must be completed and signed by the supervising partner.

3. Each attorney with a complete 203-b shall, unless otherwise noted on 203-b, require the following security settings:

Quota :	*20 MB*
Remote access: Dial-up and VPN	*yes*

With the following software allowances:

PCAnywhere	*no*
FTP	*no*
Document management	*yes*
Exchange	*yes*

a product manager for eSoft, manufacturer's of InstaGate, says, "[The] InstaGate can authenticate VPN, proxy, and mail users via RADIUS. I typically see customers using this so they don't have to duplicate their Windows user database on the InstaGate. Instead they run a RADIUS server on their Windows domain controller and have the InstaGate authenticate to it. . . . Regarding password tokens, we do not support any natively, but many can be supported via RADIUS."

5.3.2 Document access

With the inherent difficulty in securing documents, many enterprises have turned to document management systems (DMSs) such as WORLDOX, iManage, and PCDocs to provide a comprehensive solution, one that will not only protect sensitive material from casual theft, but will also provide much needed sorting and categorizing elements.

A DMS solution, such as WORLDOX, iManage, or PCDocs, has been shown to work quite well in ensuring version control, location control, and safe access to documents by remote workers. Many DMS solutions also have web interface modules that can be used to emulate a document interface at remote locations. Custom-built solutions that provide a simple intranet with a documents solution so you can log usage and then batten down the hatches and make it the only access route are also effective. Microsoft's web server platform, Internet Information Services (IIS), has a built-in user account that can be granted permission to a certain area of a server when others may not have access rights of any kind. It is, in essence, the primary operating principle of a web site—that the web server acts as an agent between the browser and the file system. Naturally, access to the server can be denied to anyone but the administrator. On a VPN, remote users can surf the intranet just as they can onsite.

Whether a firewall is developed that lets users VPN and have complete access to all network resources or access to terminal serve only to the computer in their office, the virtual office place (complete with chat utilities to replace the traditional water cooler) is rapidly becoming as much of a reality as it is a necessity. With each day, concerns over travel, time away from home, and family become bigger issues, and employers find that they must respond to the needs of employees. At the same time, they must ensure the smooth functioning of their operation. With the installation of some equipment and some time to configure, a VPN, in combination with a solid firewall and a DMS, will increase productivity and profit—for less than the cost of a new car.

5.4 Setting up a demilitarized zone: A VPN alternative?

Not really alternative in terms of the technology, but a so-called *philosophical diametric* to a VPN can be a demilitarized zone (DMZ). Philosophically, the purpose of both a DMZ and a VPN is to protect business data and resources from unauthorized access and grant access to allowed functions to outside users. A DMZ, unlike a VPN, is an area that is like a bastion between the internal network, the firewall device, and the Internet. Historically, DMZs were created through the layering of firewall devices. However, with improvements in electronics and firmware, setting up a DMZ can be as easy as plugging a Category 5 (CAT5) Ethernet cable into an Ethernet port labeled "DMZ" on the firewall. Figure 5.2 is a representation of a typical firewall/DMZ arrangement. Depending on configuration, interestingly, a VPN may even be used to connect to a DMZ.

5.4.1 Uses

A DMZ is a good place to put machines that need to be accessed via the external Internet when placing them in the internal network is too risky. This may be because the ports that need to be opened for certain types of functions (such as web and file serving) are more vulnerable, are hacker magnets, and should a single machine on the internal network be compromised, it is a hacking waterfall, and every other machine will be at risk or compromised in short order. Things such as FTP servers, file servers, web servers, and mail servers are often placed in a DMZ.

5.4.2 Theory of operation

In its simplest terms, a DMZ is a separate network that sits between two "firewalls." It takes two devices to make a firewall because it is, definitively, the more vulnerable of two networks sitting side by side.

Figure 5.2
Simple demili-
tarized zone
configuration.

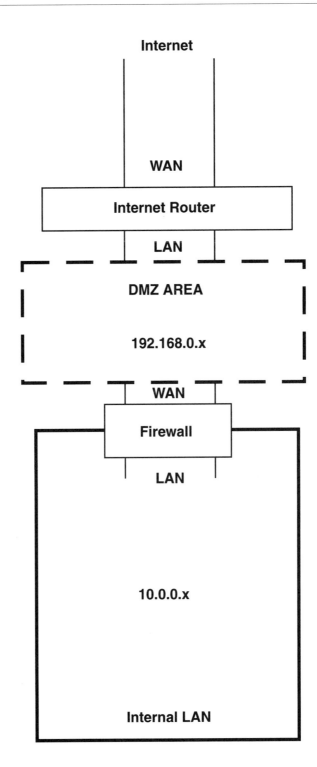

A good clear definition of a DMZ is as follows:

```
The first of two networks, in series, with the first
network separated from the Internet by a firewall or a
router and the second network separated from the first
by a firewall. Each network consists of a different
subnet.
```

Typically, most modern firewalls have a DMZ setup in which the firewall can control and create the DMZ. There are still two devices at work here; in the case of a firewall with DMZ capabilities, the second device is simply built into the firewall appliance, and the firewall becomes a bidirectional bastion server. Many administrators take the approach of simply cordoning off an area between the modem/router and the firewall; the DMZ is then a separate subnet that sits between the modem/router and the firewall. Figure 5.2 is configured in this manner. Configuration of port forwarding is accomplished at the router, and this can be accomplished in a number of ways, many of which are manufacturer specific. For example, some SpeedStream models allow configuration of a DMZ on port 1 of the router network interface ports. It may require technical assistance from the manufacturer, but here is the target checklist:

- Router WAN: same as the external IP address.
- Router LAN IP: same as the DMZ subnet.
- DMZ has subnet of 10.0.0.xx or 172.[16-31].x.x or 192.168.x.x: These subnet addresses are private set-asides. They do not exist in the public domain.
- DMZ computer gateways: same as the router LAN IP address.
- Firewall WAN is set to an address on the DMZ, with its gateway set to the router LAN as well.
- Network Address Translation (NAT) on the router is enabled in this configuration. Configuring a DMZ with NAT turned off may be considerably trickier to accomplish and may involve setting up pinholes.

The above configuration is well and good, but it may be very tricky (in other words, this author doesn't know how to do it) if not impossible to set up a true DMZ in this fashion *and* allow for internal network VPN access. Using the DMZ port (if available) on a firewall may be an alternative configuration that will achieve the same results, or using a routing table (if such a feature is available on the router) to map addresses may be another, with the DMZ existing off of a firewall that is parallel to the private subnet firewall. One thing is certain: If the above configuration is used, to enable VPN, the firewall will have to have a public IP address on its WAN port. For this to be accomplished, NAT must be disabled and the router WAN and LAN must have the exact same public IP address. This is called a *simple passthrough*, but to put a DMZ between a router configured in this manner and a firewall would contradict the definition of DMZ. It would be more like a phalanx maneuver—one that will get its head lopped off. In this configuration, most routers offer absolutely zero packet filtering or stateful inspection. Check with manufacturer specifications to be certain.

Note: Some routers are more cooperative than others, and getting oneself locked out of a router is a most simple thing to do! (See FYI 5.2.)

5.4.3   **Managing ports in a DMZ**

There are 65,535 ports that a computer uses for TCP/IP network traffic; however, only the first thousand or so are actually used by anyone. In the range of 1 to 1,023, many services and software use these for communications and operations. The primary purpose of a firewall is to centralize all communication to and from a network so that unauthorized activities and requests to these ports may be monitored effectively. For the purposes of security, many of these ports are closed or operate in a so-called *stealth mode*.

Through a number of methods, the firewall controlling the DMZ may allow certain types of traffic through, to, and from certain machines through IP address mapping. This is different than a routing table, because a routing table in a router takes *all* the communication to one IP address and passes it to another. Figure 5.3 demonstrates that through one IP address (the router), multiple machine ports are mapped to specific machines within the DMZ.

FYI 5.2 *Rogue DSL Router Rescue Operation*

When configuring a router, inevitably the inevitable happens (such is the way of inevitability—it's inevitable), and after a change to the router it is no longer accessible. Here are some tips to get through a router hunger strike:

When changing the LAN IP address, the router configuration screens (if accessed through a web interface) will be unavailable to a computer that is connected to it via a separate LAN Subnet. Change the TCP/IP settings of the connected computer to be on the same as the router, and enter the router as a gateway. Windows XP has been known to pretend not to see routers if the static configuration is set up and the DNS servers are left blank, so be sure to complete the DNS servers section of the TCP/IP configuration property sheet (networking | connection | properties).

NOTE: The Windows XP Hosts file can cause what appear to be intermittent difficulties in connecting to a router web interface. For example, if the router interface is 10.0.0.3, but there is a mapping "10.0.0.3 BG-Exchange" in the host's file, accessing the web interface may be an *interesting* experience, at best. Administrators that ply their trade on multiple networks for multiple clients should take care to document any settings, all the IP addresses, and all the system changes that are made to their laptops when the laptops are nomad. If this is done, and a router (or anywhere) is resisting or behaving strangely, then it is a simple matter of reviewing the log for a matching IP address or domain name and then taking corrective action if needed.

If this still doesn't work, and remote administration is enabled, get to a hot Internet connection and attempt to access from the WAN side.

Still can't get in? Geez, what did you do to it? Well, it's time to invest in a DB9m to DB9f straight-through cable (a whopping $4.00 at the time of this writing) and hook into the modem serial "console" port. To access the router admin screen, connect the cable between a PC (because most laptops don't have a serial port) and the modem, and (in Windows XP/2000) go to Start | Accessories | Communications | Hyperterminal. Then, (Windows 2000 only) enter an area code—you don't need it, but Hyperterminal doesn't know that and never will. Select "com3" for "connect using." In Windows XP this is simplified, and if you select com3, it doesn't require an area code. If the modem connects right away and asks for a login, it's the same as the web interface login. If the connection is stale, non-responsive, and 9 times out of 10 it will be, disconnect the power to the modem, wait a few seconds, and reconnect. Very likely, this will do the trick and the login screen will appear. If it is still unresponsive, check file | properties and hit "restore defaults" since this is the default communications method for most modems. If it is STILL not accepting keystrokes, power up and down again. Call the manufacturer if there is still a problem.

Now What?

After login, type "s i i" with spaces. This will show the configuration, and you should be able to make some determinations from it as to how bad the picture is. This will also show you what the LAN address actually is, and access through the web interface should be available on that port. Sometimes, for reasons of buggy firmware, the change to the LAN setting goes awry and the port defaults to a manufacturer setting that may be unknown. Typing "help" at this prompt will usually list available commands, with "config" being one of the more useful ones with which to become acquainted.

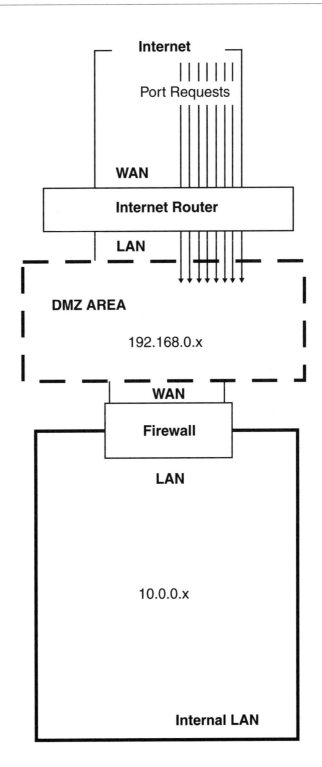

Figure 5.3
In this configuration, the router is set up to forward certain port requests to specific servers within the demilitarized zone.

In a typical arrangement, configuration settings and administrative screens would reveal that port 80 for web traffic is mapped to port 80 of a machine within the DMZ. This is useful because, should an attempt be made to open or "listen to" or "scan" other ports on the internal machine, it won't happen because they aren't there—they don't exist. The machine, except for port 80, is entirely invisible to the Internet. Additional ports, such as port 21 for FTP traffic or port 25 for e-mail Simple Mail Transfer Protocol (SMTP) traffic can also be mapped through the firewall.

A portion of this "hiding" may be achieved through NAT, where the headers of packets are converted to send IP packets bound for one address to another. It may also, in a more essential version of a DMZ, be achieved through port forwarding, where requests to a specific port on a machine are forwarded to that same port on another machine that, because of its configuration and services, may be more vulnerable to attack. The machine, a firewall, doing the forwarding should be considerably hardened. Port protection is very useful in that a machine simply sitting on the Internet is very vulnerable; it is actually impossible to close certain ports on a Windows machine!

A DMZ may also be as simple as the subnet space that exists between a firewall and a router. A router has as its LAN address 10.x.x.1, pinholes are set up in the router to allow access to machines within the DMZ subnet, and the firewall sits between the DMZ and the private LAN.

5.4.4   DMZ topology

Security, more than just a flavor of the day, is a constantly changing landscape, and as such, there are certain types of network addressing schemes that are so severely flawed that they hardly warrant mention, except, perhaps, to mention that they are inherently flawed. One such addressing scheme is called *standard NAT*. Or, to be blunt, "May as Well be Full Blown Passthrough" would be more accurate. Don't laugh—there are networks out there, with firewalls and with so-called *DMZs*, that have internal LAN machines configured with static (never changing) IP addresses. These are typically small or remote offices where NAT, subnets, subnet masks, and firewalls are poorly understood or where the administrator is naive and hails, perhaps, from a simpler time—the golden era of the Internet as it has been called (1991–1995). Or perhaps it is simply an office manager with some skill and little fear. Regardless, placing a PC with an external IP address directly on the Internet constitutes a much greater risk than anyone should ever take.

This author once had the experience of hooking up a new PC to one such network way back, back in the time of the Blaster Worm; within 30 seconds the virus scan and the RPC service had been compromised. Sometimes people aren't as familiar with the topology of their own networks as they like to think they are. There is no doubt that once cracked, these environments represent a wealth of opportunity for anyone of malevolent intent. A quick litmus test to determine if a network has standard addressing is easy. If the router does not have NAT enabled, the LAN and WAN port are the same, and the firewall (if there is one) has NAT enabled and Dynamic Host Configuration Protocol (DHCP) disabled, standard addressing must be in use. See the following list for a more comprehensive detail.

Truly, the only legitimate reason for a network to have this configuration is for leading-edge gaming where real-time responsiveness is required, security has zero relevance, or a firewall needs to be inserted with transparency in series with other devices that will negate the negatives of this architecture. The primary reason for setting up a network in this manner can often be attributed to the ease of setup, or out-of-the-box (OTB) configurations that were never changed.

Standard network addressing mode

Standard network addressing mode allows for the creation of a static subnet of public addresses on an internal LAN. It is not a recommended configuration and is listed here for identification and informational definition only.

- Router has NAT enabled or disabled. Some routers get confused if NAT is enabled and a LAN WAN IP address scheme is on the same public subnet. Many routers will assume an IP spoofing attack is underway and throw errors.

- LAN PCs are configured with the gateway as the firewall IP address.

- LAN PCs are configured with the same subnet mask as the fire-wall and with static public IP addresses.

- Firewall LAN subnet mask is the same as the internal LAN.

- WAN router address is the same as the firewall WAN address.

- All subnet masks are the same, everywhere.

Note:

> Some firewall and router configurations may have more elaborate or less controls that will either achieve the same results in a different manner or be unable to configure standard mode at all.

STANDARD NETWORK ADDRESSING FLAWS

- Ease of running continuous software directly against an IP to crack into it

- Quickness of crackability on discovery of exploit

- Ease of port listening to unencrypted traffic and associating that traffic with a specific user

- Once cracked, ease of remote management and accessibility because the IP addresses never change and are completely unique on the entire network

- Endless possibilities for reverse attacks (from the inside out)

- No restrictions, of any kind, on the sort of protocols emitted or received

- Ease of tracking users' web browsing habits

With a static IP address, tracking a user's web browsing habits is so easy that it truly is child's play. If an e-mail is sent from a particular computer with a static public IP address, chances are good that the IP address was included in the e-mail header. If a web user e-mails a company that has a web site, chances are good that the company will harvest information on a large scale so that it may track the success of its marketing initiatives, attach demographics to browsing patterns, and subsequently know who people are when they are visiting. This is not necessarily a bad thing if it is just one company using the personal info and it protects your privacy. *However,* many do not, and in the current Internet environment, once discovered, a web surfer's name and IP address and other demographic data will hit the ground running. Making sense of all the data is not child's play, however, and large data manipulation mechanisms known as *data warehouses* are implemented for exactly this sort of thing.

Network address translation

A lot has been said about NAT: some of it good, some of it bad, and some of it, simply put, untrue. NAT does not a firewall make. Most routers, in fact, do not a firewall make (and some do not even a router make). Digressions aside, NAT has its usefulness. Configuring NAT on a router means that the router will take all network traffic, entering and exiting, and alter the IP headers so that they go somewhere else. If, for example, inbound traffic is heading for 68.68.68.68, and the router is WAN IP configured to 68.68.68.68 with NAT turned on and a LAN-side IP of 172.20.15.12, all IP traffic headed for 68.68.68.68 will be routed to 172.20.15.12. The two are intertwined without bias. Additionally, a router with the most recent firmware upgrades will provide updated defense, through packet inspection, of hacking attempts in the network layer.

Network address port translation

Network address port translation is the router equivalent of port forwarding as accomplished by firewalls. It allows the designation of a particular IP address and port number combination, such as 68.68.68.68:80, to be redirected or translated to an internal IP address, such as 192.168.0.1:80. Translations such as these are called *pinholes* and are defined through router administrative screens. Pinholes are also context sensitive in that they expect certain protocols and will limit the protocols used. Some routers are fussy about which protocols bind to which ports and may not, inherently, allow certain more esoteric applications to operate.

DMZ drawback

A common drawback of the DMZ is not so much the reality but the perception that the maintenance and administration of a DMZ involves a higher level of difficulty and complexity. Administering and setting up a DMZ is no more complex a task for a knowledgeable administrator than configuring a new PC on the network. However, it does take longer to set up than a VPN, requires more machine resources, and is statistically a greater security risk.

5.5 Summary

The amount of work involved in creating a unique, custom-tailored approach to firewall security and policy should never be underestimated. Likewise, the benefits to a corporation of investing in a quality approach are infinite; these are the tools and the methods that some of the largest enterprises in the world are implementing. DMZ and VPN represent scalability in its purest essence. It is a two-edged sword, and it can and will cut both ways if it is not properly handled. There is a reason martial arts masters will not allow inexperienced students to handle edged weapons, and likewise, there is a reason that inexperienced administrators should stay away from the cutting edge of the network. An improperly configured firewall, VPN, or DMZ can gravely compromise critical and private data, can hammer the bandwidth to next to nothing, and can literally bring an operation to its knees while becoming a veritable "All ye who enter here: do not tread lightly." Look under every stone. Check every setting. Look at the log files. View the warnings. Change passwords often and change them frequently and then change them again. Implement RADIUS or similar technology. System administrators should be proven experts in RADIUS, tokens, card scanners (all of these are authentication methods), and above all, they should have verifiable experience in the management of a written, secured firewall policy.

Section III

Firewall Installation and Configuration

6

Installation Preparation

6.1 Chapter objectives

- Security options
- Choosing a platform
- Understanding ports and services
- Evaluating weaknesses
- Design and build or purchase

Once the decision has been made to invest in a firewall policy, there are many things to consider. Just like deciding to become a millionaire doesn't impart wealth instantaneously, deciding to have a firewall doesn't impart security instantaneously. The road ahead can be hard and filled with obstacles. And, just like wealth, a security portfolio (i.e., firewall policy) should be diversified. You should understand when to invest, when to act, when to consolidate, and when to diversify. "Flavor-of-the-day" security tools can actually be helpful when dealing with current threats that in time will no longer be an issue. The DoS attacks of 1998 through 2002 are one such example—firewall technology simply had not been designed with the possibility that someone would deliberately harness millions of computers with a virus and then attack a single network.

Since then, there have been many security threats, against both the physical and the cyber world that, in all their reprehensibility, were truly inconceivable, merely because sane people don't behave that way, don't reason like that, and typically can't even imagine a line of thought that is so far outside the human experience.

Of course, there are many so-called *reformed hackers* who are for hire, but one thing is certain: The truly disturbed madmen *aren't for hire*. Developing a rock solid firewall then becomes less about flavorful defense and more about where to build the cement bunker (figuratively speaking; it has been shown that cement bunkers offer very little, if any, added cyber security to a network firewall device. A nice bracket and a solid server rack do just as nicely).

6.2 Unbreakable walls

Perhaps it was the products of the 1970s that liked to leverage the concept of "unbreakable" that left consumers craving "unbreakable" things. However, everyone knows that if one of those "unbreakable" hair combs bent far enough, it would break. Any firewall appliance if not properly used, sited, or cared for will break. If the firewall is physically situated in a heavy traffic area and it gets bumped and falls off the shelf, it will most assuredly break. Much like a breakwater is built to tolerate crashing waves but will collapse if it is hit by a barge, a firewall can only be guaranteed to withstand certain types of attacks—barge strikes not being one of them. It is up to the administrator to understand the traffic patterns, the circumstances of the network mission.

The best way to prevent someone from breaking down a wall is to hide it behind another wall. If the wall can't be found, it can't be broken. Hands down, the most secure approach (and the most unfeasible in many environments) is to create a redundant network—one that pairs the LAN with an Internet-connected network. Each network coexists side by side, but there is no physical connection. The LAN would, actually, have no Internet connection or connection to other networks at all. It would be completely secure and, barring the introduction of wireless elements, should remain indefinitely secure. Realistically, larger organizations may have many firewalls and many networks living on one large extranet, intranet, or ouvrenet. An overlay-styled network, however, may have its own set of problems since, in practice, such a network would have an intrinsic inability to function properly as a communication tool. Aside from requiring that everyone (who needs Internet access) have two computers, and aside from doubling the equipment expense, the administrative efforts would also be doubled. Movement of information within such a network would be inefficient and burdensome. An overlay network is, for most of the population, unfeasible.

This brings the focus back again to hiding. A clever firewall hides things. It hides itself, hides its own ports, and effectively renders the internal network completely invisible. This can be accomplished by carefully selecting the firewall based on its capabilities, by installing it in the best location, and through the nature and type of operating system (OS). Not all OSs are created equal, but not necessarily for the reasons many people think.

6.3 Selecting an operating system

Whether building a firewall from scratch, purchasing a new firewall appliance, or taking an existing firewall and upgrading it, the OS of that appliance must be considered. Typically, an "appliance" comprises a UNIX box that has been hardened against particular types of interactions and certain services have been shut off or removed, and various types of ports have either been closed or operate in a stealthy mode and with reduced promiscuity. Only then will a machine be ready for use as a firewall platform, either as a hardened bastion or as a firewall software host, sharing its Internet connection and acting as a proxy.

6.3.1 Microsoft

Perhaps the most promiscuous of all OSs, Microsoft's OS—with its almost weekly and sometimes daily critical security updates—suffers from continuous discovery of security exploits. It is perhaps the worst choice of OS and perhaps one of the most difficult to harden. The list of services on a Windows XP system that can create vulnerabilities to external hacking, starting with Remote Procedure Call (RPC) as possibly the worst offender, would seem to be endless. The ease with which hacker-cracker software and methods can install, launch, and integrate services on the Windows platform is not merely frightening; it borders on irresponsibility on the part of its manufacturers.

But perhaps it is defensible. Windows is a very powerful OS, possibly the most powerful of them all because, with its plethora of available and native services, it is also extremely flexible. A service is usually a component of a Windows application/software. It runs in the background and usually runs regardless of the actual user account that is logged on to the system. The Code Red and Nimda viruses, in particular, exploited services that were running by default on user machines. Some viruses even install and awaken other services! But the ease with which new services can be installed and started is mirrored by the ease with which most services can be removed, negotiated, or configured. Furthermore, there is a preponderance of information available online from sites such as microsoft.com, expert-exchange.com, and annoyances.org. In and of themselves, these sites combine to provide an almost complete guide to configuring and customizing the Windows experience. Regardless, when placing a Windows server between a LAN and WAN as a firewall, extreme pains must be taken to apply critical security updates, manage file and system permissions and passwords, and find and subscribe to newsletters that discover and outline the latest security threats. The most common method of an intruder is to first compromise an exposed vulnerability and then use that "crack" to modify and subjugate additional services. For example, an intruder may crack open the RPC service and subsequently activate or install a Simple Mail Transfer Protocol (SMTP) service for the purpose of sending spam.

Navigating Windows services

Typically, the reason an administrator will choose to use a Windows system as a firewall is more one of ease and familiarity, a marriage of convenience rather than one of logic. Regardless of the reason, though, once the choice has been made, it must be supported. Here is a good place to start. Table 6.1 lists a few Windows services that must be disabled if and when a Windows machine is used as a firewall. With more than 60,000 ports and thousands of threats, listing them all would require more pages than there are trees.

Services can be viewed and configured in any Windows 2000/XP machine through the management console by right clicking on My Computer and selecting Management. If a Windows machine is to be used as a firewall, every single service that runs on that machine should be known and understood by the administrator—what its dependencies are, what its risks are, and if there is any chance that the service can be started by a successful crack into the system. It is a daunting amount of knowledge to obtain; Table 6.1 should provide a good starting point. However, this table cannot be said to be

Table 6.1 *Security Risking Services and Recommended Configuration*

Service	Port	Startup Setting	Risk	Note
Internet Information Services	80	N/A	Extremely high	Do not install, uninstall if installed
SNMP	161	Automatic	High	Uninstall/disable
Print Spooler	515	Disable	None	Needed by critical updates
SMTP		N/A	Extremely high	Do not install, uninstall if installed
FTP		N/A	Extremely high	Do not install, uninstall if installed
Background Intelligent Transfer Service (BITS)	Stopped	Manual or disabled	Nuisance	Possible software dependencies; disable at risk
Computer Browser		Disable		
Kerberos	750–754	Depends	Medium	Used by VPN technology
Security Accounts Manager		Disable	High	
SSDP Discovery service		Disable	High	
Telnet	23	Disable	High	
Terminal Services	3389	Disable or alter port used	High	Change port number (using regedit*) or use at risk
QoS RSVP		Disable		Some configurations may depend on this service; it is, however, a protocol service that opens ports on the machine and, as such, presents a security risk

*To access the registry editor, type regedit at the run prompt. In regedit, navigate to the key HKEY_LOCAL_MACHINE\SYSTEM\CurrentControlSet\Control\Terminal Server\WinStations\RDP-Tcp, and alter the value in the right-hand pane to a port value other than 3389. Further information is available online at isaserver.org.

complete because there are many services that run on machines; this list only covers a few services that are known and are extreme risks. And this table should not be used as a foundation for simply securing internal LAN PCs. This table is specifically tailored for a server dedicated for use as a firewall; that is, one that will receive firewall software to further harden the system. In and of itself, removing and disabling services *does not a firewall make*. When converting a machine for use as a firewall, the recommended procedure is to completely reinstall the OS from scratch. This is primarily because when software has been removed from Windows, it leaves behind *memories*—changed settings, modifications to dynamic link libraries (DLLs), executables, and other potentially dangerous file and system changes. It is best to start with a knowable premise rather than an unknowable one.

NTFS

In addition to the security of the ports, there are several other aspects of hardening an OS that should not be overlooked. Typically, most administrators are aware that NTFS allows far greater security of the file system than FAT. Format all drives with NTFS, without exception. Computers on the network that are FAT should be upgraded to NTFS without hesitation.

Services (Windows)

All services, generally, run under a default "system" account. Everything about how a service operates is configurable, including the service "log on." From the management console of any Windows 2000 or later machine, browse to the services console and right click on a listed service. From the Properties sheet, select the Log On tab, from which the log on can be controlled. Bear in mind, the configuration in Table 6.1 is for a dedicated firewall. Some services depend on other services that daisy chain throughout all the services. By clicking on the Dependencies Properties sheet, an administrator can work through any issues that may arise as a result of changing the log on of a particular service.

Windows XP (and Windows Server 2003) offers further understanding and configuration flexibility through a tool called the Services Controller (SC). The SC provides command line operability of all services and, to some a bonus and others a bane, scriptability.

The first question, upon review and use of this tool, is "Why? Why use this tool and not the perfectly acceptable administrative console?" The answer is that the console has a rather severe limitation: It only shows services in three states: stopped, paused, or running. This does not always actually portray the service in its true state, since there are four other modes of operation. Because of this, the administrative console may show that a service has stopped when it is actually "stopped-pending." The four other statuses are as follows:

- Continue pending
- Start pending
- Stop pending
- Pause pending

Even the net start command will show from the command line that a service is stopped when, in fact, it may be start-pending. Running SC.exe from the command line will show the true state of a service. This author has experienced a lion's share of headaches with Event Viewer errors caused by services thought stopped with the "net stop" command.

Further information about the nature of services can be obtained through the command line "portqry" command. This command does not, natively, install to the Windows command prompt. See the section Scanning for Vulnerabilities, later in this chapter, to learn more about how to install and use this tool to assist in the lock down of Windows.

UNDERSTANDING THE STARTUP TYPE OF A SERVICE

Further hardening of the OS may be necessary in cases where the firewall software requires certain services to be at its disposal. But how does one determine which services need to be configured, and how? It's all well and good to have a list to work from and to see how someone else did it, but without understanding the rigorous principles and without developing the skill to evaluate and introduce new services into the OS, an administrator is without the necessary skills to successfully administer a Windows firewall.

It may seem simple, but it's not. Things are not always as they seem on the surface, and descriptions provided by user interfaces are not always as straightforward as they may seem. The three startup types include manual, automatic, and disabled, each with its own set of quirks.

- Manual: Service starts on demand when requested by either a user or another service or software.

- Automatic: Service starts at boot up.

- Disabled: Service is turned off but can be set to manual by any user or software with the ability and the correct permissions. A better name for this would be "off."

The *hardened* approach involves the complete removal of unnecessary services, not just the disabling of them. SC.exe, natively available to Windows XP and available to other OSs through the Software Development Kit (SDK) from Microsoft, offers the administrator the ability to actually delete services. Here are some quick tips that will help with getting started using the SC:

- Run the SC by typing "SC" at the command window prompt.

- Never disable, delete, or otherwise interfere with the RPC service, because doing so will cause severe problems, and access to the administration tools to repair the damage will be impossible.

- Always make a copy of the system registry before making any changes to services through the SC.

- *Delete service name* will remove all calls to a service within the Windows registry. The only way to recover the service after deleting it in this manner is through restoration of a registry backup. *Don't do this to RPC.*

- To truly and completely remove a service, all of the file dependencies of the service must be removed by manually deleting .dll files.

- SC can be used to examine the services on another machine by including the Universal Naming Convention (UNC) path as follows:

```
c:\sc \\servername [command] [service name]
```

There are only a few Windows services that are, under all conditions, "hands off." This includes but is probably not limited to the following:

- RPC
- Windows Management Instrumentation
- Workstation

Further hardening of Windows

Much can be said, some good, some bad, about the security of a Windows server, and if this is the chosen route, then further information than is within the scope of this book should be sought. Much has been written on file system protection, and the use of NTFS as a security tool, changing of passwords, bios security, and segmenting a network are subject matters worthy of an entire book. These are all aspects of hardening a Windows environment that should be studied in depth before administering such a network.

6.3.2 UNIX

Currently, UNIX OSs are undergoing a renaissance of sorts. With the explosion of users turning to Linux (an open-source version of UNIX created and driven by Linus Torvald) as a Windows alternative, Unix has essentially gained a strong foothold in the OS marketplace. With its open source and open community of developers, flaws are discovered and repaired quickly. Many of today's appliance-based firewalls are Linux or UNIX based, prepackaged with firewall software, and hardened by firewall experts. Simply put, a UNIX firewall is to firewall deployment as fire hydrants are to dogs; it is the preferred method for disposal of unwanted network traffic byproducts. And this is the ultimate reason Linux and UNIX are better for security than Windows. There are many, many advanced and technical users who love to do nothing more than stress-test OSs. Frequently, these techs discover some flaw or vulnerability in an OS, and they may either report it to the manufacturer or use the flaw to start their own spam network. The temptation of having a network of many millions of computers at one's disposal is, for some, too great to resist. With Linux, it is a matter of community status to be the one who discovered and possibly even created a fix for a particular vulnerability. As such, flaws and vulnerabilities in Linux tend to be repaired much more quickly, reducing the possibility of zero-hour attacks.

Navigating UNIX services

As with Windows, a UNIX machine can come with its own set of inherent flaws. By its nature, however, a UNIX box is less vulnerable to intrusion. This is by virtue of how services are started and managed and how privileges are assigned. In the case of a selection of Sun as the OS for firewall deployment, a hardened version of the software comes preinstalled. Likewise, there are several Linux deployments, such as eSoft, that offer similar services. Hardening a UNIX-based system involves a greater and more technical skill set than Windows (again, another vote for Windows). For the purposes here of showing and demonstrating service vulnerabilities of an OS slated for firewall deployment, Red Hat Linux will be the OS of reference.

On any Linux box, the list of services can be obtained from either the command shell or the graphical user interface (GUI). Both the etc/inetd.conf file and the etc/services file can be affected to disable services, but simply commenting out a line of the etc/services file does not truly harden the system. The preferred method is to remove the service package by typing

```
rpm -e packagename
```

at the command shell prompt.

SERVICES (LINUX)

Two particularly dangerous services with long histories of exploitation in Linux are Sendmail and the rsh/rlogin/rcp utilities, in particular login, shell, and exec. The place to disable these is in etc/inetd.conf. They should be commented out (a number sign [#] comments out a line of code in a UNIX script) or removed completely. Typing *netstat –ta* at the command line will list all the services offered by the machine. Services such as telnet, FTP, mail, and identd should be disabled; they have no place on a firewall server.

Entering *netstat –an* will list all active Internet services; that is, it will list all services that are actively listening at a particular port for traffic to enter the system. Once a service has been disabled by commenting it out, inetd must be restarted or sent a hang-up (SIGHUP) signal to force the server to reread its configuration file.

Now, *netstat* is nice, and it will tell you if some process is listening on a particular port, but it will not tell you the name of the program running the service. Entering *lsof –I*, however, will list the command, the process id (PID), user, packet type, and protocol of each listening service. This information is invaluable in determining the strength of a system to resist penetration.

Most Linux distributions come with what is known as a Transmission Control Protocol (TCP) Wrapper Daemon (tcpd). This wrapper acts as an intermediary between TCP requests (almost all legitimate Internet traffic falls within the TCP stack of protocols) and the actual port server. By invoking a wrapper around TCP services—which means that all requests for TCP services are handled first by the wrapper and, if the host is legitimate, then tcpd passes the request to the real server—great control can be exerted over how requests are handled or if they are handled at all. However, TCP wrappers only protect services executed from inetd. When relying on TCP wrappers, care must be taken to ensure that other services are not running. If external access to certain services is necessary, an /etc/hosts.allow file must be created and configured.

Configuring tcpd to allow internal access to services is as simple as adding the line: *ALL:127* to the /etc/hosts.allow file and *ALL:ALL* to the /etc/hosts.deny file. TCP wrappers are the primary reason that Linux machines are considered by many to be easier to secure and, as a result, more secure than other more promiscuous OSs.

Services that are not run from the inetd usually originate in system boot. In these cases, each vendor is different, and to turn them off, research into the etc/rc.d1, d2, rc.d/d1, d2, or rc.d/rc1.d, rc2.d directories must be conducted. The numbers in these directories refer to run levels and contain links to programs that are active in the respective run level. Determine run level by using the *runlevel* command. To prevent a service from becoming active at system boot, remove it from the corresponding level into which the system boots at startup.

Many resources are available to help with the configuration (securing and hardening) of a Linux-based system. The previous descriptions merely provide a golden shovel for ground breaking. The real expertise comes from practice in implementation and in staying abreast of change in a very tumultuous environment (and career path).

6.4 Scanning for vulnerabilities

There are as many ways to penetrate types of networks as there are types of machine networks, multiplied by how many active and unfiltered ports are on those machines. There may exist networks that use only Simple Network Management Protocol (SNMP), that may have a need for only partial Internet access, or that may require the ability to host an over-net mail server (that is, a mail server that exists within a single private network that may be of global scope). Often, a single machine on a network (such as in a library or at point of sale) may require Internet access for the sole purpose of virtual private networking (VPN) with Point-to-Point Tunneling Protocol (PPTP) or Internet Protocol Security (IPSec) to an external resource.

Understanding this and opening only these protocols on a firewall will allow the site administrator to connect multiple computers over a wide area *without* compromising local security by enabling anyone with administrative understanding to open the computer to the web. If the firewall doesn't permit HyperText Transfer Protocol (HTTP), then users on the internal network can't connect to the web, yet the purpose and mission of the network is fulfilled.

At the social level, "scanning" for vulnerabilities merely consists of asking the right questions and understanding the environment, the mission, and the results needed by the organization leveraging the network. Only when the real critical needs of an organization are determined can a network analyst begin to frame out a solid set of firewall policy requirements and begin the process of physically ensuring that the firewall policy meshes with the social mission of the network. In a smaller network, this is not such an overwhelming task. But for a larger network, this may be truly daunting, especially if one's ability to delegate is constrained by the need for security that makes it necessary.

6.4.1 Searching for weaknesses

Beyond the socialization of firewall policies, there is the physical act of starting up various scanners and physically attempting to breach security. This step should be undertaken regardless of the firewall method chosen. Crackers are constantly scanning and searching the Internet for IP addresses running services that can be exploited. They search for ports that are active—and a port is only active if some service or software is running on that port, actively "listening" for requests.

Ensuring that there are no services running unfiltered on these ports can be easily determined. Aside from sites such as grc.com that provide a legitimate service and will scan your IP address for any vulnerable ports, there are also tools that can be downloaded and installed locally. This is particularly desirable because nobody wants to hook up an untested firewall to the Internet for the purpose of testing.

Linux comes with a tool called *netstat* that can be used by a machine to scan itself. The section UNIX, Services (Linux), earlier in this chapter, goes into some detail regarding the use of this tool for the purpose of securing Linux. Windows 2000/XP installations do not, out-of-the-box, offer the Windows equivalent of *netstat*—portqry.exe (PortQry Command Line Port Scanner version 2.0). It is a self-extracting compressed file and must be first downloaded from Microsoft's web site and, once unpacked, placed into the /Windows/ directory. A very thorough knowledge base article (832919) on Microsoft's web site is available and offers a very comprehensive overview of *portqry* capabilities. *Portqry* is quite powerful, and in addition to allowing a machine to scan itself, it can also scan other computers (see Figure 6.1 for the stages of testing using port scanning tools).

Portqry.exe is, however, quite slow, and scanning a large number of ports can be extremely time consuming. For example, to scan ports 1 through 1400, the following command line expression must be entered:

```
portqry -n [hostname] -p tcp -r 1:1400 -l log.txt
```

This command will query the name (-n) ([hostname]) with TCP as the protocol (-p) and log (-l) to log.txt. It will also take a very long time to complete if the operation is against a remote host. A final test of a firewall may be to run this command against the firewall from a remote location. In such a case, it could take most of a day to run. Typing *portqry* from the command line with no switches will show the full help page for the command; it is useful and should provide a

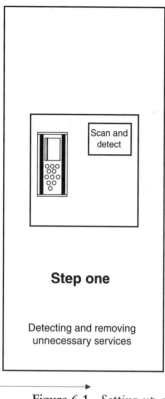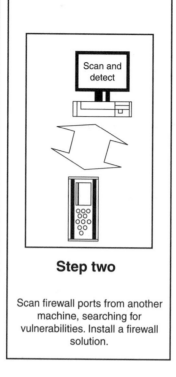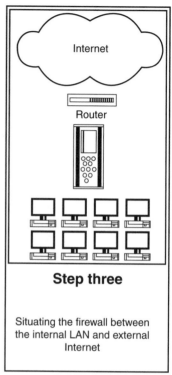

Figure 6.1 *Setting up and testing a firewall involves several steps. A firewall computer must have an active network connection to actively scan ports for weaknesses.*

full understanding of the power of this command. Here is a sample output from a log file generated by this command:

```
PortQry Version 2.0 Log File

System Date: Sun May 02 13:37:40 2004


Command run:

portqry -n 192.168.1.153 -p tcp -r 1:200 -l log.txt

Local computer name: ETHASCELLIS

Querying target system called:

192.168.1.153

Attempting to resolve IP address to a name. . .
```

```
IP address resolved to ethascellis

querying. . .

TCP port 7 (echo service): NOT LISTENING

TCP port 8 (unknown service): NOT LISTENING

TCP port 9 (discard service): NOT LISTENING

TCP port 10 (unknown service): NOT LISTENING

TCP port 11 (systat service): NOT LISTENING

TCP port 12 (unknown service): NOT LISTENING

TCP port 13 (daytime service): NOT LISTENING

TCP port 16 (unknown service): NOT LISTENING

TCP port 17 (qotd service): NOT LISTENING

TCP port 18 (unknown service): NOT LISTENING

TCP port 19 (chargen service): NOT LISTENING

TCP port 20 (ftp-data service): NOT LISTENING

TCP port 21 (ftp service): NOT LISTENING

TCP port 22 (unknown service): NOT LISTENING

TCP port 23 (telnet service): NOT LISTENING

TCP port 24 (unknown service): NOT LISTENING

TCP port 25 (smtp service): NOT LISTENING

TCP port 135 (epmap service): LISTENING

========= end of log file =========
```

The first step to take with logged results is to look for "listening" items. These items need to be researched and possibly shut down, removed, or filtered. The above results are abbreviated from a Windows XP system that has been partially hardened to prepare it for firewall installation. The following results are just a few ports after installation of the firewall:

```
portqry -n 192.168.1.153 -p tcp -r 1:200 -l log.txt

Local computer name: SCORELLIENT

Querying target system called:

192.168.1.153
```

```
Attempting to resolve IP address to a name. . .

IP address cannot be resolved

querying. . .

TCP port 7 (echo service): FILTERED

TCP port 8 (unknown service): FILTERED

TCP port 9 (discard service): FILTERED

TCP port 10 (unknown service): FILTERED

TCP port 11 (systat service): FILTERED

TCP port 12 (unknown service): FILTERED

TCP port 13 (daytime service): FILTERED

TCP port 16 (unknown service): FILTERED

TCP port 135 (epmap service): FILTERED
```

Note: | Portqry will not yield accurate results when run from the local host with a firewall on the local host. For best results, run from another computer on the same local network as the firewall. See Figure 6.1 for variations of scanning techniques. It will not run on a computer that does not have an active network connection; at least one other computer will be needed.

These results clearly show that the firewall has inserted itself between portqry and the targeted ports. Often, the first step of a cracker will be to arrange a host of machines that will first scan within a certain range for IP addresses using an automated pinger, such as Angry IP Scanner, and second, once a host is found, will scan that host for unfiltered services. It is clear from the above results that, regardless of filtering performed by a firewall, a cracker can still make many determinations about a system. If an exploit becomes known and spreads across the cracker underground community—usually like wildfire—then any system running the compromised service on the port, firewall or no firewall, may be vulnerable.

Because of the previous results, port 135 is known by us to have the epmap service running on it. Better safe than sorry! Even the very best firewalls have vulnerabilities just waiting to be discovered. The best approach is to eliminate these services completely and reduce the firewall down to the bare essentials needed for the purpose of the network it is trying to protect.

In addition to these tools, many types of scanners are available for download from reputable sites. Things such as port scanners, testers, and IP range scanners are very common and, if investigated carefully, can add a valuable resource to any administrator's toolbox. Care must be taken, however, because hackers have been known to post infected tools—they know that administrators want to use the same tools they use to test their systems. Creating fake tools that are actually Trojans and worms to be downloaded by system administrators is yet another avenue of attack. Never download a tool from a web site without a Domain Name Server (DNS) entry (a domain name such as www.google.com) or from a web site that merely provides a link to the software's executable on an FTP server with only a numeric IP address as its referrer. Always search for the original author's site, and even then exercise judicious care, scanning the file with virus scanners and testing it in a sterile environment.

Note: | The epmap service is the service that the infamous Blaster virus leveraged in its assault. It can be disabled by most software or by disabling the dcom services in the services panel.

6.5 **Summary**

Building out a homegrown firewall, an effort of noble proportions, should not be undertaken lightly. In an ideal situation, there will be a test machine with the same configuration as the firewall, where change can be introduced and tested before promotion to the production firewall. Installing software on a machine where machine services have been removed and disabled can sometimes lead to serious problems—problems that could create gaping holes in a firewall. An administrator, armed with the unique knowledge of threats posed within her environment and with a comprehensive understanding of firewall technology, should be able to successfully engineer an effective firewall policy.

7

Firewall Configuration

7.1 Chapter objectives

- Defining firewall security objects using process mapping and social querying
- Using tracert/route to validate and troubleshoot demilitarized zone (DMZ) and firewall configuration
- Differentiating trusted and untrusted networks
- Using packet analysis to sniff for security breaches

Chapter 6 illustrated the need and the methods of hardening a firewall system to protect it from exploitation. This chapter assumes that a firewall server has been built, its operating system (OS) has been hardened, and firewall software has been installed that will allow further flexibility and management of traffic passing through the firewall. This next step identifies and explicates the process through which an enterprise may define its mission as it pertains to monitoring and modulating IP traffic, and how measurement of that definition is possible.

7.2 Defining firewall security objects

An object, as defined within this section, means any piece of equipment or software with a communication need to traverse the firewall. Identifying such objects within a large enterprise-scale network may require that a checklist or questionnaire be developed to discover them. This may appropriately be considered an *object discovery process*. But discovery of a process should not immediately be cause to enable it. A network security specialist is not an *enabler*, and such actions would risk exploitation and subsequent resource compromise on any number of levels. A security specialist plays an advisory role as one who understands the enterprise mission and the pros and cons of performance impact and knows how to socialize these concerns interdepartmentally.

Beyond initial discovery, the needs and evaluations of various protocol allotments may be incorporated within the network mission through a process of evaluation, or *post object discovery evaluation*. This should be undertaken at an operational level commensurate with impact. If protocol mapping will require bandwidth and precedence allotments that exceed network bandwidth, a greater level of approval than simply that of the department manager will be necessary. Departmentally, need must be evaluated and bandwidth parceled accordingly. This author assumes that if gateways are managed, this area of implementation may not be as important interdepartmentally but still may be of concern within a particular subset of an enterprise that shares connections.

Finally, creating a policy map that reconciles firewall policies with physical addresses is critical to the maintenance process. Future troubleshooting, error decoding, and understanding the complex traffic patterns that emerge in this process will depend on the generation of an accurate policy map. Figure 7.1 is a sample policy map.

7.2.1 Object discovery process

Creating an object discovery process can be as simple as asking the right questions, reviewing software catalogs, or taking inventory. It may also include ongoing and active use of packet analysis in a fluid and deterministic method of bandwidth allotment. Unusual or esoteric software applications, from communications tools to financial monitoring packages, may have special, nondeterministic attributes and requirements. Developing a comprehensive list of all network traffic protocols that are passed throughout a secure LAN may or may not be an option. Volatile networks may be more prone to abrupt and constant change, things that can make true security nearly impossible. Such a network should focus on segregation and creation of specialized network segments that can be isolated and

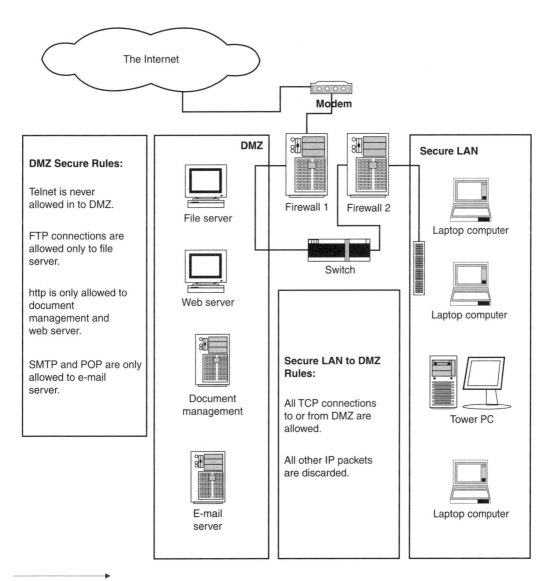

The Internet

Modem

DMZ Secure Rules:

Telnet is never allowed in to DMZ.

FTP connections are allowed only to file server.

http is only allowed to document management and web server.

SMTP and POP are only allowed to e-mail server.

DMZ

File server

Web server

Document management

E-mail server

Firewall 1   Firewall 2

Switch

Secure LAN to DMZ Rules:

All TCP connections to or from DMZ are allowed.

All other IP packets are discarded.

Secure LAN

Laptop computer

Laptop computer

Tower PC

Laptop computer

Figure 7.1 *Attached to protocol policies in a bird's eye view demonstrates a possible policy map, with physical routings of perimeter security rules.*

routed away from sensitive information (more on this in the section Identifying Trusted and Untrusted Networks, later in this chapter). An initial round of sniffing to root out the environment is critical. It probably won't cost anyone their job, but shutting down a port on someone who depends on it to complete their work will only build ill-will. Many programs, such as the Javvin Packet Analyzer 4.0, offer sensible pricing and optional support packages and provide inexperienced users with a clear understandable interface for creating a policy map. Detecting protocols that are used, and subsequently querying the user about the purpose and need of discovered protocols may seem innocent enough, but bear in mind that people can be defensive about their work, and questions of this sort should be handled with some discretion. **A general announcement that network administration plans to investigate application protocols for network security purposes should pave the way.**

7.2.2　Post object discovery evaluation

The TCP/IP protocol is the foundation on which 6 of 7 layers of the Internet network architecture is based. As such, there are many suites of protocols within the TCP/IP protocol. In the Open Systems Interconnection (OSI) 7-layer model, created by the International Organization for Standardization (ISO), there are families of protocols called *suites,* and these, in turn, are used by various layers of the OSI model. Some protocols are used on more than one layer and may appear to be subsets of another protocol, yet appear side by side with that protocol on some protocol maps. Making sense of and developing a complete understanding of the 7-layer architecture and the protocols begins here and never ends. Many times, when there are "worms" that traverse the Internet and crack security wide open, it is because someone has discovered a vulnerability in the software that "listens" at a port for a particular protocol. The worm uses the vulnerability to gain access and control of a computer, and subsequently install itself and then pass itself on to other computers. Now, all packets that are on the Internet are either User Datagram Protocol (UDP) or TCP/IP packets, but within these "suites" are hundreds of *application layer* protocols, such as Simple Mail Transport Protocol (SMTP) or Dynamic Host Configuration Protocol (DHCP). If a firewall does not offer or permit filtering and blocking of these application protocols, then it's not really a firewall; it is a router.

It is important in the evaluation process to clearly identify every port and protocol that an organization uses. New applications should be tested in an isolated environment to ensure compliance and to ensure that junkware does not install additional, undesirable communication components. As wonderful as it may seem to software and hardware marketers, a software component that sends a message to them every time a printer is low on ink does not constitute networking best practices.

7.3 Scanning the firewall and fixing vulnerabilities

Two primary tools, in addition to other tools mentioned in this book, can serve you well when testing and fixing vulnerabilities in a live perimeter. All networks consist of paths made up of equipment, lines, and signals. Tracing out these paths and ensuring that nothing is spilling into places where it shouldn't be verifies hardware and line security. Examining traffic, looking at IP headers, and observing the ports that are requested by incoming packets all involve application security and bear a heavy social component.

7.3.1 Tracing the routes

Using the policy map as a guide, all connections to all servers should be traced and mapped out. Network paths that are separate should be verified as separate, and in addition to tracing, visual and physical inspection of equipment should be periodic; after all, a CAT5 cable costs about $6.00 at Best Buy.

From a command prompt in both DOS and UNIX, the command to trace a routing path, *tracert* (DOS) and *traceroute* (Unix), allows administrators to determine the actual path through the firewall (or not!) from one computer to another. Many times when troubleshooting a firewall, *tracert* will reveal that the actual path through the system, from one machine to another, is slightly different than expected. Microsoft's DOS *tracert* diagnostic utility sends echo packets to the destination. As the packet reaches each router along the path, its time-to-live (TTL) value is decremented. When TTL values reach zero, the router experiencing the truncation returns a Time Exceeded message back to the point of origin. *Tracert* reports back to the screen or to a file each object encountered along its route. For example, running the command

```
c:\files\tracrt www.yahoo.com > trace.txt
```

yields the following results:

```
Tracing route to www.yahoo.akadns.net [216.109.118.65] over a maximum
of 30 hops:

 1    2 ms    1 ms    1 ms    192.168.0.254

 2   22 ms   20 ms   20 ms    adsl-6xx-2xx-2xx-x.dsl.chcgil.ameritech.net [xx.xx.xx.xx]

 3   21 ms   23 ms   22 ms    dist1-vlan50.chcgil.ameritech.net [xx.xx.xx.xx]

 4   21 ms   21 ms   21 ms    bb1-g8-3-0.chcgil.ameritech.net [xx.xx.xx.xx]

 5   22 ms   22 ms   20 ms    bb2-p11-0.chcgil.ameritech.net [151.164.191.182]

 6   22 ms   21 ms   22 ms    ex1-p3-1.eqchil.sbcglobal.net [151.164.240.150]

 7   25 ms   22 ms   22 ms    asn3561-cwusa.eqchil.sbcglobal.net [151.164.248.134]

 8   22 ms   22 ms   21 ms    dcr2-so-4-3-0.Chicago.savvis.net [208.175.10.237]

 9   39 ms   39 ms   39 ms    dcr1-loopback.Washington.savvis.net [206.24.226.99]

10   39 ms   39 ms   39 ms    bhr1-pos-10-0.Sterling2dc3.savvis.net [206.24.238.38]

11   40 ms   38 ms   40 ms    216.109.65.54

12   38 ms   39 ms   39 ms    vl31.bas2-m.dcn.yahoo.com [216.109.120.146]

13   38 ms   39 ms   39 ms    p2.www.dcn.yahoo.com [216.109.118.65]

Trace complete.
```

Note that *xx* represents IP addresses that have been masked to protect the privacy of this author's home network.

Notice in the previous set that there is a long name followed by an IP address in brackets [ ]. Using the –d switch will return a result set that is cleaner and easier to review:

```
Tracing route to www.yahoo.akadns.net [66.94.230.37]

over a maximum of 30 hops:

Tracing route to www.yahoo.akadns.net [66.94.230.37]

over a maximum of 30 hops:

 1        9 ms    2 ms    2 ms    192.168.0.254

 2       18 ms   21 ms   21 ms    xx.xx.x.xx
```

```
3       28 ms      26 ms     20 ms     xx.xx.xx.xx

4       24 ms      22 ms     20 ms     xx.xx.xx.xx

5       32 ms      23 ms     25 ms     151.164.191.182

6       22 ms      23 ms     28 ms     151.164.40.26

7       21 ms      25 ms     22 ms     151.164.248.246

8       71 ms      72 ms     72 ms     216.115.98.13

9       73 ms      74 ms     73 ms     66.218.64.134

10      73 ms     100 ms     78 ms     66.218.82.230

11      74 ms      74 ms     74 ms     66.94.230.37
```

Trace complete.

Adding a *–h 40* switch increases the number of maximum hops to 40. Other switches can be used. For details, type *tracert* at the command prompt with no parameters.

The > trace.txt option on the *tracert* command drops a text file into the current directory (c:\files\) and outputs the results to that file. Results will not print to the screen with this option. Beware that in a complicated trace, the screen may appear to "hang" as this command runs. If there is doubt, run the *tracert* first without the > filename.txt option and then run it again and dump it to a file. This option is especially useful when dealing with external resources that may not want to admit that something on their end malfunctions. An e-mail with a *tracert* output file attached has a great deal of persuasive powers. Here is an excerpt from an actual header from a UDP packet used in a *tracert* with a total time to live (TTL) of 24:

```
Packet Info

Packet No.: 00000004

Packet Size: 207 bytes

Timestamp: 2004-05-12 10:27:29.274

Ethernet Header

Destination: 00.90.4B.41.88.55

Source: 00.00.89.11.FC.9A

Protocol: 0x0800
```

```
IP Header - Internet Protocol Datagram

Version: 4

Header length: 5 (20 bytes)

Type of service: %0000 0000

Precedence: 000. .... (Routine)

Delay: ...0 .... (Normal delay)

Throughput: .... 0... (Normal throughput)

Reliability: .... .0.. (Normal reliability)

Total length: 193

Identification: 0x5c68

Fragmentation Flags: %000 0x0000

Reserved: 0.. (Must be zero)

Don't fragment bit: .0. (May fragment)

More fragments bit: ..0 (Last fragment)

Fragment offset: 0 (0 bytes)

Time to live: 24

Protocol: 17 (0x11)

Header Checksum: 0x7b9e (Correct)

Source IP Address: 192.168.0.254

Dest. IP Address: 192.168.0.6 (ethascellis)

No IP Options

UDP - User Datagram Protocol

Source Port: 53 (domain)

Destination Port: 3773

Length: 173 bytes

Checksum: 0x2ad2 (Correct)

Application Layer Data (Display as plain text)

Data Length: 165 bytes
```

A particular type of Internet Control Message Protocol (ICMP) packet (there are 13) called ICMP_ECHO_REQUEST is used in the tracert operation. It also requests or attempts to provoke an ICMP TIME_Exceeded response at each hop. Both the UNIX and the DOS version work similarly, but how does the trace return to your screen each step of the way? Simple: It sends the first packet with a TTL value of 1, a second with a TTL value of 2, and so forth for however many hops it has been configured, until it reaches its destination. After each stop, TTL values are decremented, so a packet with a TTL value of 1 will only make it one hop; it will return an ICMP error packet with header information about the hop. The default number of hops is usually 30. Interestingly, UNIX traceroute offers a –I switch that will change the protocol to ICMP. It's unclear how that is achieved, because ICMP is more of a routing protocol, and UDP a transport. Perhaps it is for the purpose of explicating usage of ICMP as the routing protocol, in the event that some router would choose to not comply or return a different protocol.

Sometimes, strange results may be observed and paths may not seem to flush out the way that they should. One of the ways that this can happen is because, in an environment where there are many routers, switches, and servers, patch cables may have been put into place that may serve a purpose for the moment but later serve only to create a link between two routes that preferably wouldn't be there. A thorough trace can reveal such things because packets tend to traverse the path of least hops. Adding a firewall adds an extra hop, and if it can be avoided by taking a different route, packets will surely take the shortest route. This would not be the case with packets that are routed through a managed gateway that uses routing tables to send packets of a particular type from a particular origination to a designated destination. A forgotten patch cable is one of the most common forms of network insecurity; it is also one of the easiest to detect (usually it can be spotted with a sharp set of eyes by looking around a bit).

For example, FYI 7.1 offers additional information about Internet routing and protocols. Routers are software and hardware devices that connect nodes across a network. Regardless of the physical and data link layer protocols that are used, routers are able to communicate and pass information. They are dependent only on network layer protocols, although many have web interfaces for easy configuration. Such a router would also require access to HTTP traffic.

→
FYI 7.1 *Routers and the Transport Layer*

The protocols of the Internet network layer are strictly UDP and TCP/IP. They ride the world on a carriage of routers, relays, switches, hubs, and servers. Routers are the backbone of this communication system, and they can be equipment devices consisting of hardware and firmware, or they can be software that runs on a bastion server. These routers all serve one purpose: to connect computers all over the world in, well, a global network. Even a communication satellite can be reduced to a very powerful router with a very strong solar-powered receiver and transmitter.

The Confusion

There is much confusion around the protocol barnyard. Protocols and abbreviations are slung about with little regard for who is listening. They are often used improperly or accused of doing things that they don't (and couldn't) do. Because of this, something as simple as TCP/IP is not really understood by a large number of people.

TCP is the Transmission Control Protocol and IP is Internet Protocol, but what does that really mean? The letters are there, they stand for real words, but on the surface, it just doesn't make sense.

Transmission Control Protocol is, essentially, a protocol—a set of *rules*—that governs the *how* of an Internet Protocol transmission. In other words, TCP defines how IP packets will be received and understood. Or, more appropriately, it dictates that they *will* be received and understood . . . . IP is the carrier wave, and TCP is the crystal ball that puts the pieces back together in a cogent picture. Whenever a message (a file, an e-mail, whatever) is sent across a network, it is chopped up into possibly thousands of tiny pieces. These pieces may actually be routed via different paths within the network, and logically sequenced packets may arrive discordantly. IP ensures that they all arrive where they are supposed to arrive, intact. TCP puts them back together. TCP is a transport protocol, and IP is a network layer routing protocol. Confusing TCP and IP is like confusing the telephone wires with the signal. The two are not the same.

Almost all protocols within the TCP/IP suite use IP and TCP to transmit and receive packets. The exceptions may use only one or the other, and they are rare.

Part of the confusion is that IP is a protocol, and it is usually defined as IPv5/6 within the TCP/IP suite under network layer routing protocols, as are other protocols, such as ICMP (the error protocol) or RIP. There are six layers of the OSI standard, and all six of them use protocols that are subsumed by IP. Additionally, TCP and UDP are defined as transport layer protocols.

7.3.2 Perimeter packet analysis

There are two components to packet analysis: *capture* and *analysis*. In addition to the protocol analysis, *reconstruction* of the packets is a desirable feature, especially in perimeter security. Sniffer is the leading brand in packet sniffing, but use of tools such as Sniffer and Wildpackets requires weeks of expensive training. Add in the cost, and these tools can run anywhere from $2,000 to $40,000, and it may be that such tools don't provide the level of reconstruction desired or are too expensive. They offer many features and toolsets that are clearly outside the scope of establishing a secure perimeter; they are troubleshooting and trouble-finding tools and are perfectly qualified for this sort of work. Just bear in mind that they require a great level of expertise.

Some may say there is a *monitoring* component of analysis. Really though, monitoring entails just doing capture and analysis simultaneously. Many system administrators avoid undertaking packet analysis because, facing the facts, it is a difficult and confusing subject that once learned needs to be practiced and studied frequently. Many people consider it nearly an art form, a discipline in and of itself.

There is a ray of hope, however. Packet analysis tools are becoming more powerful, easier to use, and less expensive. In 2001, a decent packet capturing and analysis tool costed almost as much as an expensive workstation from Dell and extremely difficult to use. With the growing popularity of open source and Linux, there are some new and emerging tools that are worth looking into. Snort from snort.org is completely open source and offers the ability to capture all TCP/IP packets that pass through a network. It also has a very comprehensive set of documentation and a published book. However, it (like many other packet capture tools) requires additional software, comprehensive expertise, and much training to decipher and render the captured packets as useful data. Tools such as Barnyard and SnortaLog provide such analysis and are often used in tandem with capture tools to provide real-time security, alerting users to attacks as they occur.

For most administrators, purchasing a tool that offers a consolidated interface for analysis, monitoring, and capture is the ideal solution. Key requirements of a packet analysis tool include the following:

- Packet capture of all TCP/IP packets
- Packet filtering
- Export of indeterminate packets
- Packet analysis of at least TCP/IP, UDP, HTTP, HTTPS, SMTP, POP, TELNET, and FTP
- Ease of use and integration with other software (such as Internet Explorer and Outlook) where needed

Packet analysis and monitoring are routine tasks on any large network. Many of the more experienced system administrators will already have a favorite analysis and capture tool, and some of them have even written entire books on their use. The Javvin software, so far, is the only reasonably priced and comprehensive sniffing and analysis tool on the market. It offers plain-English views of all TCP and UDP headers, as well as packet reconstruction at the application level for the most common application protocols. Future releases of this software may allow reconstruction of instant messages; as a comprehensive and affordable security and monitoring tool, both socially and technically, Javvin meets or exceeds most requirements.

7.4 **Identifying trusted and untrusted networks**

There is nothing, nothing, about the Internet that is trustable. Eavesdropping at a port is almost child's play. With a little indiscretion, discontent, and a healthy dose of disregard for federal and state laws, a small investment in software and equipment and some IP addresses, anyone can sit and watch everything that passes over the Internet.

Note: | The Internet is not a trusted network.

7.4.1 **The firewall stops here**

By this time, it should be clear that at least 50% of a firewall policy is social. LAN users need to be trained in security policy. Conveying a clear understanding of firewall capabilities is the first step in successfully delineating trusted and untrusted networks. Whether this training occurs in a classroom format, an occasional casual briefing, or in a handbook is purely subjective. It depends on the environment. Regardless, the content of the knowledge base is the same. This brief list of items illustrates the many ways in which firewall security can be completely bypassed:

- E-mail is never secure.
- HTTP (web) sites are never secure.

- Clicking an unexpected attachment, no matter who it is from, is strictly prohibited.

- Files from office computers and files from home computers should never commingle.

- Home computers used for work should be held to the same standards as office computers.

- A computer not owned by the enterprise should never be connected to the enterprise.

Establish clear and understood consequences. Without understanding the consequences of their actions, users will click on anything. For example,

- Clicking on attachments can introduce harmful viruses, worms, and Trojans into the network, even a protected network can get sleeper viruses and spyware that will cause extreme difficulty when they activate.

- The firewall, if it has been skillfully configured, will detect and stop traffic from these viruses from escaping, but it will not protect internal bandwidth from choking.

- Downloading applications from unknown and untrustworthy web sites can introduce new and unpredictable vulnerabilities that can destroy network performance and trash a computer.

- Some employers dock employee pay when spyware and adware hotels have to be removed, equivalent to the cost of removal.

- Halting the spread of Trojans that have gained access and subsequently repairing damage caused by a rogue computer is expensive, with costs that can in some cases never be truly gauged.

- Lost productivity, missed opportunity, damaged OSs and software, compromised corporate data, and damaged reputations are only some of the effects that clicking on a single harmful attachment can unleash on an enterprise. In particular, beware last day mischief. Some employees, on their last day of work, decide that every rule ever put in place may now be broken. For this reason, it is advisable to either ask an employee to take their last day off on the day before their last day, or to simply cut off their Internet access.

Allowing oneself to be distracted by web site pop-ups and banner ads that boast of free tools is *hazardous*. Establishing a clear verbal or written policy regarding these things is an essential part of mapping out a comprehensive security policy. These "free" things, and any that follow suit, may be socially engineered attempts to infiltrate otherwise secure LANs:

- Offers of free DVDs
- Free virus scanners
- Date managers
- Screen savers
- Download tools
- Music file sharing
- "We have detected your computer is vulnerable . . ."
- Etc. . .

Users must understand what a firewall can and can't do. There is a razor's edge between trusted and untrusted. User *knowledge* walks on that edge. (Wear hard-soled shoes!)

7.4.2   Creating trusted networks

In some cases where resources are shared, two networks may "overlap" in a way that creates some security risks. For example, in a university environment, it may be necessary to create a student computer lab that exists on the same network as the administrative network. Sometimes, printers, scanners, and other equipment may need to be shared between two networks. Creating policies that reflect this need and the need for privacy and that show how this privacy will be achieved is not only a useful foundation for deployment, but it serves as an excellent tool for budget defense (if ever needed). The administrative network would be considered a trusted network, whereas the student one should be considered a hostile untrusted network. It must be protected from the Internet. At the same time, other networks must be protected from it as though it were as dangerous as the Internet. A simple litmus test to distinguish a trusted network from an untrusted one includes the following:

- Sensitivity of data: segregate sensitive data
- Promiscuity of user base: Multiple, potentially anonymous users on a single machine in a single day would be a highly promiscuous machine.
- Uncontrolled access to machines: A reception computer may not be a trusted network device.
- Risky software development practices. Isolate!
- Unsecured previously known compromised areas

Organize the network accordingly. From a chaotic mash of trusted and untrusted computers, multiple networks can emerge. Subsequent organization and policy mapping will allow a higher level of security.

7.5 Summary

There are many harsh realities involved in deploying a security policy. There is a certain level of privacy that many people perceive that they have with their computers. This is an illusion, and it shouldn't be encouraged. The Internet is no more private (in fact, even less so) than the watery trenches at Wrigley Field. Establishing a security policy, mapping it to firewall functions, and deploying it successfully can be successfully executed by first creating a process and then following that process. Half of that success is contingent on the introduction of a well-formulated socialization approach. The other half depends on the careful scrutiny and construction of the physical hardware components and software configuration.

Section IV

Supporting Outgoing Services Through Firewall Configuration

8

Simple Policy Implementation

8.1 Chapter objectives

- Firewall traffic control and policy configuration
- Understanding port orientations
- Web access control and filtering HTTP sites
- Allowing/disallowing dynamic content on dynamic port ranges

Everything about a firewall is about traffic control through the opening and closing of ports or the filtering and inspection of traffic. This is done, as discussed in the previous chapter, through policy management. This chapter, and Chapter 7, provides *in situ* deployment tactics. Read both of them to gain a comprehensive understanding of deployment conditions. Having developed a policy and an understanding, it is time to ensure that the firewall reflects that understanding accurately.

There are many, many types of traffic. It would be an epic task to write a comprehensive transport lexicon. More purposeful, perhaps, would be to review the most common types of traffic that often require special handling. The phrase "open up a port" has been used quite generously in this book, and herein explains exactly what that means.

In many enterprise environments, such as large law firms, corporations, consultancies, and manufacturing support facilities, the requirement exists for Internet connectivity. We've discussed, at length, the risks of opening up a network to the Internet. The focus, so far, has been on the transport and network layers. This chapter moves up a level, shifting the focus to the application layer.

8.2 Policy configuration

As mentioned in Chapter 7, a firewall policy is a physical manifestation of a business need. Particular types of network or application protocols may be deemed counterproductive to business objectives. As such, the firewall is the place where business objectives become practical reality.

8.2.1 Interface

A firewall has two avenues of approach: LAN and WAN. Traffic requests may originate from either side, and as such, policies must be developed that correspond to each side. For example, HTTP traffic may be permitted from the WAN side, but not from the LAN. Denying LAN HTTP traffic would, effectively, prevent an employee from setting up a web server and running a competing business from his desktop. This happens mostly in large offices where supervision is loose and firewall access controls are never configured. A common question that arises with respect to "closing ports" has to do with the way in which a server and a client negotiate a connection. Most people, initially, think that port 80 on the server talks to port 80 on the client. This is not the case. Below are three sample packet headers from a secondary HTTP packet:

1.

```
TCP - Transmission Control Protocol

Source Port: 80 (http)

Destination Port: 4889

Sequence Number: 0x00d85110

Ack Number: 0x80c3aef7

Offset: 5 (20 bytes)
```

2.

```
TCP - Transmission Control Protocol

Source Port: 80 (http)

Destination Port: 4882

Sequence Number: 0xf334bc6b
```

```
Ack Number: 0x80b372d6

Offset: 5 (20 bytes)
```

3.

```
TCP - Transmission Control Protocol

Source Port: 80 (http)

Destination Port: 4890

Sequence Number: 0x00d92fee

Ack Number: 0x80c434a6

Offset: 5 (20 bytes)
```

Clearly, the port on the client (*Destination*) computer is port 3762. This is a random number between ports 1024 and 65535 selected by the requesting agent. Closing port 80 on the LAN side to all HTTP traffic will, therefore, not block internal users from establishing port 80 connections to external servers. RFC 2616, the standard for HTTP 1.1, is interesting reading and contains more information about the behavior of the protocol. RFC 793, for example, details TCP/IP. Many of the Request for Comments (RFC) document series contain useful information. They are the ultimate authority on the manner of behavior for many aspects of the Internet Protocol.

8.2.2 Source

Additional control over the source IP address may be required. Simply put, this allows highly localized control over "trouble spots." Oftentimes, this can be applied to a particular problem spot where a computer may be engaging in some inexplicable, yet harmless, protocol transmissions. A policy that targets a particular IP address can be useful in balancing load usage or simply preventing undesirable activity. Don't micromanage your firewall, though! Care should always be taken to address as many issues at the macroscopic level as possible.

8.2.3 Destination

In the context of a policy configuration, a destination will be either the LAN or the WAN. For example, the source for Point-to-Point

Tunneling Protocol (PPTP) may be set to *Any* and the destination set to the WAN IP address of the machine. Simultaneously, on the LAN side, a policy may be configured for the purpose of preventing internal machines from acting as mail servers—a common tactic of viruses. Such a policy would have a LAN destination, with a source of *Any*. Actual restriction of the port and protocol would be configured under Services.

8.2.4 Services

There are many services, such as FTP, HTTP, PPTP, etc., that are preconfigured for convenience on firewalls. These services are well known, and may or may not be cause for concern. Much depends on established business policies. However, there may be a case where, through the use of a sniffer, an unusual level of activity is noticed to be traversing between particular ports. An administrator of a highly secure network may want to immediately disable this traffic. If the service is already defined, then the configuration of a custom policy will immediately put an end to the trouble. If it is not, then there are several pieces of information that must be obtained from the packet header:

- Protocol
- Source port
- Destination port

Most firewalls present protection from the perspective of defending against the external world. Yet, a custom policy may be applied to either an external or an internal traffic pattern. What this means is that the configuration of a custom policy is done from either the frame of reference of an *inbound packet* or an *outbound packet*. If the packet being examined is an inbound packet, the source and destination will be one way, and if it is an *outbound* packet, then the source and destination reverse themselves.

Some firewalls may not explicitly define the context of *inbound* or *outbound* and *primary* or *secondary*. Figure 8.1 demonstrates that typically the world of connections is viewed from the point of view of the firewall. However, this may not always be the case, as some manufacturers, in a misguided effort to oversimplify administration, have

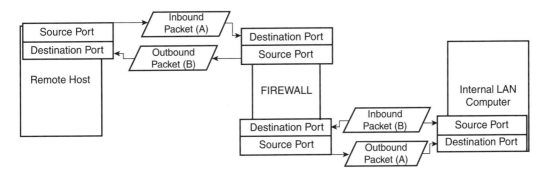

Figure 8.1 *Many firewalls are egocentric. Regardless of context, all packets directed at the firewall are referred to, within the administration utilities, as Inbound. This orientation is with respect to the firewall. In this diagram, inbound packets to the firewall from the external server become outbound packets to the internal LAN computer. Inbound Packet (A) becomes Outbound Packet (A), and on the right side, Inbound Packet (B) becomes Outbound Packet (B).*

been known to regard *all* traffic that is heading toward the LAN as *inbound*. In these cases, trying to decipher which way is which from the firewall perspective is a matter for simple experimentation. If the illicit packets are still flowing after the rule has been created, delete the policy and recreate it with the numbers transposed. It's usually a good idea to restart a firewall after a policy has been deleted. Oftentimes these configurations are made to text-based configuration files that are only examined on startup.

8.3 Supporting HTTP

HyperText Transfer Protocol is a very lightweight, application-level protocol that is used globally. According to w3c.org, Tim Berners-Lee invented the world wide web in 1989 when he wrote the first www client and the first www server. He wrote the first GUI browser called *"WorldWideWeb"* and it allowed for color and inline images. It wasn't long after that the National Center for Supercomputing Applications (NCSA), in Champaign, Illinois, came out with their own version of a web browser, called Mosaic. As a youth, this author had the amazing opportunity to spend an entire day testing the prototype of Mosaic. Not very many people at the time really knew or cared about any of it, however, since Mosaic hadn't really hit the marketplace yet.

Later, the creators of Mosaic would splinter from the NCSA and attempt to form their own company and launch Mosaic as a brand. However, the NCSA fought and won rights to the product and the name, and subsequently it sold the rights to Microsoft. There is more, much more to that story, and it is a shame to reduce it to a single paragraph, but this a book about firewalls, not software development intrigue.

Historically, the relevancy of these facts pertains to the main reason HTTP has become one of the primary business application communication protocols that exist. For nearly 15 years, since its inception, HTTP has been and continues to be a protocol that captivates with its simplicity while carrying the flexibility of scale to provide a worldwide architecture of communication. The list of applications that are able to interoperate with and generate HTML pages is staggering.

Nearly all, if not all, commercial firewalls provide the capacity to either permit or deny HTTP traffic. Ones that don't are not true firewalls.

8.3.1 Web access control

A typical firewall may have an administrative utility that allows for a web proxy server. This feature, often called *Web Access Control,* allows the system administrator to manage and control each user's Internet access privileges. Through this utility, the administrator may enable general web access by filtering, disabling, enabling, and requiring password protection. He may also enable logging to monitor and track usage. These are the types of tools that allow the administrator to create and effectively administer an *acceptable-use policy* in accordance with business requirements.

With a proxy server enabled, the firewall stores web pages on its local hard drive. This is especially useful because these files are then available to other users as needed or requested.

Use of the password feature will typically require that each web browser be configured to use the firewall as a proxy. This prevents the user from "clearing" his or her cache to mask Internet activities; all activity is logged and recorded with the username on the firewall.

Other types may allow for automatic detection of the proxy settings based on the gateway in use. Additionally, site filtering products that are designed to prevent access to particular sites or types of sites may be run on the firewall as plugins that are context sensitive to either individual users or groups of users. Web site lists may also be created where, if a user enters a URL that is not on the list, the filter will block access to the site.

Site filtering is not dependent on the creation of individual user proxies. A good firewall will allow for the creation of separate site lists, Deny and Allow, which are universally applicable. For example, an employer may want to limit employee distractions by denying access to a particular site that employees may be accessing to check their personal e-mail. Such a filter should include all computers to prevent "desk hopping." Other categories of sites that may be filtered include criminal activities, games, sex sites, drugs, hate sites, finance, sports, gambling, and news. If it's an addiction, there is a category for it and there will be a service available to either help people find it or prevent people from getting to it. Black lists that are subscription based are common and, when used judiciously, can benefit productivity and reduce outages.

Policy creation is an integral component of web access. For web access filtering to work, a policy has to be created, either automatically by the system or manually by the administrator. This policy will direct outbound HTTP traffic to a Web Access Control module on the firewall; the web site will, therefore, be filtered (prevented) at the *request* level.

8.3.2 HTTP as a policy

As mentioned previously, in addition to Web Access Control, HTTP must also be configured as a policy. The creation of a policy in a firewall, though differing technically between various firewall products, generally consists of several areas of interest. Typically, an HTTP policy would be created on the WAN side of the firewall. Web Access Controls are usually configured in tandem with a policy that creates a rule to pass all outbound HTTP requests to the Web Access Controls. A firewall that is servicing multiple subnets will require individual policy creation for each subnet. Where a policy is not created for a subnet, it is likely that the subnet will default to the default rule. Defaults for traffic are almost always set to *Any*.

HTTPS

HyperText Transfer Protocol Security (HTTPS) is an encrypted derivative of HTTP. It allows for the secure movement of HTTP traffic across the web. It would take many computers and many days, if not years, to crack a secure certificate. A good firewall will allow for independent differentiation in control between the two protocols.

8.4 Dynamic content

When a computer talks to another computer, the rules of Transmission Control Protocol (TCP) break the connection into two components: a primary and a secondary connection. The initial connection is made to the standard port, such as port 80 for HTTP, and the secondary, subsequent TCP connection occurs on one of a range of dynamically assigned ports (1024–65535). This is the *dynamic port range* of the TCP network layer.

The manner, or the mechanism, whereby a firewall will or won't pass through traffic on this dynamic range may or may not be a function of your firewall. If there is a list of questions that could be compiled, listed in order of importance, "will it or won't it accept dynamic port, secondary TCP connections?" ranks near the top of that list. For most types of activities such as simple web browsing, an inability to configure dynamic port ranges is not an issue. However, if a firewall cannot manage these types of connections, many dynamic content services, such as Net Meeting (see FYI 8.1), will need to be accommodated. This may mean hours of special handling and painful configuration that, in the end, may render a colander-like appearance to enterprise security.

Firewalls that permit configuration of dynamic range policies will adapt to the deployment area with greater ease than some of the more basic proxy-styled firewalls. Configuration of a dynamic range will require the following settings:

- Port or range: 1024–65535
- Type: TCP
- Direction: inbound

FYI 8.1 *Details of the Net Meeting Firewall Requirements*

Most providers of dynamic content services will provide technical materials detailing firewall configuration requirements.

Net Meeting and Configuring a Firewall for Delivery of Dynamic Content

Net Meeting, a Microsoft service, requires the use and configuration of several TCP ports. To enable Net Meeting, which offers program sharing, Whiteboard, Chat, file transfer, and directory access, a firewall need only allow primary TCP connections on established ports. However, the audio and video features will require secondary TCP and UDP connections in the dynamically assigned port range. Firewalls that only allow primary connections will not permit the audio and video features. An organization's security policy and firewall capabilities will determine the final configuration. Table 8.1 lists the ports, functions, and connections used by Net Meeting.

Table 8.1 *Net Meeting Port Requirements*

Port	Function	Connection
389	Internet Locator Service	TCP
522	User Location Service	TCP
1503	T.120	TCP
1720	H.323 call setup	TCP
1731	Audio call control	TCP
Dynamic (1024 – 65535)	H.323 call control	TCP
Dynamic (1024 – 65535)	H.323 streaming	Real-Time Transfer Protocol (RTP) over UDP

The ports listed in Table 8.1 must be configured to pass through primary TCP connections on the static ports, as well as secondary TCP and UDP connections on dynamically assigned ports (1024–65535).

Figure 8.2 demonstrates the sequence of events that lead to the establishing of a Net Meeting event. The result is that the firewall creates two dynamic ports on both the LAN and the WAN side of the firewall.

Continued

8.5 **Summary**

Conclusively and clearly grasping all the ins and outs of packet traffic, the types of traffic, the protocols, and the passing and controlling of connections requires much study and hands-on experience to be truly understood. Setting up a firewall is almost always an enterprise-wide effort, and maintaining the policies that are generated can be very time consuming. However, for some, the intrinsic

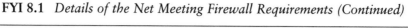

FYI 8.1 *Details of the Net Meeting Firewall Requirements (Continued)*

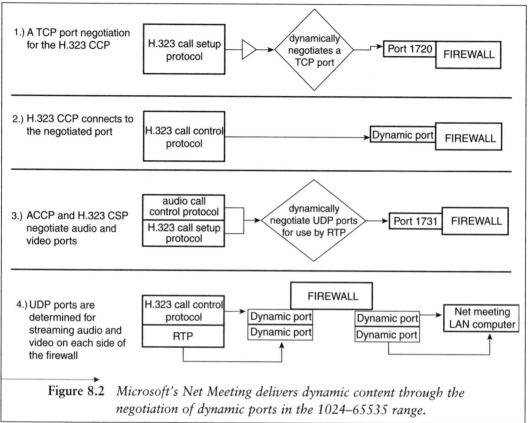

Figure 8.2 *Microsoft's Net Meeting delivers dynamic content through the negotiation of dynamic ports in the 1024–65535 range.*

reward of developing and maintaining a profound firewall solution lies in the exercise of philosophy, technical skill, management ability, social skills, and time management. Success in this area of IT bears the fruits of the labor: It is a much loftier and worthier task as opposed to the alternative—the desperate and frenzied activity of constant desktop support calls where the technician is not so much a valued member of a team as merely someone to blame.

Remember, *users will click on anything*. Opened ports or poorly managed firewall solutions merely present even more opportunities for click-happy people to, well, be happy. In this, the technical world, Nana of Babylon can be *anyone*.

9

Complex Web Services Management

9.1 Chapter objectives

- Understanding protocol vulnerabilities
- Vulnerabilities of wireless access
- Streaming audio and video
- FTP and Telnet

Each of the many application protocols possesses inherent weaknesses. There is a battle zone raging on the Internet; you can't see it, and you can't hear it, except in the occasional cubicle groans or shouts for desktop support personnel. Traffic of the highest criticality is deeply encrypted and passed from firewall to firewall, with each firewall offering independent reception of the encryption. Open keys are never passed. Other application protocols ride piggyback across these encrypted "tunnels" of Point-to-Point Tunneling Protocol (PPTP) or IP Security (IPSec) or L2P and provide slow but secure transfer of data. However, despite these precautions, malware applications pass cloaked datagrams inside of HTTP, disguise themselves as other protocols, search for open ports, take over operating systems, and redirect critical traffic.

It's a war, and it is a war with no clear lines; on some issues, this book doesn't even take a stance. Some networks will want to allow traffic that other networks would consider highly destructive and disruptive; they spend thousands of dollars to *prevent* the exact protocols this book explains how to permit. To come out and say, "This protocol is bad, never allow it!" wouldn't be appropriate.

Regardless of whether it is wanted, the administrator's job is to provide security. So often, though, despite all the best efforts, undesirable channels of communications are established, and sensitive information gets exposed to the elements. But Internet communications have their own special set of vulnerabilities that must be considered. Much like a chain of dominoes, a packet of information falls across the Internet as a series of relays. Each router in the chain receives the packet and then retransmits it to the next link in the chain. If that router happens to be mirroring all of its traffic to a single port connected to a computer with a packet analyzer, then your unencrypted information has just been compromised. Often, the most convenient location for unsightly network components is the phone room or a maintenance room. Getting access to these rooms is not a problem for anyone posing as a maintenance worker. With a little knowledge of operations and a couple of dropped names, even a supposedly secure telephone room in a bank may offer walk-in access. This author knows of a room in one particular branch of a major bank where the door to the communications room frequently stays propped open with a fire extinguisher.

Then where should the security focus be? A firewall policy is, of course, as much a policy about locked doors and equipment locations as it is about software and protocols. But beyond locked doors and firewall policies, certain risks warrant a serious look at the protocols going out the door.

Failure to pay attention to the activities of these protocols can have dire consequences. Here are a few of the bad things that can happen if things like Telnet, FTP, POP3, gopher, finger, etc., are left open:

- Denial of Service (DoS) attacks

- Compromise of sensitive passwords and login information

- Network traffic redirected away from intended recipients

- Intercepted e-mail

- Theft of corporate data, files, databases, programs

- Loss of bandwidth

- Interruption of service

- Staged attacks—attacks launched from your system that make you look like the perpetrator

Note: Many of the port numbers that are assigned to well-known services can be viewed in the services file in the windows/system32/drivers/etc directory. When in doubt, this file offers a good starting point to discovery. This file lists the well-known services—it does not list the services that are in use by your computer. Microsoft provides no such convenience.

9.2 Telnet

Telnet access allows remote access to computers via a command prompt, or shell, style of access. Both UNIX and Windows systems run services that allow this style of access.

Both the Windows command (DOS) window and Internet Explorer offer the ability to run Telnet. To start Telnet in a command window, simply type *telnet servername* at the prompt. The computer will then attempt to request the Telnet service from port 23 of the host server. If Telnet has been disabled, it should not respond. If it has been enabled, you will be prompted for a login and password. Many servers offer free Telnet access to anyone who comes knocking. For example, the Library of Congress provides a free library research service that uses Telnet access to search catalogs and legislation copyright information. It is accessed by simply typing *telnet locis.loc.gov* at the command prompt.

The Telnet protocol sends passwords and login in clear unencrypted text. As such, the decision to allow Telnet access to internal computers must be one made with extreme caution, because it is unsafe. The locis.loc.gov telent site does not even bother to prompt the user for a login or password.

9.3 FTP

Perhaps the great grandfather of all protocols (because it is one of the oldest and should, by all accounts and reasoning, be dead), File Transport Protocol (FTP) specifies the mechanism whereby files may be transferred from the file system of one server to another. It is a client/server protocol that requires the installation and setup of FTP server software. It requires FTP client software on the client computer as well as a software service running on the providing server. Ipswitch offers a shareware FTP program, as do most web browsers.

Both UNIX and Windows offer command prompt FTP access as well, although the DOS version is basically a bad joke, at best. IIS, Apache, and Netscape web server products offer optional services to provide FTP capabilities.

If external trusted access needs to be established through the firewall, then great care must be taken to configure the FTP server properly so that it may run securely. Since FTP lacks encryption capabilities, this basically means that FTP, as known and loved, cannot be run as it is usually run: wide open to the Internet.

Note:

If an NT server with FTP access shares a FAT-formatted volume, it cannot be made secure.

In many cases, disk access is best permitted only over a secure IPSec or PPTP encrypted tunnel. In other words, if the firewall creates a secure point to point tunnel using Point to Point Tunneling Protocol (PPTP) and the external user joins the network, FTP access in an intranet style would be feasible. Direct directory browsing offers another option, but it involves far greater bandwidth consumption than FTP directory browsing. If a remote computer attaches to another network via PPTP, we call this style of connection a Virtual Private Network (VPN). Computers on a VPN may browse the directories of shared network drives simply by typing "\\xx.xx.xx.xx (the IP address of the target computer) into either a web browser or an explorer window. FTP over a secure tunnel is the *only* way to implement secure FTP, short of using entirely different products and methods that offer the same outcome—the transfer of files. Where bandwidth usage is critical, or scarce, FTP browsing offers a light-weight alternative.

9.3.1 The role of FTP

What purpose does FTP serve? It allows the creation of drop-box–styled archives where information can quickly be retrieved or distributed. It is quick and allows the transfer of files in a hybrid environment, where perhaps Macintosh, UNIX, and Windows machines coexist. Anonymous access, unless desired, should also be removed. On a Windows server, these features, and many more, are available and can be configured through the management console. Access by a right-click on My Computer | Manage and then drill into Services

| Internet Information Services | Default FTP Site. Right-click to access properties. A good book on Internet Information Services (IIS) will have several chapters devoted to this topic.

9.3.2 FTP access

There are several types of login access that can be established when setting up an FTP server. In UNIX, if secure FTP is desired, there are commercially available FTP products. In Linux, the FTP service is configured through the /etc/inetd.comf file. Suffice it to say, neither Linux nor UNIX offers a standard secure version of passing FTP passwords and logins. Furthermore, if the FTP service is enabled, it automatically grants access to the FTP directory to any (this host) machine account.

Regarding Windows, FTP logins and passwords may be based on NT security. Built-in security then provides a secure method of authentication. Passwords and logins will not be compromised. However, anyone running a packet sniffer can capture and decode any and all files that are transmitted. This is because the session itself does not encrypt traffic.

9.3.3 FTP sessions

When an FTP client connects to a server, a request is passed to port 21 for a TCP session. If there is, in fact, an FTP service "listening" at the port, a TCP connection is established that remains in place until it either times out from lack of activity or the client or the server requests a disconnect. Port 21 provides the control circuit for the connection. Port 20 provides data transfer of either American Standard Code for Information Interchange (ASCII; the standard used by software and computers to interpret Latin characters from machine binary. There are 128 standard ASCII codes, each represented by a seven-digit binary number: 0000000 through 1111111) or binary data. It opens and closes only when data are transferred.

FTP client computers, much like HTTP, have ports dynamically assigned to them. Again, as in the previous chapter, these port numbers are assigned in the 1,024 to 65,535 range. Observation of activity with a packet sniffer will reveal these ports, which may be different for each file that is transferred. The control port, on the client side, will be dynamically assigned but will stay the same for as long as the connection remains open.

9.3.4 **FTP and firewalls**

In Windows, passing FTP port requests through the firewall to an
FTP server in the demilitarized zone (DMZ) is probably the best
security solution. A business requirement for an FTP service to a
known and trusted audience means that the FTP server may have
Windows authentication enabled and IP address–restricted lists.
Having the restricted list won't, of course, stop a hacker from trying,
and if there are many open ports, simultaneous and repeated
requests to all the ports from many machines simply increases the
risk of a successful penetration once the hacker guesses a trusted
IP address. However, for less commercially visible enterprises, the
risk is a calculated one: One must calculate risk and make a
judgment call. Should absolute security, with all files encrypted, be
necessary, then some sort of Secure FTP (SFTP) server should be
purchased.

9.3.5 **Netstat**

No discussion of Windows FTP would be complete without discussion of the *netstat* utility. This utility allows administrators to
observe active FTP connections and accompanying activity. At the
command prompt, enter *netstat –p tcp*. This will show all active connections, listing their protocol, local address, foreign address, and
state (active or inactive). Local address and foreign address will also
show the port number in use.

9.3.6 **FTP security**

Conclusively and clearly, FTP of neither the Windows nor the UNIX
flavor is secure. FTP lacks the ability to encrypt anything; logins and
passwords are sent in clear text. In an environment with high threat
anticipation the greatest danger comes from the inside when an IT
manager believes, for any extended length of time, FTP can provide
a viable and secure file transfer solution.

9.3.7 **Alternatives**

Without question, FTP is a vital part of operations for any web site,
remote office, or organization that wants to share files across the

Internet without giving away the keys to the kingdom. And here we are, telling you not to use it. Alternatives exist. Many sites, where security is not a wholesale concern, continue to use FTP to upload changes, download files, etc. Many sites get defaced also, but that is neither here nor there. The most intelligent choice is to, instead, create site user logins. Create (or purchase) utilities that allow transfer of files over HTTPS. Web site directories are entirely capable of using Windows or Digest Authentication to permit access to a directory, and on the server side, these directories can be mirrors where the directory index default file name/type is set to "none" (this will allow directory browsing, even when an index file is present). VanDyke Software (www.VanDyke.com) offers a comprehensive suite of SSH FTP security products. It also boasts a secure shell (SSH1 and SSH2) product for both Windows and Unix that offers Telnet-styled terminal emulation.

9.4 Handling port numbers

Much has already been said, and much more will be said, regarding port numbers. Earlier, reference was made to a file in the Windows system folder that lists port numbers and related protocols and services. Here is that file, listed for your convenience:

```
# Copyright (c) 1993-1999 Microsoft Corp.

#

# This file contains port numbers for well-known
services defined by IANA

#

# Format:

#

# <service name>  <port number>/<protocol>  [aliases...]
[#<comment>]

#

echo            7/tcp

echo            7/udp

discard         9/tcp    sink null
```

```
discard 9/udp sink null

systat 11/tcp users #Active users

systat 11/tcp users #Active users

daytime 13/tcp

daytime 13/udp

qotd 17/tcp quote #Quote of the day

qotd 17/udp quote #Quote of the day

chargen 19/tcp ttytst source #Character generator

chargen 19/udp ttytst source #Character generator

ftp-data 20/tcp #FTP, data

ftp 21/tcp #FTP. control

telnet 23/tcp

smtp 25/tcp mail #Simple Mail Transfer Protocol

time 37/tcp timserver

time 37/udp timserver

rlp 39/udp resource #Resource Location Protocol

nameserver 42/tcp name #Host Name Server

nameserver 42/udp name #Host Name Server

nicname 43/tcp whois

domain 53/tcp #Domain Name Server

domain 53/udp #Domain Name Server

bootps 67/udp dhcps #Bootstrap Protocol Server

bootpc 68/udp dhcpc #Bootstrap Protocol Client

tftp 69/udp #Trivial File Transfer

gopher 70/tcp

finger 79/tcp

http 80/tcp www www-http #World Wide Web

kerberos 88/tcp krb5 kerberos-sec #Kerberos

kerberos 88/udp krb5 kerberos-sec #Kerberos

hostname 101/tcp hostnames #NIC Host Name Server
```

```
iso-tsap 102/tcp #ISO-TSAP Class 0

rtelnet 107/tcp #Remote Telnet Service

pop2 109/tcp postoffice #Post Office Protocol - Version 2

pop3 110/tcp #Post Office Protocol - Version 3

sunrpc 111/tcp rpcbind portmap #SUN Remote Procedure Call

sunrpc 111/udp rpcbind portmap #SUN Remote Procedure Call

auth 113/tcp ident tap #Identification Protocol

uucp-path 117/tcp

nntp 119/tcp usenet #Network News Transfer Protocol

ntp 123/udp #Network Time Protocol

epmap 135/tcp loc-srv #DCE endpoint resolution

epmap 135/udp loc-srv #DCE endpoint resolution

netbios-ns 137/tcp nbname #NETBIOS Name Service

netbios-ns 137/udp nbname #NETBIOS Name Service

netbios-dgm 138/udp nbdatagram #NETBIOS Datagram Service

netbios-ssn 139/tcp nbsession #NETBIOS Session Service

imap 143/tcp imap4 #Internet Message Access Protocol

pcmail-srv 158/tcp #PCMail Server

snmp 161/udp #SNMP

snmptrap 162/udp snmp-trap #SNMP trap

print-srv 170/tcp #Network PostScript

bgp 179/tcp #Border Gateway Protocol

irc 194/tcp #Internet Relay Chat Protocol

ipx 213/udp #IPX over IP

ldap 389/tcp #Lightweight Directory Access Protocol

https 443/tcp MCom

https 443/udp MCom

microsoft-ds 445/tcp

microsoft-ds 445/udp

kpasswd 464/tcp # Kerberos (v5)
```

```
kpasswd 464/udp # Kerberos (v5)

isakmp 500/udp ike #Internet Key Exchange

exec 512/tcp #Remote Process Execution

biff 512/udp comsat

login 513/tcp #Remote Login

who 513/udp whod

cmd 514/tcp shell

syslog 514/udp

printer 515/tcp spooler

talk 517/udp

ntalk 518/udp

efs 520/tcp #Extended File Name Server

router 520/udp route routed

timed 525/udp timeserver

tempo 526/tcp newdate

courier 530/tcp rpc

conference 531/tcp chat

netnews 532/tcp readnews

netwall 533/udp #For emergency broadcasts

uucp 540/tcp uucpd

klogin 543/tcp #Kerberos login

kshell 544/tcp krcmd #Kerberos remote shell

new-rwho 550/udp new-who

remotefs 556/tcp rfs rfs_server

rmonitor 560/udp rmonitord

monitor 561/udp

ldaps 636/tcp sldap #LDAP over TLS/SSL

doom 666/tcp #Doom Id Software

doom 666/udp #Doom Id Software

kerberos-adm 749/tcp #Kerberos administration
```

```
kerberos-adm 749/udp #Kerberos administration

kerberos-iv 750/udp #Kerberos version IV

kpop 1109/tcp #Kerberos POP

phone 1167/udp #Conference calling

ms-sql-s 1433/tcp #Microsoft-SQL-Server

ms-sql-s 1433/udp #Microsoft-SQL-Server

ms-sql-m 1434/tcp #Microsoft-SQL-Monitor

ms-sql-m 1434/udp #Microsoft-SQL-Monitor

wins 1512/tcp #Microsoft Windows Internet Name Service

wins 1512/udp #Microsoft Windows Internet Name Service

ingreslock 1524/tcp ingres

l2tp 1701/udp #Layer Two Tunneling Protocol

pptp 1723/tcp #Point-to-point tunnelling protocol

radius 1812/udp #RADIUS authentication protocol

radacct 1813/udp #RADIUS accounting protocol

nfsd 2049/udp nfs #NFS server

knetd 2053/tcp #Kerberos de-multiplexor

man 9535/tcp #Remote Man Server
```

Firewall administrative utilities often offer a configuration screen that is used for the purpose of allowing and disallowing these application protocols. Here, the application protocol and protocol name (User Datagram Protocol [UDP] or TCP) can be entered along with the destination and source ports. Source and destination ports for protocols such as FTP are configured as follows. Typically, administrative screens offer the ability to either place the range as xx-xy in a single field or allow definition as an <u>xx</u> to <u>xy</u> range. They may allow the source port—the port requesting the connection—to be defined as *Any*.

- Name: FTP
- Protocol: TCP
- Source port: any
- Destination port: 20-21

Alternatively, separate services may be set up for each connection. Some configurations may work better in one firewall than in another.

9.5 Deploying Real Audio

Much like any of the other services and ports described in this and previous chapters, Real Audio relies on the intrinsic ability of computers to receive and assign communications to ports and ranges of ports. Configuring Real Audio does present an opportunity to understand, at a greater depth, some of the configuration options available.

9.5.1 Outgoing versus incoming

If a Real Audio server is deployed within the DMZ of a business, the connections should be set up as follows on the external facing firewall.

TCP port 7070 is a client port used by the remote computer to initiate the connection with the external RealServer. It authenticates the player to the server and acts as the control connection, or channel, much as port 21 does for FTP. It handles pause, stop, play, and other actions. Incoming connections to the firewall will have no reason to access this port. However, if internal access to real audio is desired, internal computers must have this port open. If internal computers are running personal firewalls, or if the internal facing firewall is configured to block requests with certain source ports, then creating a service and an accompanying policy will be required on both the internal facing firewall LAN side and the DMZ facing side of the external facing firewall.

UDP is used by the RealServer for the data connection. RealServer uses two custom application layer protocols, Real Time Streaming Protocol (RTSP) on port 554 and Progressive Networks Audio (PNA) on port 7070. HTTP is also used for some data.

Note: UDP is a one-way–only connection protocol. Unlike TCP, this protocol does not perform error checking, so it is much faster than TCP and, though less accurate, can deliver streaming data much more efficiently.

Some firewalls (or their administrators) strictly prohibit all forms of UDP traffic. Bearing this in mind, RealServer allows for its protocols to work across either UDP or TCP.

9.5.2 Flexibility

Real is flexible, and if firewall monitoring is an ongoing activity, observation of a RealServer trying to connect to a network may almost look like a hacking attempt. *Any port in a storm,* and Real is no exception. This breakdown of the connection process elucidates the various actions that a RealClient will take to attempt a connection to a RealServer. Clearly, the main concern of a firewall administrator will revolve around allowing or disallowing Real access from the internal network to the Internet.

Note:

> By its nature, its aggressive tactics, its advertising niche, and its redundancy, to some people Real presents a very real threat to internal security. It gobbles bandwidth usage, distracts employees from work, and buries itself very deep in the registry, and certain functions can be very difficult to disable. Tea Timer from Spybot will show the Real installer attempting to place itself into the startup long after installation.

A control connection is established, attempted first using port 554 (RTSP) and then port 7070 (PNA). If TCP on 554 is restricted by the firewall, the client will attempt to hide what it is doing by cloaking the TCP in an HTTP wrapper. Devious? Maybe. Devious is as devious does. This is called *HTTP cloaking,* and Real doesn't have the monopoly on this practice.

If the firewall is smart, it sees this happening and puts the kibosh on it. The client's next attempt will be to download the REAL file via HTTP download. This is where user quotas can come in handy; someone who is consuming vast amounts of bandwidth can be allotted a certain quota per day, and once that is exceeded, all connectivity terminates.

Usually, however, the RealServer host will not want to permit an HTTP download, because then the client will have the entire file, which may be in violation of the copyright. Or, if it is a live broadcast, the "whole file" may never actually exist.

In a case where Real traffic is to be permitted, the control channel on 554 opens, with UDP on 6,970 through 32,000 as the protocol of choice for the data stream. If UDP is not allowed, the client will attempt to use TCP on 554 and will cause a much greater stress on bandwidth. The thicker and heavier TCP protocol uses much more bandwidth for the exact same transmissions as UDP. This can, conceivably, bring the network to its collective knees.

If the request is for live content, three options are attempted by the client. First, the client attempts a multicast type connection. A special attribute of particular firewalls allows multicast so whether or not this connection type succeeds depends on the firewall. If multicast is not available, the client will attempt to open a UDP channel for RTSP or PNA on ports 6,970 through 6,999. If UDP is not allowed, the client falls back on TCP over port 554.

9.6 Summary

Many legacy technologies, such as FTP and Telnet, have been rendered obsolete not only by emerging replacement technologies and methodologies, but more so by the dire need for increased security on the Internet. Unfortunately, when it comes to FTP, this industry-wide problem continues to propagate. "Obsolete" begins to describe these technologies, but much like a chicken with its head cut off, FTP does not realize it is dead yet. Macromedia, Microsoft, et al. continue to develop software products with embedded FTP abilities.

The solution, as with many things that are popular, but not right, is to hold a steady course and spend wisely. Ultimately, the direction product development takes boils down to market demand. If there were not continued demand for increased features and functionality made by consumers, software development would grind to a halt. Software manufacturers don't usually come out with new versions of their software so that they can then make money; rather, they make money because they come out with new versions of their software. Likewise with security. Purchase products that offer the ability to swap FTP traffic off of FTP ports and over to SSH ports. Uninstall FTP services and install SFTP products.

Every day, as new technologies emerge and old technologies submerge, the ports and the protocols they use appear in, and fall out of, the protocol barnyard. Every time a new version of Real comes out, the port ranges change and the protocols adapt, particularly where marketing is concerned. American marketers are relentless; getting their message out and in front of as many faces as possible is how they survive. We exist in a culture of marketing saturation. On the Internet, at least, there are many who devote much time and energy to countermarketing. For many network administrators, preventing the plethora of spam, malware, spyware, pop-ups, self-installers, and socially engineered Trojans starts the day. Staying sane in a tumultuous sea of crashing applications breaking against your security shores finishes the day. It is a discipline; it is an emerging science. Long hours of study and dedication are required not just to learn about it, but to keep up with the change. A thirst for knowledge and an unquenchable curiosity are the best friends a security practitioner can have.

10

Content Filtering

10.1 Chapter objectives

- Understanding critical protection offered by content filtering
- Understanding the types of attacks
- The types of filtering
- What the future holds: Adaptability is key

Content filtering, defined, provides a level of network traffic examination that prevents harmful content from entering or leaving a network. This content may be cloaked within seemingly harmless HTTP traffic, it may be HTTP traffic, or it may be some other hijacking attempt trying to socially engineer itself past firewall defenses. It may be a full-blown Denial-of-Service (DoS) attack, or it may be someone internally using a web site e-mail account to drop sensitive documents. There are many types of content filtering and many types of covert and overt attacks. This chapter explores enough of them to establish a trailhead, with a map of known routes and avenues. Learning them well ensures that when a new avenue opens or emerges, recognition comes naturally.

10.2 Filtering out dangerous content

A solid firewall implementation will provide the ability to detect, block, and filter application protocols. Many application protocols represent extremely undesirable forms of traffic over a private enterprise subnet for various reasons:

- High bandwidth usage

- Unpredictable routing

- Frequent socially engineered hack attempts

- Unsavory content (pornography, gambling, hate, racist, etc., web sites)

Unfiltered content, in this author's experience, offers the easiest and most promising path to hackers. And let's be crystal clear about this: Hackers roam the Internet like mayflies on a windshield in May. One only has to sit and observe a firewall filter for a few minutes to view a constant barrage of port scans, probes, and automated tests that crawl all across the Internet, incrementing and decrementing through all known private and public subnets, searching for an opening. Why do they do this? Because they are finding *holes*—gaps in security that allow them to download content from illegal sites, gaps that allow them to run the code of their choice on remote computers and gain control of those computers (imagine the sorts of things you could do with a thousand slave computers at your disposal). Gaps that allow them to feel powerful when, socially, they may feel hurt and inadequate.

With control of a thousand networks, a criminal-minded hacker can almost be guaranteed a payoff. Here's a laundry list of fun activities for a hacker at 2 a.m. on a Saturday morning:

- Hack into and download an entire, real web site

- Make some slight alterations to the site's commerce engines

- Crack into a business network

- Load stolen site onto local computer

- Alter the host's file, pointing the real domain name to the bogus, internal site on the local computer

- Spam all business users, and provide a link to the site with "free" offers

- Spam again, and again, and again, rotating out different hijacked sites until credit cards are captured or network admin spots the intrusion

- Drink a Mountain Dew, and eat some Fritos

- Purchase additional network scanner equipment and order an additional DSL line

- Repeat, with various modifications to enhance automation

It's almost laughable in its simplicity, yet heinous in its implications. Imagine ordering computers and office equipment from a cleverly hijacked web site. Individual businesses spend thousands of dollars a year in business-to-business (B2B) expenses on the Internet. If a hijacker knows which sites a business frequents, and has internal access to the business network, a hacker may unleash any of a variety of socially engineered methods whereby to gain easy, and unknown, access to business dollars. The majority of hackers don't go for the big payoff that will be discovered. Rather, a steady trickle of income reaped from the harvest of personal information and spending habits has greater appeal. In the case of the hacker that loads large, and bogus, websites onto local networks, content filtering could have halted this activity. Simple quotas would have prevented the 2 a.m. loading of 300 MB of pornography web sites onto local computers. Content filtering would have alerted or stopped FTP or shell types of activities.

10.2.1   Scanning e-mail

A scanning e-mail filter scans e-mail for confidentiality breaches, pornography, and missing or forged headers. This type of scanning runs in both directions, analyzing Simple Mail Transport Protocol (SMTP) and POP3 traffic in both directions. Unless an e-mail server is running internally, SMTP traffic from WAN to LAN should be blocked. POP3 from WAN to LAN should be blocked. Outbound (LAN to WAN) SMTP and POP e-mail requests should be fully filtered. More information on scanning e-mail is presented in the following sections.

10.2.2 **Web filtering**

Three types of web filtering are discussed here: content blocking, site content filtering, and URL keyword blocking. They cover most business and private web surfing–related issues. There are others, but they are either a less general description or a rehashing of these items.

Content blocking

Blocking services, such as those offered by Cerberian, are a type of web filtering that provides access to a privately managed rating service. Such a service, some sort of subscription database available on the web, allows the firewall to intercept the request and pass it to the rating database. With certain time constraints (where sites not responding are blocked), the rating is sent back to the firewall. As demonstrated in Figure 10.1, depending on the granularity of control offered by the web filter, the site may be blocked based on its rating.

Note: | If the network is compromised, the site being requested may actually exist *within* the network. The request will never pass through the firewall and will never pass to the rating service.

Some firewalls may offer a configuration screen that allows the administrator to control access and block objectionable sites based on their Acceptable Use Policy (AUP). Here is a list of a number of categories of sites that may be desirable to block:

- Drugs and drug paraphernalia
- Gambling
- Militant/extremist
- Religious
- Hate sites
- Disturbing or gross depictions
- Sports
- Hardcore pornography
- Nudity
- Artistic nudity

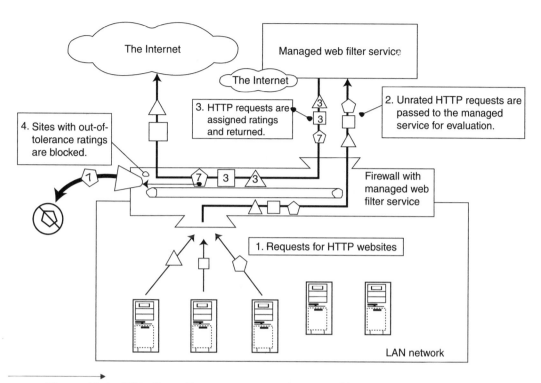

The Internet

Managed web filter service

The Internet

3. HTTP requests are assigned ratings and returned.

2. Unrated HTTP requests are passed to the managed service for evaluation.

4. Sites with out-of-tolerance ratings are blocked.

Firewall with managed web filter service

1. Requests for HTTP websites

LAN network

Figure 10.1   *This firewall sports a service base site filter. Requests for HTTP web sites are passed to the remote service, rated, and returned to the firewall. If the rating is out of limit, the request is tossed out and the user receives a "page not available" error from the firewall.*

These sites constitute a vast and always growing portion of the Internet, so blocking them on an "as-discovered" basis would be impossible. Many of the filters offered as software plugins for firewalls depend on page scraping technologies or externally managed services. Access controls may provide the ability to assign blocking to particular users or groups of users.

Web site content filtering

Many types of unsafe web content can be blocked. Blocking all web content from a particular web site or category of web sites may not be a viable component of your Acceptable Use Policy (AUP) strategy. Regardless, every AUP should consider that most malicious content arrives in the form of e-mail and web site ActiveX controls, cookies,

Java applets, HTTP downloads, and other active scripts. Prevention of these types of activities is called *content filtering* because the firewall allows portions of the content to pass while removing unsafe components. Ideally, this protection also extends to e-mail content. The filter will examine SMTP and POP traffic that passes through, reassembling the packets at the application level and examining the content for unsavory executable directions.

Other content filtering activities that are ideally centralized at the firewall include blocking of pop-ups, banner ads, referrer tracking, redirects, and auto-installers in both e-mail and web content.

Note:

No firewall can protect against a user who has access and knowledge of routers, firewalls, and wiring. Most firewalls can be bypassed by a smart user with a single length of CAT5 network cable and 15 seconds of access to the equipment room. Organizations with a strict AUP should have secure access controls for equipment rooms. Install key card or palm print access to doors, and physically block all unused ports on routers and switches. A pack of RJ45 connectors (crimp it first or it won't fit) and a small tell, such as a very small dab of carpenter's glue or a piece of tape as a seal, work very nicely for this.

URL keyword blocking

Also called "site filtering," the URL keyword blocking feature allows the blocking of Internet web sites based on partial and full matches to certain words. It can be enabled, disabled, or set to a particular scheduled time. Maybe there is a shift of workers who come in during a certain time that cause trouble, or maybe certain sites need to be blocked only at a certain time. Whatever the reasons, blocking by scheduled times can be a valuable feature if bandwidth usage of certain sites at certain times of the day causes a bottleneck at the router. Keyword blocking operates through the creation of filter strings. For example, by entering the character string "g?mbling" into the filter, any web site that matches gambling, with any letter in place of the "a," will be blocked. The following are examples from a HotBrick that will block several sites. First, here are the rules of blocking:

- "**" blocks multiple wild-card characters, including "."

- "*" blocks multiple wild-card characters with the exception of "."

- "?" blocks single wild-card characters with the exception of "."

The following are examples that use these rules. Any similarity to actual web sites, either real or imagined, is purely unintentional and coincidental. No poodles were harmed in the typing of these rules. We all love toy poodles.

- **p??dles**: Blocks any sites with *poodles* or derivative spellings of *poodles* anywhere in the domain name.

- **p??dles*.com: Blocks out any dot-com sites with *poodles* or derivative spellings of *poodles* anywhere in the domain name.

- **toy*p??dles*.net: Blocks out any dot-net sites with an exact match on the word *toy* and any derivative spelling of *poodles* in the domain name.

- **toypoodles**: Blocks any site that includes the exact string *toypoodles* in the domain name.

Currently, in the web environment and spam e-mail that are being sent, a lot of damage to your network can be avoided with some very simple exact matching on the word *sex,* such as "**sex**." Users should be informed of such rules when they are in place, because there are a number of exceptions that will occur—for example, legitimate sites that should not have been blocked but were because they contain a partial match on the blocked string. The HotBrick does not offer filter exceptions; there are better filters out there that can be purchased and installed on a beefier firewall than the HotBrick.

Oftentimes a site that contains malicious content will run across a range of up to 100 IP addresses, and often these IP addresses change day to day; for a single administrator, keeping track of thousands of IP addresses and address ranges would be overwhelming. As a solution, In addition to the blocking of web sites by Internet Protocol (IP) address, or by a range of IP addresses, services can be located that will provide, for free, a constantly updated IP address list of known offensive sites. On the topic of free lists, there are also many community-maintained lists of ad providers that avail in the form of pac files for use in either a browser proxy configuration or a black hole hosts file approach. Manipulating the hosts file causes pages to load slightly slower than a proxy file. Either methods are nice if they are maintained but the ad makers are wise to this approach and change their server names frequently. A smart administrator sets up a network-pushed hosts file to each computer that works to completely block blinking and pushy banner ads. Optimally, this file is updated daily.

10.2.3   Application filtering

Application filtering, often confused with port filtering handled at the network layer, usually takes the shape of a piece of software resident on the firewall. The need for distinction between network layer and application layer protocol filtering is mandated by the pervasive level of cloaked protocol threats. Concerned administrators can best prevent objectively malicious user activity by removing permissions to install and configure software from computers. *Objectively* in this sense simply means relative to corporate AUP.

When adding a user to a computer user list, setting them as "restricted users" either at the local computer or through active directory permissions will effectively block individual user installation of unauthorized software. Blocking all known ports for unauthorized software protocols will prevent unauthorized activity when permissions management is not an option. When selecting a firewall product, the keywords *Application Filtering* should be present. Policy and port management do not, truly, constitute true application filtering. The firewall has to be able to look inside the application protocol and make the determination: "Is it what it says it is?"

Obtaining a list of application protocols and the ports they use is a good starting point. Bear in mind, however, that these things change with each version of the software. Furthermore, cloaking and spoofing can allow applications to evade port countermeasures by sneaking in on something commonplace, such as from port 80. Certain types of firewalls, such as those run on local machines, can block and filter application activity based on the name of the process that requests the access; unfortunately, this information does not get attached to the port traffic stream—control is in the hands of the user. Most users will allow anything because the process requesting the access is unfamiliar. We have already established that *people will click on anything*.

What then can be done? Application Layer Filtering (ALF) is an intelligent technology that compares header messages of TCP packets with a dictionary of known application headers. It may be referred to as *stateful multilayer inspection firewalls*. Their primary disadvantage is that a bottleneck may be created when application layer traffic is heavy if the firewall stops often to thoroughly inspect every packet that passes through. Some of the types of application security features that one expects to find with any self-proclaimed application filtering firewall include the following:

- Blocks unwanted e-mail and SMTP buffer overflows
- Allows secure Exchange server connections
- Protects from DNS and POP3 buffer overflow
- Prevents intrusion
- Prevents attacks inside SSL tunnels

For any office with remote virtual private network (VPN) users, utmost importance rests in the ability to detect activity passing to the internal network through a VPN tunnel. Typically, administrators have little or no control of an employee's home computer. This may be a communicable (oops, communal) computer—everyone in the household uses it—and as such, it has a high incidence of transmittable, viral, computer dysfunction. That is to say, it is scrambled eggs and it just jumped on to your pristine network. Without application layer inspection that penetrates incoming tunnels, whatever nonsense is installed on it by the resident 16-year-old will now spread to the corporate LAN. And who knows, the 16-year-old may be the one actively spreading it, *on purpose*! But don't let that encourage the widespread belief that most hackers are pimply 16-year-old boys in their mother's basements. After all, some of them are girls, too.

Ideally, a "working from home" computer will be company property that must be brought in regularly for scheduled checkups. A laptop is the *ideal* unit for this scenario. And if the option of application filtering of VPN traffic does not exist, there are interim solutions. So, in cases in which the Powers That Be have Issued Orders that defy common sense, placing resources needed within a DMZ poses an excellent work around. And acquiring the funding for proper security tools does not usually present a problem when properly presented. Here is an excellent and known successful dialogue when confronted with supervisory incoherence regarding matters of security: "Sorry, our LAN edge firewall security policy simply doesn't support VPN tunneling. In other words, I can do it, but you run a very real and immediate risk that all data on all computers and servers can be destroyed." But never, ever, present a problem without a solution. "However, the caveat to that is product X. Installed, it would provide the necessary security; it costs $xx, requires xx hours to implement, and requires xx yearly hours to effectively support."

10.3 Summary

Distinction between protocol policy creation, port filtering, and application protocol filtering must be made. Applications may cloak themselves within other application protocols that are deemed safe and are accepted by filtered ports. Things such as URL filtering based on keyword regular expression filtering and external services are a boon to network administrators who simply want to stop the obvious threats and present a layer of defense that stops first timers. Computers using PPTP, SSL, HTTPS, and IPSec used for VPN technology to attach a network remotely create an application layer chink in the armor that often passes undetected. Be sure to speak with tech support before purchasing a firewall to find out for sure whether the firewall supports application filtering of VPN traffic! This will truly be the future of firewall security—intelligent application protocol filtering that can be upgraded, configured, and adjusted so the target applications are actually receiving the traffic requested.

Section V

Secure External Services Provision

Publicly Accessible Servers Implementation

I I.I Chapter objectives

- Types of server environments
- Remote versus self-hosted
- Types of web server–specific attacks
- E-mail servers

I I.2 Securing your organization's Internet site

Connecting to the web can be hazardous. Even when all precautions are taken—firewalls installed and regularly updated, policies created, and application protocols filtered—it only takes one user clicking on something hazardous to open the door to mayhem. For now, though, attention must be turned to the outside, to that which lurks just outside, on the "doorstep" to the Internet. Many organizations have both the technical and the financial resources to host their own web site. Budget aside, there are many points that need to be considered when deciding whether to host a web server *on-site*. Figure 11.1 demonstrates the difference between a locally hosted web site and one that is co-located and possibly managed by an external service. Budgets have a way of doubling and tripling as unexpected problems arise that must be addressed. What may seem like a small equipment and time investiture can escalate into massive overtime and software and capital expenditures.

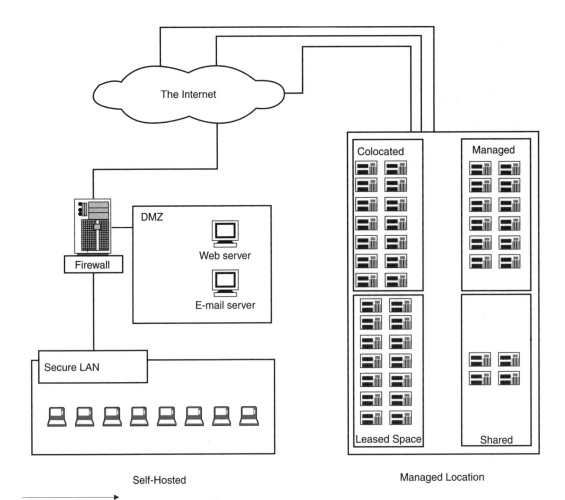

The Internet

Colocated

Managed

DMZ

Firewall

Web server

E-mail server

Secure LAN

Leased Space

Shared

Self-Hosted

Managed Location

Figure 11.1　*A web server in a demilitarized zone (DMZ)–style arrangement, tandem to a private network, contrasted with a privately managed web site provider. Distinct advantages and disadvantages exist in either method.*

11.2.1　Pros and cons

Most often, evaluating business Internet requirements with respect to the decision of hosting *on-site* entails less a question of bandwidth and equipment and more one of support personnel and skill sets. That is not to say that consideration of bandwidth and equipment are not critical questions. But these *are* easier questions that involve adjusting the budget to accommodate for the investment, or allocation, of funding. An internally hosted site requires management by a skilled set of hands. The primary advantage of a co-managed, co-located, or managed web site lies in the skills of the business providing the service. It is also one of security because co-locating means placing the entire operation in a rented or leased situation at a hosting facility, like those owned or operated by companies such as Level(3), Intermedia.net, Interland, or any number of others. A number of questions should be reviewed:

- *Physical security*: Will the server be on a system with other web sites, or will it be a dedicated machine in a locked cabinet?

- *Power*: battery UPS or failover diesel generator?

- *Fire*: inert gas injection or sprinklers?

- *Physical security*: hand print or retinal scan access controls or Simplex combination? Maybe both?

- *Redundancy*: multiple backbones with large pipe connectivity or two T1 lines from the same carrier?

- *Software and hardware costs*: lease, own, or share?

These questions do, of course, lead to other questions. The differences between co-located, leased, co-managed, managed, and shared hosting beg to be defined. The aspects, advantages, and disadvantages of each item need to be understood. What is the advantage of a backup generator over UPS? And there are cost, security, and business logic considerations with each solution: How will the web site connect to the accounting system? Does it need to? The preceding list truly only represents the tip of the iceberg.

Some would, and will, jump to the conclusion that an *on-site* solution is the cheapest, the most secure, the most logical, and the easiest route. That would be jumping to a conclusion, though. Most conclusions are best approached with a slow walking gait. No jumping!

The best approach to making a decision about whether to host internally is to hire an external consulting service—a service that you will not use to perform the work (and make sure they know it)—and let them spend 40 to 50 hours analyzing your business needs, capabilities, and budget. The consultant can then make an educated recommendation that may prevent much grief. After all, Custer and his men certainly didn't wake up that morning with "last stand" and "Custer's" in mind. They all had positive *can-do* attitudes, and that is what got them into trouble. With just a quick technical review and a glance into the mountains at all the Indians, any consultant at the time worth a penny, and with no self-interest in making Custer look good, could have told them to stay home that day. No administrator or manager desires a Custer-styled approach to internal management of web applications.

For the do-it-yourselfer, be prepared to adapt a personal integrity with great objectivity and be prepared to lay the evidence out in an understandable format. Table 11.1 lists the attributes, with respect to the ability to effectively firewall and maintain a web server, of each of the types of hosted services. *High security* means that it exists, and access and configurability are complete. *Low* means that firewall security may not exist, and if it does, then it cannot be configured or managed by the customer.

Expensive web hosting solutions always consider security. Inexpensive solutions rarely do. It is expensive to maintain an up-to-date, secure web site. Web sites rank as the most desirable attack launch platform for hackers. Cracking open and gaining access to one server can mean an island-hopping excursion that will lead to bank accounts or free stuff. And the actual content and code on a web site can often be attractive bait. The more highly visible, the wealthier the owners, or the more politically oriented a site, the more likely it is to be attacked and the greater the need for hardening and securing the server. Brochure sites, or innocuous sites that serve few pages certainly have their own worries, but they may not be business-critical worries. Table 11.2 lists some attributes of the various types of hosting that should provide some understanding of what they entail.

Table 11.1 *Firewalls and Web Hosting*

Firewall Security	Low				High
Co-located					X
Leased					X
Co-managed					X
Managed					X
Shared	X	X			
Self-hosted	X	X	X	X	X

Table 11.2 *Types of Services and Firewall Policy Concerns*

Service	On-site Management	Machine Access	Firewall	Facilities	Cost*
Co-located: Customer owned equipment co-located at a secure, hardened, failover facility such as Level(3). ISP and rack space services provided by either the actual location owner or a reseller.	Power and reboot only. Locked cabinet access.	Full and absolute. Facility staff has little or no access, depending on if an entire rack space is purchased.	Rack space permitting, the sky is the limit.	Failover power, inert gas fire extinguishing, air conditioned, secure access	$30K+ annually
Leased (co-located): Reseller provides the rack space and equipment along with various other, bundled services.	May be managed, co-managed or co-located.	May be full and absolute, or the lease may be a contrivance of the contract, a way for the ISP to charge more.	Depending on the level of co-location service provided, firewall information may or may not be available.	Failover power, inert gas fire extinguishing, air conditioned, secure access	$50K+ annually
Co-managed: Co-located and management assistance provided by on-site personnel.	Typically, leased or rented equipment and access to the equipment are provider only.	PC-terminal services access to server should be available. Physical access may be allowed, but will probably be supervised.	Firewall services are usually optional and cost extra.	Failover power, inert gas fire extinguishing, air conditioned, secure access are usually available from more reputable providers.	$40K+ annually

*Bandwidth usage drives costs upward.

Table 11.2 *Types of Services and Firewall Policy Concerns (Continued)*

Service	On-site Management	Machine Access	Firewall	Facilities	Cost*
Managed dedicated service	The provider owns the equipment, but the server will usually be dedicated to a single client.	Console-styled access only. Software installation allowed, but only by provider's on-site staff. Machine access strictly prohibited.	Firewall service usually available, but may be a cheap unit with expensive monthly rates ($300–$400 a month charge for a firewall appliance unit that costs only $600).	Failover power, inert gas fire extinguishing, air conditioned, secure access from more reputable providers	$15–30K+ annual
Shared	Provider only access. Multiple accounts exist on single machines. Shared SQL services may have as many as 200 databases on a single server. Web servers may have as many as 500 web sites on a single server.	FTP only. Some possible controls through a web based management console.	*Not* the place for an e-commerce web site. Little to no firewall protection may exist. Shared machines are the machine purgatory of ISPs.	Location dependent, many fly-by-night shared hosts provide very little extras for their cheap, shared accounts.	$20–$300 per month charge. SQL server, exchange services, bandwidth usage, etc., increase costs.
Self-hosted (leased or owned)	Full and complete control of access.	Full and complete access to machine and software installation capabilities.	Owner-controlled budget and staff technical skills are the only constraints.	15–30 minutes of failover UPS battery power. Fire protection as provided by location.	$10K+ is the initial first-year cost for self-hosting. Things like dual WAN, load balancing, e-mail servers,

*Bandwidth usage drives costs upward.

Table 11.2 *Types of Services and Firewall Policy Concerns (Continued)*

Service	On-site Management	Machine Access	Firewall	Facilities	Cost*
Self-hosted (leased or owned) *(Continued)*					remote access, elaborate backup systems, and power failover increase the cost dramatically.

*Bandwidth usage drives costs upward.

Linus Pauling, one of the great thinkers and physicists of the twentieth century, once said (paraphrased) that the only *impossible* is the impossibility of *impossible*. It is highly unlikely that a hosted shared web account at $4 a month will provide adequate firewall protection. However, simply raising the question of security to support personnel or to sales staff may be the wind in their sails needed to drive the point home to management.

Take the concerns about security to heart, discuss them with providers, and seek answers before spending money. Such an approach helps everyone by raising issue awareness.

11.2.2 Special concerns

Web servers run an entire gamut of specialized and targeted attack types. This is not to say that these same attacks don't get launched against all networks. Web servers are, however, particularly vulnerable because they freely and openly engage in communication with the Internet. There may be massive amounts of traffic coursing through a web server farm where 10 to 20 web servers are clustered to provide the needed equipment for a single web site. With such massive amounts of public traffic, no single human could look at it and see trouble. Firewall tools must be extremely sophisticated to provide a strong defense from the many types of attacks. The following sections list and define the most common and effective tactics used by hackers, the consequences of attacks, and possible countermeasures.

IP spoofing (DoS attacks)

Many, many protocols were designed and implemented before the advent of the Internet and, as such, were not really designed with any sort of security in mind. TCP happens to be one of them. As discussed in previous chapters, TCP is the backbone of the Internet network protocols. To launch an IP spoofing attack, an attacker uses an option called *sock_raw,* which allows the manual creation of a packet. Header fields, such as those shown in Chapter 8, must be manually entered. Denial-of-service (DoS) attacks are IP spoofing attacks and consist of two types:

- Land attack
- Smurf attack

A *land* attack is one in which the forged, or *spoofed* packet has been altered so that its source address actually duplicates the victim's server IP address. The source port gets set equal to the destination port. The server gets confused and starts sending the packet back and forth to itself and thus appears to be busy because it will stream to itself endlessly and without interruption. Firewalls stop this sort of attack because the firewall will reject any packet sent to it with its own IP address in the source field. Even a stateful packet inspector can halt this sort of activity.

A *Smurf* attack is based on the Internet Control Message Protocol (ICMP) *ping* function. The attacker must have prior knowledge of the internal IP address structure. This information gets coded into a bunch of forged packets that appear to the server to be ping request messages from the internal LAN. The victim then becomes preoccupied with sending ping responses to the entire LAN. This can be most easily prevented by using a firewall that allows for the blocking of ping requests. There are also other filtering options, and many modern filters can block IP spoof attacks rather easily.

Packet sniffing

A hacker may install a sniffer on the network to obtain a plethora of data about the network. With a packet sniffer and solid analyzing skills, a hacker can view *all* the data that is transmitted from an enterprise over the Internet. Always treat every e-mail as though it could be published on tomorrow's front page. Who do you suppose pays the hackers to do these things?

OS fingerprinting

Even a hacker is helpless until she knows the operating system (OS) flavor of the victim; knowledge of the victim OS reveals the types of flaws and exploits that may render the victim into a willing slave computer. There are several ways to identify the type of OS of the victim. Some OSs will either respond, or not respond, to incomplete packets sent to particular ports. Such differences in behavior are like a gambler's *tell*. Some applications, such as Internet Explorer, may even go so far as to expose the information in the header of all TCP packets.

SYN attacks (DoS flooding attacks)

TCP synchronization (SYN) packet attacks are both the grandfather and the grandchild of DoS attacks. They are responsible for many highly publicized turn-of-the-century outages, as well as outages that, as recent as last week (from this writing), have driven some high-profile ISP networks into the ground for as many as 4 hours of outage. SYN packets are the initial packets sent by one application to another. They are responsible for saying "here I am, I am about to send you more stuff, please wait for more stuff and open a connection on port so-and-so for me." The hacker arranges for hundreds (if not thousands) of computers to simultaneously send these requests to a single network. The aforementioned recent attack was believed to have originated in the Middle East and is under investigation with the FBI.

Some firewalls will prevent novice SYN attacks by preventing a single IP address from going nuts with SYNs, but by diversifying the attack base or by forging/spoofing packet headers, this countermeasure is easily countered. There are other measures, but most of them only reduce the attacks, and they can't be completely prevented. Oftentimes, SYN floods fill a server's request queue as it waits for responses that will never arrive, and nothing can be done until the attack stops. These attacks only last a few hours because, given enough time and cooperation, the source of the attack can be traced through global network traffic analysis. In combination with a land attack, the original SYN attack is made one step nastier by making the attack look as if it has originated from your own network.

Routing vulnerabilities

In this scenario, an attacker broadcasts false routing information to make a router appear to be an IP address that it is not. ISPs are able, for the most part, to detect and prevent these sorts of attacks from occurring; however, on larger and unregulated Internet segments (which exist in every major city or communications center), such introspection is not as common, and for a while this can be easily accomplished. By broadcasting fake routing information, a bogus router can capture network segment traffic intended for another host. The higher risk associated with this sort of attack prevents it from commonplace occurrence because it normally involves the physical cracking into routing networks. This sort of attack yields similar results to DNS poisoning.

DNS cache poisoning

When a web address is requested, a packet, called a *DNS Query,* is sent to the DNS server of record. That DNS server then looks to the actual DNS server that contains the real information about that request. For example, if a hacker sends a DNS request to an SBC DNS server for yahoo.com, the DNS server then looks to whichever server contains the lookup information for that site. Not all DNS servers contain databases of the entire Internet; rather, they contain metadata that tells them how to find out. Unfortunately, the response packet is rather easily predicted, and before the *real* server can get a response back to the victim DNS server, the attacker "guesses" what the response packet will look like and forges it with the data of his choice. Thus, yahoo.com, on that particular DNS server, becomes whatever IP address the attacker suggests. From that moment on, until the cache updates, that particular DNS server has what is called a "poisoned" DNS cache.

Fragment attacks

Fragment attacks all bear one common trait: They involve the purposeful sending of packet fragments that when reassembled turn out to be much larger than the victim thought they would be. Victim computers will crash, hang, or even spontaneously reboot.

Ping of death (fragment attack)

Prevent ping and this attack is prevented. Ping-of-death attacks involve the reassembly of packet fragments into a single packet that is far larger than the maximum allowed ping packet size.

Teardrop attack (fragment attack)

As a server or router receives packets, they are fragmented and must be reassembled. To do this, the server relies on the addition and subtraction of numbers. By reason of design, these numbers will never be negative. If they are negative, the server may hang or crash. This attack sends fake packets that when reassembled result in negative numbers that are interpreted as very large integers. Firewalls can prevent these sorts of attacks because they are more adept at packet examination.

Tiny fragment attack

By not placing certain data into the first packet, this attack slips packets past filters. Stateful packet inspectors should be able to halt this sort of attack if they are configured properly. Minimum first-packet sizes must be enforced so important information that is contained within the first octet of a packet is reviewed.

11.3 Separating your Internet site from your intranet

First of all, the difference between an Internet site and an intranet should be clarified. An Internet site is one that exists on the public subnet. An intranet may be a series of web sites and resources that exist on an internal LAN, or private subnet.

Note: *Intranet* is often pronounced "in-TRUH-net," whereas *Internet* is pronounced "IN-ter-net" to provide clear distinction in discussion.

The most common use of an intranet site is to provide resources to internal business users. Such resources may be web-based accounting system reports, human resources information about things such as benefits, health plans, employee directories, manufacturing systems, document management, internal tracking systems, etc.

Business users often have many of the same needs for types of web services internally as commercial users do on the Internet. Business users may be required to file requisitions, reports, and employee data all online. Such web sites would be of little use on the public Internet.

It's easy to see that in an extremely large or global enterprise, security presents as real a risk as it does to public Internet sites. It serves no purpose for a company to provide a rock-solid layer of firewall security for its Internet sites and then suffer an attack launched by an internal hacker. Much like the credit card fraud committed by employees who acquire easy-to-get jobs as counter staff, some types of fraud are committed by employees whose only purpose in working somewhere is to gain internal access to sensitive information. Personal information is valuable. Using credit cards and identifying information on the web at any site that "looks" legitimate is a guaranteed way to get into trouble. Companies should take great care to ensure that security around internal Internet sites meets the same high standards as external sites.

Separating your Internet site from your intranet site pretty much happens as a matter of course. One exists within the LAN, and the other exists outside of it. Placing both the Internet and the intranet sites within the same subnet on a demilitarized zone (DMZ) can, physically, be done. Small companies do it all the time and there are no violent repercussions.

Companies with 14 or fewer employees have few security concerns. The following will most likely be true:

- Employees have personal history that is known.

- A large percentage of employees are either blood or in-law relations.

- Employees are trustworthy, and the percentage difference between the lowest and the highest salary is not inordinate.

- Jealousy of the company's success or a failure to understand limited resources is not widespread, if present at all.

- If the previous items aren't completely true, enough of them are true that personnel security is intrinsic; it is built in to a group of people who are intimately concerned with and loyal to the owner.

- Technical abilities will be concentrated in one individual.

- Security policies may not be written, but they may be understood by all and communicated verbally.

- Budgets will be tight, and until something happens that causes a need to arise, security will not be a major concern.

The many companies that operate in this fashion, though they suffer from no threats from internal personnel, are usually very poorly protected from the Internet with as little as a single stateful packet filter between themselves and the Internet. It is companies like these that have been cracked and provide the beach-head for hackers and spammers to launch assaults on the Internet at large. The level of automation of hacking tools necessitates that all businesses take the appropriate countermeasures.

Note: | From residential homes to small business to global enterprises, a firewall can offer much-needed protection and security of both corporate and personal data.

Generally, security breaks down when the employee count reaches 15. The fifteenth employee will be the first employee to be hired through an agency or an external service. Typically, less than half (or none) of the other employees will know the fifteenth. A background check will probably be considered too expensive. Often, this hire illustrates one of the first (and rarely the last) hiring mistakes made by a company. So it obviates the need for greater security precautions, both in hiring and in technology. Companies of 14 or more employees must begin to take precautions. Servers should not be left in the open. Passwords should be complex and not shared openly. Meetings about technical and sensitive information should be held behind closed doors. Internet and internally sensitive servers will require firewall protection, from both the outside *and* the inside.

11.4 Supporting SMTP mail architectures

Self-hosting e-mail can be one of the best things a company, even a small company, can do. It offers greater control, less expense, redundancy, and provides much greater levels of security than are available in any other configuration. Ideally, such self-managed e-mail servers will exist in a secure co-located environment. Machine requirements, even for large organizations, can be relatively modest. When considering self-hosting a web site, self-hosting an e-mail server can be a good place to start. Mail Exchange (MX) domain name service (DNS) records are relatively easy to change and permit the configuration of separate e-mail and web server records.

Firewalls and SMTP e-mail traffic have an intrinsic relationship: E-mail is the hacker's favorite way of gaining socially engineered access to a network. Therefore, one thing becomes abundantly clear: Self-hosted or ISP-hosted e-mail *must* be inspected for viruses. The single greatest threat to networks is unfiltered e-mail virus attachments and malicious spam. Within seconds of clicking on an infected attachment, the entire network can be poisoned, and the damage and the cleanup of that damage can be more expensive than even the best firewall and e-mail system. Many hybrid products offer gateway e-mail sniffing as well as mailbox antivirus software for e-mail systems that inspects e-mails after they have arrived but before they are opened.

Outsourced e-mail hosting can cost as little as $100 a month for 10 user accounts, and the only risk is that a total stranger will decide to spend an afternoon by reading your corporate e-mail. Administrators of such systems rarely have the time to do such a thing, but if a bunch of stray e-mail arrives, the administrator may *have* to look at it just to see where the intended delivery went afoul.

If the expertise exists on staff, it is well worth the effort to self-host the e-mail server. The control over this, what is today one of the most critical of business communication tools, will easily pay for itself and grant a level of business flexibility that is unimaginable with most of the hosted services. Some of the benefits include the following:

- Unlimited e-mail accounts
- Unlimited mailbox sizes
- Unlimited e-mail forwards
- Unlimited attachment sizes
- Virus scanning

- Spam filtering
- Ease of acceptable-use policy enforcement

One warning, though: Just because you can receive unlimited attachment sizes doesn't mean that everyone can. Recently, this author tried to send a very large file (as requested) to a client on an AOL account. As a result, AOL barred future e-mails to the client from the author's domain name. All e-mail to AOL began to fail because AOL filters the ability to send e-mail to its customers based on past activity. The client, consequently, moved to a self-hosted e-mail system.

11.4.1 Internal e-mail

E-mail servers may also be situated internally. Some enterprises may not have any need for their employees to communicate with the external world. Such business populations may be segmented, and their e-mail servers may be positioned on an internal LAN DMZ with ports for SMTP and POP3 enabled.

E-mail should never exist on the same server as a web server. Large attachments, as they enter the system, can clog things up a bit and demand CPU resources as the file copies to disk. It is far better to have this sort of thing happening on a dedicated server than on a web server where such a thing could cause an e-commerce failure when a customer abandons a shopping cart due to sluggish response times. People can, and do, wait for e-mail without much complaining. Customers, on the other hand, do not wait for unresponsive web sites.

11.5 Summary

Setting up and maintaining a web server presents a very complex challenge, especially if the web site receives a lot of traffic and has high visibility in markets or search engines. The methods of attack include DoS, SYN, packet forging and spoofing, DNS poisoning, host file tampering, etc. Sometimes, why the Internet continues to exist is a confounded mystery. Many sites go along unnoticed and unattractive to attackers. Sites that have heavy traffic, take extreme political or religious stances, or make lots of money are precious targets. Many attackers see themselves as Robin Hood, stealing from the wealthy and giving it to themselves. E-mail servers, though similar to web servers, are somewhat easier to manage and should be isolated from web servers; that is, they should exist on separate machines. The benefits of hosting an e-mail server internally are far greater than those of hosting a web server internally because of lower expenses and greater security.

Architecture Selection

12.1 Chapter objectives

- Choosing an effective architecture
- Perimeter and demilitarized zone (DMZ) subnets
- Blended defense
- Dual-homed host firewalls
- Understanding the security risks of each architecture

12.2 Types of screened subnet architectures

A screened subnet, built singularly of packet filtering routers, can easily be the cheapest and easiest solution where security requirements are minimal. However, most of the more advanced, effective firewalls will incorporate into their architecture provisions for additional application protocol filtering. A screened subnet will typically involve more than just two routers creating an empty-space subnet. That space will likely be filled by something. Situated within a screened subnet, a server that performs some traffic regulatory function becomes part of the firewall policy and is referred to as *a bastion host* or a *dual-homed host*, depending on implementation and equipment configuration. Both configurations are explored in this chapter.

Ultimately, a screened subnet firewall without application filtering may not provide adequate security where a broad range of protocols need to be filtered and where ranges of ports need to be dynamically accessed. If minimal access to the external network fulfills business objectives, a screened subnet can be simple and quick to establish. However, be sure to establish, upon deployment (or before), the immediate rules of acceptable use with respect to the capabilities of a packet filtering–only network. Truly, such screened subnets are only good for internal firewall applications where internal network segmentation may be required, but many people throw caution to the wind every day and readily accept the concept that a single router can provide adequate security.

Each of the architectures discussed has its flaws. They all boil down to single points of access, which, if compromised, will permit complete access to the internal network. If data theft is the fear, nothing should be placed on the adjacent network that could cause severe or crippling damage to the network if compromised. All the time, on the news and in the media, we hear about this memo or that report or this e-mail that says that this company was doing this, that, or the other. *Where do you think those memos, e-mails, documents, and reports came from?* The first thought is that they come out through the front door, but the possibility that they come out through side, back, and trap doors is just as real as front-door access. An internal employee would much rather drop a file out over the Internet than print it and carry it out as paper, or risk being caught with a disk, or even worse, faxing it.

Segmentation of internal resources is as much a part of the firewall policy as everything that sits on the perimeter. Movies and books are chockablock with tales and plots of intrigue and treachery. Art imitates life: In the real world, jealousy and anger and childishness combine to present very special and very real risks. A consultant's phone *never* rings more often than for an office where there is a lot of infighting. The best management technique to solve this problem and to save both consultant and management headaches usually involves a round of pink slips. The honest consultant usually knows where the problems are and, if asked directly: "I'm going to fire three people to make these security issues go away, who are they?" will usually say "Just look at my billing." Employees that explore out of bounds areas on the network often cause damage to their computers as they experiment with settings in attempts to bypass security. A consultant or IT manager can provide valuable insight and is usually in the position he is in because he is trustworthy. And by creating internal network segments that implement screened subnets in the private LAN, many problems that may arise due to unauthorized file access will be avoided, thus *preventing* barnyard politics in the first place.

12.2.1   The perimeter

A perimeter network is a network with a different subnet that sits outside of the local network, separated from the internal network by either a router or a firewall. Sounds a lot like a DMZ, doesn't it? With respect to addressing scheme, on paper it may even look exactly like a DMZ. In fact, a DMZ is a type of perimeter network. The critical difference is in the way IP addresses and traffic are handled.

In a perimeter network, the external facing router may have an internal LAN Dynamic Host Configuration Protocol (DHCP) service configured that broadcasts and assigns IP addresses to all the computers within earshot. Typically, this would be either every computer that is either configured with the same subnet mask and IP address prefixes, or any computer with DHCP configured that is plugged into a switch that is plugged into the router. DHCP typically allows a mixture of both, with the ability to configure a static range and a dynamic range of IP addresses. Often, things like mail servers and file servers will require static, private IP addresses so software configured to access the machines can be permanently configured. Also, a routing table in a router may be configured to point different external IP addresses to static perimeter network IP addresses.

For some people, as soon as this is done, the perimeter network may be classified as a DMZ. This is because, as illustrated by Figure 12.1, although a perimeter network may not be a DMZ, a DMZ—if it is situated at the perimeter of a network—is a perimeter network. A DMZ offers the exact same features as the perimeter network, with one exceptional difference: In a DMZ, all traffic to and from the DMZ is controlled by a firewall. Through the use of a policy table, different protocols that come into a single IP address are mapped to the correct DMZ IP address. If DHCP is needed within the DMZ for some reason, a firewall should be configured or purchased to provide DHCP on the DMZ side. If you aren't sure that what you have is a DMZ, then it's not.

One thing is certain: If a perimeter network contains external IP addresses, it can't be a DMZ. This is because the computers are then, actually, a perimeter network sitting on the Internet. If these machines are not firewalls, then the technical term for these computers would be "sitting ducks." This author has actually seen an entire small office in a perimeter sitting-duck situation. In 2003, when the Windows RPC exploit that caused immediate system

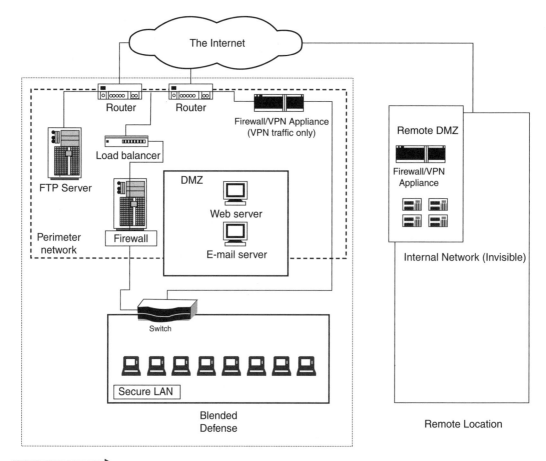

Figure 12.1　*Multiple screened subnets exist, as well as a demilitarized zone (DMZ) and a single-box configuration. A firewall/virtual private network exists for peer-to-peer virtual private networking (VPN) communication to a co-located server. Technically, anything inside the dotted-line box and outside the secure LAN should be considered "on the perimeter." The items grouped here, within the dashed line, all share a physical connection. If each grouping or single piece of equipment has a private subnet address, there are as many perimeter networks on the perimeter as there are unique private subnets.*

shutdown raged across the Internet, a new computer plugged into this sitting-duck network caught the virus within 30 seconds of completing the boot cycle.

12.2.2 Two routers

The two-router configuration consists of an external router, a bastion host, and an internal router configured on a perimeter network. The interior router provides connectivity to a bastion host/proxy for the purpose of filtering IP traffic. Routers typically offer something called *pinhole routing* or *port forwarding,* which is similar but less effective because it may only offer stateful packet inspection, is difficult to configure for functionality, does not always work properly, or may simply forward all traffic to the destination machine without looking at it. Successful pinholing requires an in-depth knowledge of the protocol communication for the particular protocol being forwarded.

By placing the bastion host coupled with the external facing router, compromise of the bastion will not immediately compromise the internal network. After all, the hacker needs a few minutes to install the hacking tools onto the bastion server. The bastion server may provide a complete array of proxy services for things like Telnet, HTTP, FTP, and SOCKS. Internal traffic is filtered to the bastion server through the internal router and packet filtering. Services such as FTP that require special considerations of port handling may force the opening of a range of TCP ports to allow the acceptance of traffic. Because routers typically only provide packet inspection, anything can come through on these ports, and internal machines will be vulnerable to SYN attacks and other various methods of crippling and overtaking a host.

This is where the concept of using a bastion host with routers begins to break down. If the external router is somehow compromised, the internal router may be susceptible to attacks. Why? Because the router rules may only allow the configuration of *allow* or *deny* based on the direction of the traffic, the source address, and the destination address. Some may also check the ACK bit value for validity (this prevents some types of fragmented packet attacks) on TCP packets. Clearly, source addresses can be forged, and if the bastion host is compromised, it may merely offer a convenient staging server for launching a full-scale attack on the internal network.

Compromise of the internal router won't even be necessary. Many of the "attacks" will take the shape of seamless web site hijacks, pop-up serving, and other guerrilla marketing tactics that are so prevalent in day-to-day life. Compromise may, in fact, not even be immediately apparent.

It's a matter of opinion, but when time and money are an object, a bastion host in a two-router–screened subnet, as shown in Figure 12.2, provides moderate thin-curtain security. It is really more appropriate for internal subnet segmentation. However, in a router–bastion–firewall scenario, security would be *greatly* enhanced when the internal facing router is actually a full-fledged firewall. Such a combination of proxy servers and firewall possibly provides the highest level of security available.

12.2.3   Single router

A single-router–screened subnet implementation provides adequate security only where a greater level of security already exists. For example, a screened subnet may exist in a situation where a firewall sits inline with the router, between the internal LAN and the router. Some specialized routers offer three faces, and these can be used in the same manner as a two-router approach with a bastion host acting as a proxy to mask internal IP addresses from the external world.

12.2.4   Multiple screened subnet architecture

Again we return to Figure 12.1, which typifies the arrangements present deep in the network bowels of most medium-sized enterprises—especially ones that have experienced rapid growth. Time and money are so slippery that oftentimes the best solution involves a quick trip to CDW for a $500 box that will do what is needed. Managers often demand instant results. This often means a bumper crop of multiple screened subnets aggregating on the perimeter. Consolidation of these elements, a critical security task, must not be delayed. More access points do not necessarily mean weaker security, but they do mean more work for the administrator and more opportunities for mistakes.

Ultimately, a multiple screened subnet architecture with a complex structure—if it can be successfully maintained—provides the best network security approach. Isolating network tasks and

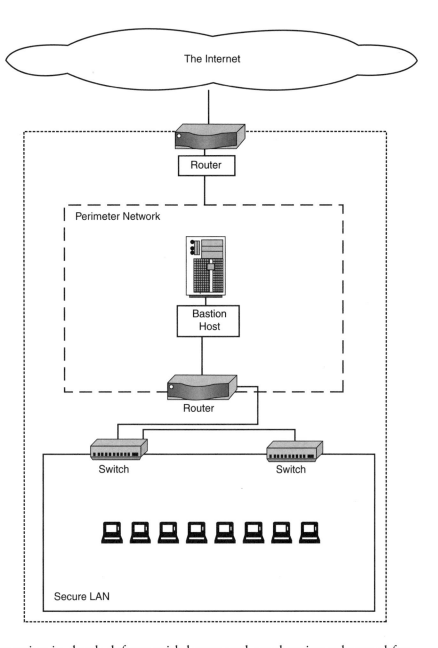

creating in-depth defense with layers and overlapping subnets obfuscates and hides the internal LAN servers that must, at all costs, be protected. Further steps may include the installation of internal firewall security products on file, application, and database servers that represent the greatest risk to business if compromised.

12.2.5 Screened host

A screened host architecture consists primarily of a bastion host with a single network interface card (NIC) situated within the internal network. This server provides the only point of access to the Internet, and the router is configured so that this bastion host is the only server that it is allowed to see. It may do this through simple Internet Connection Sharing (ICS) or other software methods of packet filtering and routing and sharing out the Internet to other internal systems. This differs from a dual-homed host in that a dual-homed host has two network cards, and packets from the external network cannot reach the internal network. A screened host has no perimeter subnet.

With a screened host architecture, it is necessary to configure the router with a high level of complicated packet filtering rules. The screened host is actually rather vulnerable; furthermore, if it fails, the entire internal network may immediately be compromised. Packet filtering rules governing inbound and outbound packets will be necessary.

Screened hosts are often used in networks where a costly firewall cannot be obtained. Its greatest advantage over a dual-homed host with proxy services is that it offers the ability to pass traffic for which proxy software may not exist. Figure 12.3 shows a typical screened host implementation.

12.2.6 Dual-homed host

The dual-homed host architecture is often, at first, most appealing to the do-it-yourselfer who would like to have his Internet and use it, too. In some cases, a dual-homed host may provide a very convenient approach to running some proxy software for Internet connection to the internal facing LAN card and running additional external facing services (such as a web site) on the external facing card. This is how many current *off-the-shelf* solutions are rigged. Some may even provide a third network interface for the creation of a DMZ. Figure 12.4 demonstrates a dual-homed host by itself, providing Internet application filtering to its LAN subnet. In configuration, the internal facing NIC and external NIC are logically bridged by translating the packets with a software agent, or daemon.

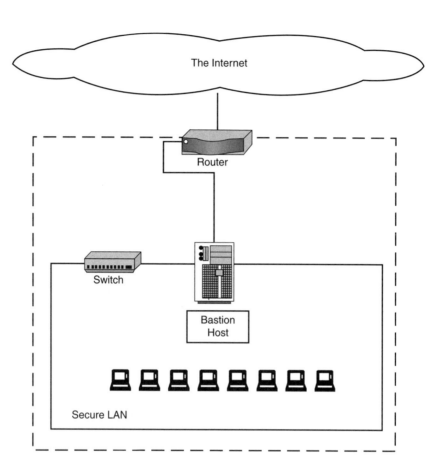

Figure 12.3
A bastion host is situated as a screened host. It provides single-point access to the Internet and may or may not provide proxy services.

Bridging the gap

A dual-homed host creates a physical break in the network. Logically, anyone connecting to either machine can see shared drives and folders on the host, but they can't see each other. From the desktop of the host, the user can browse either network, but *tracerts* and *pings* will never resolve without some configuration and useful software tools. On a UNIX box, this can be accomplished by editing the kernel configuration file and recompiling the kernel. Subsequently, the *natd* service, a network address translation (NAT) daemon, must be initiated (created) to use DHCP and provide translation.

This is a very insecure firewall at this point. Further configuration of the *ipfw* file (on FreeBSD) must be accomplished to complete the security of this machine. Furthermore, proxy software must be

Figure 12.4
*A dual-homed
host provides
Internet access
and proxy
filtering for an
internal network.*

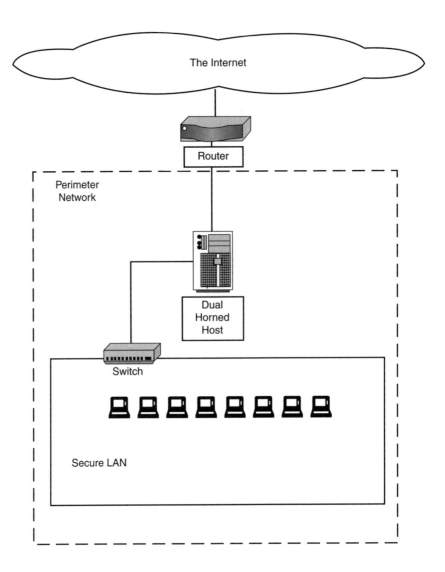

investigated. A complete firewall solution means that one side of the
dual-homed host emulates the Internet for the other, with all packets and protocols filtered at the application level and the network
layer. Anything less tempts fate. This author has seen fate. Fate can
be very nasty and can cause much indigestion and sleepless nights.
Don't tempt fate.

On a more cheerful note, there are many resources available on
the web that will assist with pointing the do-it-yourselfer in the right

direction. Reading this book six times, buying a copy for each of your friends, and reading any and all available resources on the subject will be a good start. However, just like oil painting, reading a book on the subject will not produce an expert. Getting elbows deep into a dual-homed host configuration while knee deep in users baying at the gates may not be an option, either. Late nights, after hours, are best for developing this art. Firewall configuration, from scratch, takes many hours of concentration, and frequent interruptions can be unnerving and detrimental to the process.

In the end, a packaged solution may be ideal. The phone and e-mail technical support team is usually excellent, and software updates for a thriving company will be frequent. Beware of purchasing from up-and-comers, because oftentimes they get bought out, and although they seemed like a bargain at the time, you will lament a great deal when the new proprietor opts to discontinue the product line in favor of another.

12.3 Single-box architecture

Much of what has been discussed in these past few chapters relates to single-box architecture. This refers to the concept of a single unit, such as a dual-homed host or a souped-up router, used to provide gateway security. The advantage of such consolidated systems includes the following points:

- Easier to understand
- Easier for management to understand
- Simple to purchase
- Well supported
- Quick to implement
- Easy to maintain

Alternatively, some would suggest (and as the name implies) that a single-box firewall presents a security risk because in the event of a breach, a potential for system-wide enthrallment exists. However, if in-depth defense is the goal, then a comprehensive single-box architecture can be just as capable as multiple component systems of a multiple, layered defense. In some cases, such architectures may incorporate series, parallel, or series and parallel defense strategies, wherein multiple firewalls and DMZs exist on the perimeter with specialized functions. This can lighten the load of network traffic on a single machine, easing a bottleneck, or it can merely be that the one-box solution provides *better security* in some particular area than another. Multiple firewall devices and appliances may end up grouped at the perimeter and providing a range of security services.

Single-box architectures and blended defenses are common; many are the IT security centers where a stack of mismatched boxes and appliances serve in a variety of security roles. Again, Figure 12.1 shows multiple single-box points. There is a box for FTP service, secure virtual private networking (VPN) from the DMZ to another DMZ, gateway e-mail firewall, proxy service, and stateful packet inspection. Network tasks have been broken out and isolated to provide additional security. Connectivity to the remote host actually requires a workstation attached to the VPN firewall device; it's not even accessible from anywhere in the internal network. Sometimes security is less about the physical approach and more about best practices.

Such a system as the one in Figure 12.1 can be very complicated. It follows, then, that physical security precautions become more important, because tampering may not be immediately evident. Systems such as these, often on busy and mutating networks with diverse missions, also may be subject to frequent physical alteration. A component may fail, and rerouting may be necessary. New appliances may be introduced and removed and patch cables may be added and removed or added and forgotten. For this reason, network diagrams should be detailed and kept current. Such modularity may be appealing to some, but the complexity and the distributed nature increase maintenance, and management costs can be prohibitive to others. However, the nicest thing about this structure is the ease with which systems can be brought online and offline without affecting other enterprise systems.

Often, a single-box implementation will be just that—a single box. In these cases, there may be no screened subnet or perimeter network at all. NAT is disabled, and both sides of the router are set with the same external IP address. This turns the router into little more than an authenticating device that assures the ISP that the network attached to its network is, in fact, authorized to be there. Other than that, it passes all traffic to whatever sits on its internal side. In a *single-box* architecture, the firewall attaches to the router in this fashion. Setting up a subnet between the firewall and the router won't hurt anything, but if the firewall is to be receiving any significant application traffic that requires the use of an external IP address for security reasons, such as SMTP, the simplest solution will be to enable passthrough.

12.4 Summary

Firewalls are ever-evolving systems. As companies grow, they change. They gain resources that allow them to provide many costly services internally, at what may be bargain-basement discount prices. And, as companies grow, security risks from both internal and external networks become greater. Perimeter security often shifts and alters itself in response to situations.

External events also affect configuration; a change in how large ISP e-mail providers receive and authenticate e-mail may force change. Buy-out of a company that provides load balancers may cause a discontinuation of support for your favorite product, and as time passes and the Internet changes, the product—with no firmware upgrades available to it—may one day cease to function, or some aspect of it may no longer operate properly. Nobody in a technology services career should expect to find and implement a firewall solution that will always be appropriate; environmental and technological changes virtually guarantee that the landscape of a firewall perimeter will mutate frequently.

13

External Servers Protection

13.1 Chapter objectives

- Web site strategy
- Secure server communications
- Secure application development
- Server performance
- Using Secure Socket Layer (SSL)
- Internet server virtual private networking

13.2 Siting external servers on a perimeter net

Without doubt, placing and managing servers on the Internet for external use involves a high degree of skill and proficiency. The ever-increasing tide of malicious traffic alone will discourage many, but the rewards and cost savings of self-hosting can, for the proficient, make this a worthwhile endeavor. Chapter 12 detailed the various methods of protecting internal systems from the Internet through placement of proxy servers in perimeter nets or demilitarized zones (DMZs). This chapter explores methods to protect those servers that are placed on the perimeter, whether FTP servers, mail servers, database servers, or web servers; failing to ensure the protection of these critical business components only produces a full and healthy yield of *disaster*. The type of protection varies depending on the mission of the server, the operating system (OS) of the server, and the location of the server. Almost *any* web server placed on the Internet will experience intentionally malicious intrusion attempts.

Once upon a time, long before placing servers on a perimeter net required such consideration, somebody famous once said, "The only thing we have to fear is fear itself." With respect to *edge* server deployment, this describes the general psychology of paranoia and fear that seems to plague many server administrators. As they watch their machines in normal operation, the *edge*—the servers on the perimeter—often causes them to jump to radical conclusions. There are many, many stories that this author has experienced first-hand, heard, or seen that corroborate this theory: One server administrator was convinced his machine had been compromised and had commenced to acting as a slave in an army of slaves attempting to bring down the entire government. In reality, a developer had just posted a script to the site that checks a government time server every 100 milliseconds instead of every 100,000 milliseconds. Another server administrator became convinced his server had been compromised when, for no apparent reason, the indexing service stopped working properly and site searches no longer yielded results. In reality, a different service had been reconfigured (improperly) by someone else and this caused a conflict. This is not uncommon. Web developers are infamous for their exuberant inexperience, a trait that often leads to web servers behaving in radical ways that give server administrators bad cases of the jitters and, for lack of a better term, a general *shell-shocked* management approach. Web developers do things that break site indexing, spawn multitudes of processes, poison DNS caches, create connections to other servers, bring a server to its knees, cause excessive file accessing, and create endless loops that rapidly fill up RAM and can consume disk space like the Chicago fire consumed lumber yards.

Such nuisance phantom web outages caused by the oh-so-often maligned web developer are easily prevented. Implementing a web page/code promotion schedule that follows a calendar cycle, relegates code promotion to one person, and involves a stepped approach of promoting content creates a more predictable server environment. By doing this, the administrator will simply *know* when erratic behavior may occur. Stepping the content through from development, to test, and then to production will prevent the disruption of service caused by prematurely deployed scripts. These things occur in the natural course of operating a web site; their impact can be minimized, and possibly fatal security flaws can be safely avoided, by careful testing and reviewing of code.

Access to the production web server should be strictly limited to the person who can take responsibility for the promotion of all code. By following a calendar-based promotion schedule, non-promotion days when errata are observed are greater cause for concern. A buckshot approach to web development can cause such frequent and common errata that an administrator may be completely unable to differentiate hacker activity from the normal hysteria of day-to-day web development! Using something like Visual Source Safe and integrating it into procedures for web development can provide a very secure and solid foundation upon which to implement acceptable use and development policies.

Operating a SQL server in a development environment creates a level of chaos that can only be untangled by the most proficient of database administrators. As explained in FYI 13.1, further complications with a web server can arise from improper equipment architectures.

13.2.1   Security of SQL and web servers

Someone once suggested to this author that secure communication between remote web servers may be possible over HTTPS. Coming right out and saying that HTTPS between two servers is impossible would be one sure way to receive many letters proclaiming, "Look here, this is what and how we did it." Things happen all the time that defy explanation; however, the primary use of HTTPS is to provide a security protocol for the transmission of data from an authenticated client. This is usually triggered when a user browses to a URL beginning with *https://*. Together, the client and the server negotiate a connection and then exchange authentication information.

How or why this could work between two servers depends on the task that the designer of such a link had in mind. What is the objective? If it was some sort of XML application that retrieves content from another server through HTTP, then yes, HTTPS is an entirely possible and plausible method. But what is the direct security benefit?

In the situation where a TCP/IP connection is using a Data Source Name (DSN) to query a remote SQL server, getting an HTTPS link

Often, for budgetary reasons or whatever, the wrong type of equipment architecture is chosen for servers placed as external servers. Server architecture is important, not only from a security standpoint but also from simple performance requirements. The software OSs, such as UNIX or MS Server 2003, are much better equipped to deal with and address the security concerns of running a web server. Furthermore, the performance of a server equipment architecture will prevent things such as disk hotspots and slow response times that may outwardly imply a breach but are in fact poor performance under heavy load. Desktop workstations are not designed to act in a server capacity, and neither are desktop PCs with server software installed on them. The architecture and equipment are ill equipped, at best, to deal with the strain of acting as an Internet workhorse. Disk response times are significantly slower, and the chipset is simply not designed for a multi-user, high throughput environment.

Primarily, aside from slow responsiveness, slow disk access times, and slow information transmission, if something should happen to the hard drive, should it crash or burn up (something that happens often to single hard drives that suffer from overuse), important data may be lost. If a tape backup has failed for any reason, double the damage. A sincere server architecture would be equipped with SCSI hard drives, which are far superior to PC parallel ATA IDE (what most PCs have), and it would be equipped with several of them at some level of Redundant Array of Independent Disks (RAID), which would allow, if there is a failure, replacement of the drive without interruption to service. Serial ATA (SATA) drives are the latest HDD technology to arrive on the market, and drives such as Western Digital's Raptor boast near SCSI access and response and latency speeds at half the price of SCSI and 4 times the disk space, and will probably render the parallel ATA drives obsolete. As of this writing, the technology market still awaits the introduction of a server architecture based on serial ATA.

Additionally, if tested and proven reliability is needed, such reliability cannot usually be found in PC architectures. Granted, new advances in Serial ATA hard drives, such as Seagate's Barracuda or Western Digital's Raptor drives, shatter the glass ceiling of ATA drive limitations in areas such as armature shake, access time, and RPM. These drives are also priced far beneath SCSI drives of comparable storage size, making them desirable on both levels. Regardless, there are aspects to information handling at the mainboard bus server architecture that should not be overlooked. Although in minimal-use applications, a beefy desktop with a server OS may suffice, the industrial strength of a true server architecture can't be beat.

to work would be much more challenging, and creating a custom application program interface (API) or COM object to translate HTTP traffic would be required. If they were standard queries, then the content could be posted to an IIS directory on the SQL server and the other server could retrieve it via HTTPS that way, but still the authentication method and session management via the web server would be necessary. This might be unwanted overhead.

Although rigging HTTPS to transfer data or to serialize XML data may be a possible solution for cross-Internet secure communication between servers, the best bet for that sort of communication is a virtual private network (VPN). There are other issues involved as well, especially if one of the servers is tucked away behind a firewall. In such a case, you can tunnel out from behind the firewall, as long as you have an Internet connection at the machine and providing a policy has been configured on the firewall to allow the VPN port to communicate freely and establish a VPN, regardless of where it is.

However, in that case, the machine behind the firewall has to be the one initiating the connection. If the connection is broken, then it also has to be reinitiated by the hidden machine. I think that having a service running that monitors the VPN and ensures it is active is wise and probably easier than trying to create an HTTPS device that, basically, acts like a VPN. If you use HTTPS, then you also have to consider the rules that you will have to create to keep just anyone from connecting to your HTTPS port. Remember, HTTPS merely authenticates the server and encrypts the resulting connection traffic. It does not particularly care about the client—it only cares that throughout the conversation, the client stays the same (this is done by carrying a piece of the original request from the client throughout the transaction). Anyone with a web browser can connect to a secure port unless his or her IP has been blocked, an obstacle easily overcome by IP spoofing. Alternatively, client layer applications, such as ASP or ColdFusion, can be used with HTTPS to develop custom interfaces that will authenticate with codes. However, such *open, interpretive* languages reside on the servers as plain text, in which case a hacked server becomes an island hopper, opening a gateway to other servers "up the chain" because passwords are stored in open, unencrypted directories and files.

More than likely, what the person who posed the question probably had in mind was the use of SSL, which is a protocol security that can be used with many application protocols and is not relegated strictly to HTTPS. SQL Server supports the use of SSL for various types of communication. Microsoft and Linux both offer a Certificate Authority Service that allows you to create your own certificate, but it will not be one that is publicly trusted and should not be used for public facing applications. More information about how SQL can communicate through SSL and how to install the Certificate Authority can be found in *SQL Server Books Online*. In Windows, under Add remove Windows Components, there is an option to add Certificate Services. Adding a certificate as a Root Certificate Authority will allow your machine to run SSL without paying for a public certificate. Again, although this is just as secure as the public version, it does nothing to identify you as friend or foe to the casual user who may be connecting to the server for some advertised service. Root Certificate Authority should not be used for anonymous access. Furthermore, once installed, the name of the machine will be unchangeable, and it will not be allowed to enter or leave the domain. It is for these reasons that often other security measures are desired.

Finally, the platinum standard of Internet, interserver secure communication is a VPN. Depending on the configuration, the availability, and the purpose of the communication, often the easiest solution is to set the servers up as dual-homed hosts and connect them via secure VPN tunneling. This allows the remote servers to be in constant communication and to move information, and it preserves bandwidth and security. This also allows the two servers to maintain a direct network connection that will potentially support any of the network layer protocols. Either PPtP or IPSec VPN handle the link effectively. Some schools of thought believe that IPSec VPN handles security with both stronger encryption and less bandwidth consumption. IPSec VPN, based on public key and private keys stored on the server, are only as secure as the server. IPSec has little regard for the authenticating client. PPtP leverages either MS-CHAP or MPPE methods of authentication, and care should be taken when configuring the VPN client to ensure that it uses the correct versions.

13.2.2 Search engines

One of the considerations of a web server is also the prying tentacles of search engines. A search engine is also a "bot" that is designed to crawl and creep into every nook and cranny of a web server so that all linked (and sometimes unlinked) pages are indexed. The impact on a site from search engines can be minimized by placing a text file, called *robots.txt*, at your root directory that provides instructions to (most) bots as to where to index and where not to index. Generally, the traffic caused by a single search engine such as Google would be minimal, but there are lots of bots crawling the web and not all of them are as well designed as they should be. It's generally a good idea to keep an eye on the statistics logs for problems, and if there is a problem with a particular bot, usually the problem can be eliminated by configuring IIS to deny the originating IP addresses.

Using the following rules to control bots that visit your site may also alleviate the problem:

To exclude all spiders and bots, enter the following code into the robots.txt file. It will be found by the bot if it is placed at the root of the web server's public directory:

User-agent: *

Disallow: /

To exclude only certain directories from bot scanning, place the following instead. For multiple directories, add additional *disallow* lines. For a particular file, enter the name and directory path of the file:

User-agent: *

Disallow: /aboutme/

To prevent a particular search engine indexing your site, you must first know the name of the engine's bot:

User-agent: Bot_Name

Disallow: /path/

Search engines usually provide the information on their sites about their robot methods, schedules, and attributes. Examining a hits log may also provide some clues.

Other alternatives include creating a script as a site interface that will deny certain types of requests. This author did something similar for a site that kept getting punched out by code red requests. A script that can periodically create a site index of pages, a sort of registry, is required. Another script can then be positioned as an application script for the entire site. ASP and ColdFusion both offer the ability to place a script that intercepts any and all requests to the site before any files are ever served. These *requests*, once received, can be handled just like any other environmental variable on a web site. If the web server requests an unlisted page, the script serves up an error. Granted, IIS is supposed to do this for you, but the code red problem was a problem for that very reason; certain types of requests that came in caused the server to choke. A script can also be created that will allow access to only certain IP Address ranges, and anything else that comes in will receive the error of your choice—like, "site not found," etc.

13.2.3 SQL server security

Running a SQL server on a perimeter net can pose its own set of both security and performance problems. If a SQL server is running unthrottled, with no performance tuning on a shared space with other web applications and services in use, detecting and removing a security concern can be tantamount to finding a needle in a haystack. The following items, if true, are of particular concern with respect to SQL performance:

- A database's tables will be poorly indexed if it is not truly relational; a table that is 82 fields wide, with half of the columns empty wasted space, will perform very poorly.

- Poorly indexed tables tend to generate disk hotspots like a burning pile of tires generates black smoke.

- Are the indexes clustered? Sometimes a clustered index causes problems, sometimes not clustering an index causes problems. If it was performing better a week ago, have any new indexes been created?

- All user queries are saved in session in RAM.

- The ldf and the mdf files are on the same drive.

- IIS is sitting on the same server as the SQL database. While the SQL server is working, trying to put together data, IIS has to wait (disk hotspots and delays).

The following items are some of the main security concerns. They should be addressed to ensure the server is operating with the full measure of security available to SQL servers:

- *Ensure organizational security*: Make sure that the right people have access and that there is a written security policy.

- *Use both levels of SQL security*: SQL server and database—a Windows login that has been granted access to the SQL server and a SQL server login maintained by SQL server.

- Configure SQL server to use Windows authentication mode.

- Depending on the access needed, servers should be grouped and assigned database roles that allow or prevent things like Delete, Select, and Insert rights.

- Restrict physical access to the server.

- Rename the SQL server Windows administrator account.

- Disable the guest user account.

- Use intrusion detection software to analyze trends, detect DoS attacks, and notify administration of possible breaches.

- Filter data used in queries to prevent users from using SQL injection to execute SQL commands against the database. This can also be accomplished in part by leveraging stored procedures to run the actual SQL commands.

- Logins of employees who leave the organization should be dropped immediately from the database, because they may have unlimited access to sensitive data.

- Use the EFS feature of Windows to encrypt database files. This will prevent unauthorized theft of the two main SQL database files, the ldf and the mdf.

13.3 Deploying packet filtering to control access to your servers

Almost all forms of Internet servers, whether they are SMTP, web, FTP, POP3, or other, will allow the creation of access lists. These access lists allow the creation of either accept or deny lists. Simply put, within the administration properties of any of these servers, there is a tab for site security. This tab will allow the manual entry of multiple IP addresses that can either be allowed or denied access to the resource. In addition to this, if the server is situated behind a firewall, the firewall can be configured to block or grant access to lists of IP addresses.

Typically, these filters allow two basic configurations. The filter can allow access to everyone and then asks that you configure exceptions, which are those to whom you wish to deny access. Alternatively, the filter can be configured to deny everyone and then the acceptable IP addresses must be entered. For a web site that is a confidential resource only to be used by a handful of people, configuring the server to "deny everyone" is the wise choice. For public servers, in which a few nuisance IP addresses are causing trouble, it is best to configure the filter to "accept all" and then deny the nuisance sites.

But what about those who don't have access to the properties and configuration of the web server? Some shared host plan web sites may experience unusual levels of hits activity in their web logs and may simply want to deny access to their site to certain IP addresses. If the site can run scripts, then any competent web consultant should be able to insert a script onto web pages that checks a file or database for a list of IP addresses that should be denied access to resources. This is, of course, a reinvention of the wheel, and if such tasks have become necessary, it may be time to self-host or to consider managed or co-location alternatives that provide more adequate resource controls.

13.4 Router packet filtering

Often, for reasons of performance, budget, time, etc., the only thing standing between a web server and the Internet is a router. Situating a server in this manner, regardless of the level of filtering performed by the router, is not for the fainthearted. Extreme care must be taken to ensure that OS and application updates and virus definitions are always exactly up-to-date. All of the foibles and follies of the OS must be understood. For example, by default, Windows 2000 does not block packets from source TCP port 88 or UDP port 500. A more advanced hacker who knows how to forge packet headers can easily spoof the source port to make it look like a legitimate port 88 (Kerberos) packet.

Things like this are common and widespread (and not well known, either), but this is the type of knowledge that must be sought. It would be nice if everything could be listed here for convenience, but unfortunately the knowledge is so extensive that it would require a book of its own to be complete, and even then it would never be complete because it always changes. There are many Registry tweaks that can be made that will halt such behavior—behavior that is oftentimes perfectly legitimate and even desirable in shielded network computers. Ultimately, if speed and performance of the connection are sought, constant maintenance of the server, constant monitoring, and constant upkeep of router filtering rules can deliver the desired performance. For gaming servers, this is often the rule, not the exception.

13.5 Using router access control lists

Using router access control lists (ACLs) to control access to the server, though not a true firewall, can provide adequate protection if properly configured. ACLs serve as filters that control all traffic entering or leaving a router interface. Information about an IP address and/or a port number can be entered, depending on the router, through either a configuration interface or terminal access. Cisco, for example, provides ample documentation explaining and providing lists of example ACL entries. Things such as the Tiny Fragment attack and the Overlapping Fragment fragmented packet attacks can be blocked with the proper ACL entry. Typically, ACLs are the weak point; they are the reason that fragmented packet attacks are able to penetrate perimeter networks. Cisco has updated its firmware to provide better protection against fragmented packet attacks. Not all routers will provide terminal access to configuration options, and many of them will not offer the granular control over packet types (level 3 or level 4 packet inspection), IP addresses, and ports offered by Cisco. Look before you leap, and if ACL is an important feature and will play a pivotal role in your firewall policy, be sure to pay attention to the details.

Note:

Most router manufacturers practice the philosophy that their job, first and foremost, is to route packets. Filtering is a secondary concern.

13.6 Summary

Placing servers on a perimeter net can provide easy and profitable access to company resources such as web sites, file servers, e-mail, extranets, images, and applications. But it comes at a price. Maintaining security on these servers ranks as one of the most labor intensive and costly endeavors involved in network management. Specialized training, application and equipment firewalls, and security precautions should be in place before servers are even situated. Databases present their own particular sets of security concerns, and in addition to great care in handling credit cards and personal information, it has been shown that e-mail can also be a risk factor. As recently as 2003, AOL experienced the theft, by a trusted employee, of more than 93 million e-mail addresses. This is particularly noteworthy because despite precautions taken to limit file size download and to monitor Internet Messenger (IM) traffic, the employee used VPN access and encrypted IM to plan and execute the heist. In 2004, the perpetrator is on trial, but at what cost? The price tag associated with loss of business, court costs, damage to reputation, etc., will easily run in the millions of dollars.

Access lists should be treated with the same level of security as government threat codes. They should change frequently (daily), should be token driven, and the storage of critical information (including and especially e-mail addresses) should be encrypted at the data level. Merely protecting these items from access is not enough. Special encryption algorithms should be *required* for even simple examination of the data. Only the full gamut of security measures will ensure the protection of critical data—data that, if compromised and released to the public, may cause the annihilation of public trust when the data fall into the wrong hands. Such flagrant heists as the AOL breach give spammers and hackers a veritable gold mine of information. AOL users are, typically, novice users and are the most likely to fall prey to spam scams, or "scam mail" as some call it. By carefully and thoroughly monitoring traffic and engaging the full capabilities of ACLs, application firewalls, and inherent database security, much of the problem traffic present on the Internet today could have been avoided. Being "aware" of the precautions that need to be taken does not serve anyone; security is less about *understanding* and all about taking *action*. Being sorry after the identities of thousands of loyal customer identities have been stolen will not stop the civil suits suing your company for damages.

Section VI

Internal IP Services Protection

14

Internal IP Security Threats: Beyond The Firewall

14.1 Chapter objectives

- Addressing the major threats to networks
- Using a layered security strategy to address internal security threats
- Assessing risk to your organization
- Examining inside attacks
- Locating the saboteur
- Finding the leaky mails
- Dealing with new threats

At this point in the book, it is time to take a step back for a reality check. Firewalls in themselves are not the end-all security solution. A more complete approach is to integrate firewalls with other effective security tools. Let's take a look.

Today the Internet has become a key tool for business communication and information sharing, and many organizations would cease to function if e-mail and web access were denied for any significant period. All Internet content you read, send, and receive carries a risk. The number of potential security risks has increased at the same time as that dependence on information technology has grown, making the need for a comprehensive security program even more important. Likewise, the job of those persons tasked with network security, often system administrators, has never been harder.

The number of reported security incidents continues to grow. There is little indication that this trend will reverse any time soon. According to industry analysts, in 2003, there were 208,870 reported incidents. By the end of the second quarter of 2004, there were already 312,981 incidents reported. A reported incident can be as simple as a single computer being compromised or as severe as a complete network compromise involving hundreds of client computers. The number of reported security vulnerabilities has continued to grow at the same alarming rate, with 8,659 vulnerabilities reported in 2003 and 12,760 reported by the end of the second quarter of 2004.

Many companies, unfortunately, have stopped short of implementing a more secure layered approach to network security and have chosen to rely solely on the firewall/virus scanner approach. Although firewalls and virus protection are necessary, by themselves they address only one portion of potential security risks and may contribute to a false sense of security. A more complete approach integrates these technologies with other effective tools including web and e-mail filtering, intrusion detection, PKI, and artificial intelligence tools. Advanced tools can automate many tasks and increase the efficiency of a security program while reducing demand on network administrators.

14.2 Network threats

Almost every day, experts discover new security vulnerabilities. These newly discovered vulnerabilities may be due to flaws in software or they may be the result of software configuration errors. Hackers or other malicious individuals can exploit these vulnerabilities to gain access to network assets. Administrators must spend a lot of time and energy just staying informed about and dealing with new vulnerabilities. Often the result is that they are unable to take the time to monitor and educate the staff. Enforcement of security policies may be nonexistent or may rely on the honor system. Failure to defend against the key threats to data and network assets can result in disaster.[1]

14.2.1 Behavior of employees

Because of the behavior of their employees, companies can face significant risk. Whether malicious or accidental, security incidents caused by insiders are becoming more common. Insiders may present a more likely threat to many organizations than an attack by hackers or other malicious outsiders. Even when internal security compromises occur, many organizations decide not to report the incidents because of fear of negative publicity. Failure to address employee behavior as part of internal network security leaves an organization exposed in a variety of ways.

The organization can be exposed to litigation by employees accessing offensive or illegal material from a company's network. Employees visiting porn sites or sites with other offensive content create a hostile work environment, affect morale, and may lead to costly litigation. If personnel access illegal material, such as child pornography, an organization may be held liable, have network assets seized in an investigation, and suffer negative publicity.

Tens of millions of people subscribe to free web-based e-mail services such as Hotmail and Yahoo! mail. Allowing personnel to access web-based e-mail accounts from a corporate intranet increases the risk of damage to data and assets by a virus. Although an organization may scan for viruses at its e-mail gateway, employees downloading attachments from web-based accounts circumvent this protection and may unwittingly receive and execute malicious code.

What really poses a threat is software downloaded from the Internet and installed without consent. Employees may inadvertently create a security hole by using ICQ (not an abbreviation, but Internet slang for "I seek you") or chat software. Disgruntled personnel can download and install hacking software that may allow them to circumvent security and delete or steal data. Downloaded games can contain malicious code, and illegal copies of software can result in fines and litigation.

The productivity of the entire organization can be affected negatively by employees who are abusing or misusing e-mail to forward jokes, chain letters, or hoaxes. Organizations can be liable for forwarding of material that is threatening, harassing, or defamatory or that violates human resources (HR) policies. Companies must educate employees about security and information technology (IT) policies to avoid many of these problems. Usually this burden to instruct and notify personnel falls on the IT staff, adding to their workload and frustration. Advanced tools automate these and other functions, freeing IT staff to do other projects.

Employees who are disgruntled may share intellectual property or competitive information with the press or with the competition. Customer lists, proprietary data, financial data, research, and other types of confidential information are also vulnerable. Employees can easily undermine a company's competitive edge with a few forwarded e-mails.

When designing a layered security program, you should consider employee behavior a prime risk. The potential damage done by an insider is often considerably greater than the risk posed by an external threat. Later in this chapter, there will be a discussion about tools that will mitigate these risks and make management of a layered security program easier and more efficient.[2]

14.2.2 E-mail

The Internet's killer application or the application that has driven adoption of the Internet to the greatest degree is definitely e-mail. Most people depend heavily upon e-mail, and many organizations could not operate effectively without it. Although employee behavior can account for the majority of serious abuse, it is not the only threat to this resource.

Spam or junk mail can be an excessive burden to e-mail resources and quickly fill up inboxes. It is often difficult to stop spam despite attempts to legislate against it. Employees should be discouraged from posting or using their work e-mail addresses for Internet shopping or special offers.

To replicate and spread from inbox to inbox, many new Internet worms exploit bugs in Microsoft Outlook and other e-mail software. Virus scanners at the gateway can minimize the risk but may not always intercept new viruses. You should instruct personnel to avoid opening unidentified or suspicious e-mail attachments.

14.2.3 Viruses

Devastating to network assets, data, and productivity are viruses and other malicious code. Each year, viruses grow more sophisticated and programmers who create malicious code are creating more viruses, worms, and Trojans that take advantage of and exploit software vulnerabilities. The Sasser worm is a recent example of this trend.

The numerous virus hoaxes are almost as damaging to productivity. Well-meaning employees forward warnings for nonexistent viruses to other members of the organization, as well as friends and family, compounding the problem of this false information, wasting mail server resources, and creating an additional burden for the IT staff, which must respond. Perpetuation of virus hoaxes can be limited or stopped by addressing employee behavior in your security program and using the proper screening tools.

14.2.4 Spyware

Spyware can be defined as any software that covertly gathers user information through the user's Internet connection without his or her knowledge, usually for advertising purposes. Spyware applications are typically bundled as a hidden component of freeware or shareware programs that can be downloaded from the Internet; however, it should be noted that the majority of shareware and freeware applications do not come with spyware. Once installed, the spyware monitors user activity on the Internet and transmits that information in the background to someone else. Spyware can also gather information about e-mail addresses and even passwords and credit card numbers.

Spyware is similar to a Trojan horse in that users unwittingly install the product when they install something else. A common way to become a victim of spyware is to download certain peer-to-peer file-swapping products.

Aside from the questions of ethics and privacy, spyware steals from the user by using the computer's memory resources and by eating bandwidth as it sends information back to the spyware's home base via the user's Internet connection. Because spyware is using memory and system resources, the applications running in the background can lead to system crashes or general system instability.

Also, because spyware exists as independent executable programs, they can monitor keystrokes; scan files on the hard drive, snoop other applications, such as chat programs or word processors; install other spyware programs; read cookies; and change the default home page on the Web browser. This information is consistently relayed back to the spyware author who will either use it for advertising/marketing purposes or sell the information to another party.

Licensing agreements that accompany software downloads sometimes warn the user that a spyware program will be installed along with the requested software. Nevertheless, though, the licensing agreements may not always be read completely because the notice of a spyware installation is often couched in obtuse, hard-to-read legal disclaimers.

14.2.5 Hackers

An individual with a great deal of technical knowledge about computer systems and their security is known as a hacker. Originally, the term had no negative connotations; in fact, it was a compliment in recognition of a great deal of technical prowess. Today, the term is frequently applied to cyber criminals, to the dismay of legitimate hackers. Hackers prefer to call criminal hackers "crackers" and wish that the press would do the same.

The most publicized threat to enterprise security are hackers. Hackers make great headlines and companies have spent millions of dollars improving existing security programs or creating new ones in reaction to the threat. Although malicious outsiders are a risk to an enterprise, in comparison to other risks faced by an organization, it is less likely that an outsider will compromise network assets.

Focusing entirely on hackers may lead an organization to overlook a more likely threat, that of an insider compromising security intentionally, due to mistakes, or through negligence. Even in cases where an outsider actually penetrates network security, more often than not, someone within an organization has enabled the attack intentionally or through negligence. Adding additional layers of security that complement firewalls and virus protection will allow an organization to mitigate internal risks.

14.3 Organizational risk assessment

Most companies would privately admit that their IT security is not as comprehensive as it should be. Security policies and procedures are often far behind technological advances, and adequate staff education is rare. In fact, many organizations only develop or update policies and procedures in reaction to a security compromise. As a result, many companies are vulnerable, despite spending large sums on security products and consultants. A more proactive approach involves identifying risks specific to your organization, regularly auditing, addressing known risks, and dealing with new risks proactively rather than reactively.

An organization has to know that it is at risk before it can protect something. It is impossible to plan for the security of assets if you do not know the threats against them. Risk analysis is a process of identifying assets that need protection and evaluating the threats against those assets. Risk analysis can be simplified and broken down into five steps:

1. Identify assets.

2. Determine the value of each asset and identify the cost associated with its loss.

3. Identify threats to the asset.

4. Determine the vulnerability to those threats.

5. Prioritize assets by level of importance.[3]

By following the preceding steps, you can identify assets that are at risk and plan for their protection. You should also not overlook the possibility of threats from within your organization. Too often, organizations emphasize external threats, specifically hackers and viruses, and ignore the more likely threats from within an organization. Most threats come from within a company, and recent trends demonstrate this.

Malicious action, negligence, disdain of security practices, and ignorance of security policy and practices are sources of insider security problems. Misuse of computer systems by employees may result in liability if they use internal systems to access illegal or offensive material or to commit computer crime. Intentional or accidental public dissemination of sensitive information can result in lawsuits or loss of revenue. Laws concerning protection of privacy data make monitoring employee behavior more important than ever before.

How is internal network security addressed by your organization? What is the liability involved if your organization's data are compromised? Your level of exposure to internal risks will dictate the steps you must take to mitigate the risks. A security policy and program must include steps to mitigate the risks from disgruntled employees, risk of liability due to employee behavior, or damage to systems from employee error. As mentioned earlier, the job of enforcing the policy and educating personnel usually falls on the shoulders of an already burdened IT staff. Automated security tools can inform and enforce, making a security program more efficient while reducing the cost in person-hours.

14.4 Examining inside attacks

Recent industry surveys indicate that security breaches originating from within an organization may account for up to 90% of all incidents. These same surveys indicate the losses suffered from an external intrusion amount to $90,000 on average and that the average "inside job" cost is in excess of $5.9 million!

The risk from within certainly seems to outweigh the seemingly more dangerous threat posed by hackers. An insider often has the motive, knowledge, and opportunity to do far greater harm to IT assets than any outsider. A hacker must spend a great deal of time and effort to gain significant intelligence on a well-protected network. An insider has intimate knowledge because of his or her position in the company and can often compromise security or destroy data even after he or she no longer has physical access to the network. Consider this threat a prime risk to network security. The following real-world examples demonstrate why.

14.4.1 Saboteurs

On August 3, 1999, a software time-bomb went off on the primary file server of an engineering company's Bridgeport, New Jersey, manufacturing plant. The malicious program deleted manufacturing programs that the company depended on to conduct business, causing it to lose an estimated $13 million in business and $5 million in programming costs to resume business. The company suffered loss of market share and had to lay off many employees. Even now, it is still recovering from the sabotage.

A systems administrator who worked at the company for more than 14 years wrote the software time-bomb. He had intimate knowledge of the network and critical systems and was able to use that knowledge to cripple his former employers. Lloyd, a trusted and loyal employee, had access to senior management. As the company grew, he became disgruntled at his own loss of influence and eventually lost his job. This apparently prompted his act of sabotage, and no procedures were in place to protect against an individual with his level of access from damaging the systems from within.

A jury convicted the systems administrator, and a federal judge sentenced him to 44 months in federal prison and $5 million in restitution. But the damage inflicted on his former employers can never be undone.

The company has put security systems in place to mitigate the risk of future sabotage, as well as multiple backup systems to provide for recovery of data. However, reacting to a security incident has certainly cost the company far more than a proactive security program would have ever cost.

14.4.2 Leaky e-mail

In Japan, the U.S. Army was embarrassed when an anonymous employee leaked the contents of an e-mail message sent by Brigadier General Jack O'Niell (not real name) to the local press. Relations between the U.S. Military and the local citizens were already strained because of several incidents involving U.S. Army personnel, including the rape of a schoolgirl by four soldiers. Brigadier General Jack O'Niell conveyed his thoughts about local officials in his e-mail. "I think they are all nuts, and a bunch of wimps," he stated in his e-mail. Of course, this aggravated an already volatile situation and damaged relations between the Army and the local citizens even further.

A single forwarded e-mail further damaged public relations and cast the U.S. military in a bad light both in Japan and in the United States in this case. A proactive content security program may have prevented a sensitive (or insensitive) communication from being compromised.

14.5 Handling new threats

Almost on a daily basis, new threats to networked computers appear. Hackers may discover weaknesses in software and post these exploits on several web sites. There is a good and a bad side to this activity. The good side is that the information is available to everyone and security personnel or system administrators can act to secure computers with the security hole. The bad side is that the information is available to everyone, and malicious hackers can attempt to use it to exploit and gain access to systems before system administrators patch them.

Often the threats are variants of previous threats (modified worms and viruses), in which case they will take advantage of known weaknesses in operating systems or applications. This underscores the need for personnel to stay aware of software vulnerabilities that may affect their systems and update software accordingly. Security applications that automate updates to their own databases can significantly improve efficiency in this regard by assuming responsibility for this task and freeing IT personnel for more important duties.

14.6 Antivirus software technology: beyond the firewall

Firewall is the first and last word in security for many companies. Many administrators regard the firewall as a magic bullet that will somehow make their networks impervious to risk. A firewall is a necessary and important part of any security program. It can limit access to your private network from the public Internet and divide your internal network into zones, thus limiting employee access to network areas that they require to perform their jobs. However, a firewall by itself cannot effectively deal with most insider threats.

Antivirus software is the second ingredient that makes up one of the most popular security programs. With the proliferation of viruses, worms (see FYI 4.1) and other malicious programs, antivirus software is also a necessary part of network security. Even a simple e-mail worm (the Love Bug) can waste bandwidth and crash mail servers or entire networks. Some worms, such as the Code Red worm and its variants, inflicted unexpected collateral damage on many networked print and storage devices, causing them to crash or hang despite that it did not target these devices specifically. Properly maintained and updated antivirus software can go a long way in protecting a network from this damage, but insiders can intentionally, or inadvertently, circumvent antivirus applications, thus leaving your network vulnerable.

As prevalent as the firewall/antivirus security model is, it cannot adequately protect organizations from the risk of an external attack

FYI 14.1   *MyDoom Worm Variant Hits Google and Other Search Engines*

Major Internet search engines were crippled by a variant of the MyDoom worm, rendering Google inaccessible to many users and slowing results from Yahoo. The attack also affected smaller engines, including Yahoo's AltaVista and Lycos.

The MyDoom worm affected performance of the search engines. The effect on Yahoo was limited because of the company's backup procedures. However, AltaVista, a search engine that Yahoo owns and that relies on different technology, experienced more problems.

MyDoom was kind of an inadvertent distributed denial-of-service (DDoS) attack. The sites were being knocked out in the search for more e-mail addresses. This is a twist on MyDoom: Earlier variants looked for e-mail addresses on the host hard drive. The latest version is now running queries on search engines.

Once infected, a machine might send thousands of requests. If a computer is only a few years old and connected to the Internet via broadband, the user probably won't notice the slight decrease in his or her machine's performance. Google users were especially taken aback by the search outage.

and does little alone to provide security against malicious insiders. The answer to this problem is the addition of security layers using advanced tools that complement the firewall/antivirus approach while addressing the areas of greatest risk.

14.6.1   Layered approach

Using successive layers of protection allows an organization to provide adequate protection against most threats it faces, thus minimizing risk. Implemented technologies should complement one another, with one component addressing threats that other components do not and securing paths around (or through) other components. This comprehensive approach can mitigate risk more effectively and improve the efficiency of the security program.

You should take care to carefully select tools that perform the required functions without adding unnecessary complexity to the system. Increased complexity often results in decreased security, not in a more secure network environment. You should also avoid unnecessary redundancy. This is not the goal of a layered program and may increase complexity or create conflict between components of the system. If one antivirus package is good, that does not mean that two running on the same gateway would be better. A duplicating function would most likely result in conflict and wasted computing resources.

For an example of complementary technologies, let's look at antivirus software and content security using web filtering.

An antivirus product installed on an e-mail gateway may provide adequate protection from e-mail–borne viruses and malicious attachments. However, if employees can access web-based e-mail accounts, they can circumvent this component and compromise the network by downloading attachments. A web-filtering solution can prevent employees from accessing web-based e-mail accounts, closing this backdoor past the antivirus solution.

This is the strength of a layered program: Each component acts to protect the network against specific threats while adding to the effectiveness of the other components. The different tools, like layers of armor, work to exclude unauthorized access and prevent compromises from within the network.

You should select automated tools that will handle reporting and enforcement of the security policies. A web-filtering tool that informs users that they cannot access a specific web site and notifies the administrator of the attempt saves time and allows fewer IT personnel to invest time in monitoring and educating employees. Real-time reporting is especially desirable, because it allows an administrator to detect and react to attempts to compromise security before they succeed.

14.6.2 Intrusion detection tools

An intrusion detection system (IDS) monitors systems and analyzes network traffic to detect signs of intrusion. An IDS can detect various attacks in progress and attempt to scan a network for weaknesses. An IDS can be a dedicated network appliance or a software solution installed on a host computer. A network intrusion detection system (NIDS) monitors all traffic on a network segment and is most effective when used with a firewall. If placed near remote access servers and on wide area network (WAN) backbones, traffic on a WAN backbone may be too fast for an individual NIDS to keep up with.

An NIDS/IDS can detect attempts to scan a network for intelligence gathering purposes. Hackers often scan networks to detect services running on ports of specific hosts. This can allow a hacker to identify the operating system of the host(s) and detect any exploitable services. There are many types of port-scanning applications. Some can bypass a firewall and attempt to scan hosts within a private network. An NIDS/IDS can detect these stealth scans, complementing your firewall and providing an added layer of security.

An NIDS/IDS may use anomaly detection to discover intrusion attempts. This involves monitoring resource use, network traffic, and user behavior, as well as comparing the levels of these to normal levels. If a user that normally accesses the system only between 9 am and 5 pm suddenly logs on at 3 am, this may indicate that an intruder has compromised the user's account. An NIDS/IDS would then alert administrators to the suspicious activity.

14.6.3 Public key infrastructure

Public key infrastructure (PKI) enables organizations to communicate securely using software and services that rely on public key encryption. PKI systems use digital certificates and digital signatures to identify parties in a transaction and allow for secure signing of messages, confidentiality of communication, and secure remote access to network assets.

Public key encryption uses pairs of encrypted keys (public and private) to allow parties to communicate securely. Using an individual's public key, anyone can encrypt (scramble) a message that can only be decrypted (unscrambled) by that person's private key. A digital certificate is a digital ID that certifies that a particular public key belongs to a specific individual or organization. PKI relies on trusted third parties called *certificate authorities* (CAs) that issue digital certificates to identify individuals and organizations over a public network.

Much of the software already in daily use supports PKI, including browsers and e-mail clients. Properly used, PKI can secure remote access to systems, communications, and financial transactions. Digital signing of software can ensure that software downloaded from the Internet has not been tampered with and establish who wrote the software. Digital signatures can ensure the integrity of a message so that recipients know that a third party has not altered it. By ensuring the integrity of documents, digital signatures can satisfy legal requirements for non-repudiation in some states.

PKI can be an important part of a comprehensive security program, but it is not a cure-all for security woes. PKI solutions vary in complexity, and no single approach is right for every organization. PKI has its weaknesses, and some PKI solutions are more secure than others. By itself, PKI does not adequately address the threat posed by malicious insiders.

14.6.4 Security content

Content security using filtering technology provides the key protection against risk posed by employee behavior and abuse of IT resources. Filtering solutions can protect an organization from employee error, including the following:

- Accessing illegal or offensive material
- Compromise of information due to negligence
- Compromising security by downloading unauthorized software
- Inadvertent disclosure of confidential or sensitive information
- Malicious compromise of information[4]

Filtering solutions allow management to control who may access and distribute information. This limits the amount of damage that individuals can do and aids in the enforcement of both security and privacy policies. Even when an acceptable-use policy (AUP) is in place, administrators often lack the means to enforce it. Filtering solutions enable management to enforce security policies, privacy policies, and AUPs while managing staff productivity and minimizing wasted network bandwidth.

Filtering the web

Internet access is necessary for many employees; however, abuse of this access can waste network bandwidth, decrease productivity, and expose an organization to legal liability. Internet filtering manages harmful and unnecessary web and e-mail content according to your policy. Web filtering can increase the security of a network by preventing circumvention of other security software (antivirus software via the Internet) and blocking the download of unauthorized or illegal software.

To maximize the benefits of a filtering solution, it is essential that the chosen solution is configurable and gives administrators maximum flexibility in managing content security. Administrators must be able to configure blocking by user and group. There is no such thing as a one-size-fits-all policy, and organizations differ in their need for blocking even between individual departments. A solution that does not allow this level of customization will quickly outgrow its usefulness, or worse, administrators may circumvent it if it seems to be a burden.

Software should allow for blocking by file extension or true MIME type. This is extremely useful if your staff collaborates on documents via the web and you want to allow Microsoft Word and PowerPoint documents, but not executable files or image files. Again, if the choice is all or nothing, the result will be that administrators will block no files if the software prevents the staff from doing their jobs.

Administrators should be able to define rules for blocking for maximum flexibility. Management can predetermine the level of trust for each employee or group of employees and allow selective blocking based on employee need and level of trust. Flexibility is one of the most important factors relating to acceptance of a filtering solution.

Automated reporting increases the efficiency of policy enforcement, allows management to stay informed of employee activities, and reduces the workload of administrators. Reports should be customizable to allow for different information requirements and reporting to different levels of an organization. Automatic scheduling of periodic reports and real-time notification and reporting of abuses are essential and will increase the ROI of the program.

Many filtering applications block web addresses based on a list of keywords or phrases. These keywords may indicate obvious offensive or illegal material such as porn, sex, or words that are more explicit. Keyword blocking is limited in its effectiveness and can result in overblocking or erroneous exclusion of sites. An example of this is a breast cancer site blocked because of the word *breast* appearing on the page. Such obvious mistakes have become rare as the technology has improved, but software that blocks based on keywords alone is an insufficient tool in an enterprise security program.

Software intended for use in an enterprise security program will usually rely on an extensive database maintained by real people, in addition to blocking based on advanced artificial intelligence and keyword recognition. These databases consist of millions of sites prescreened by professionals to determine their content. The best solutions organize sites into groups and categories that allow administrators to define access to very specific types of web sites while blocking others. Because of the nature of the Internet, updates to the database should be available frequently (daily is best).

By implementing content security through web filtering, an organization will minimize the risk of litigation, reduce wasted network bandwidth, and improve productivity. The use of advanced automated tools will increase the ROI, reduce the burden on IT staff, and improve the enforcement and efficiency of security, AUP, and privacy policies.

Filtering e-mail

The second key component in the content security program is an e-mail filtering solution. Access to e-mail is necessary for arguably every employee in a company. E-mail provides an efficient means for all levels of the organization to communicate and collaborate on projects. However, abuse of e-mail will result in loss of productivity, exposure to liability, wasted bandwidth, and an increased burden on mail servers.

Often abuse of e-mail leads to the termination of personnel. In 1999, the *New York Times* fired 24 employees for sending inappropriate e-mail, and the U.S. Navy disciplined more than 600 sailors for sending sexually explicit e-mail. Clearly, an AUP or security policy will not enforce itself. Depending on the honor system for enforcement increases risk and undermines the credibility of policies and procedures.

An e-mail–filtering solution must allow managers to control which employees can e-mail particular information and to whom they may send it. The software should provide real-time monitoring and quarantine of suspect messages. The software must be configurable to allow managers to review e-mail, remotely if necessary, and provide automated notification so administrators can monitor attempts to send unauthorized information or attachments.

Advanced text and content analysis is necessary to reduce the likelihood of users sending sensitive information to unauthorized parties. Analysis should be customizable and allow for examination of attachments including those that are compressed (zipped files).

Solutions that allow for multiple dictionaries are context sensitive. They include the ability to filter by keyword and phrase, reduce the number of false false-positive alerts, and increase the efficiency of the system. Customization is key, as in web filtering, and the solution that allows administrators the most flexibility in determining rules will be the most successful.

E-mail–filtering tools are the most reliable way to enforce e-mail procedures and policies while reducing the workload on IT staff.

This is the best technology decision for mitigating the risk of employee abuse of e-mail services and possible liability resulting from that abuse. Together with a web-filtering product, an e-mail filter provides a complete solution to secure content in an organization. Securing content is necessary to prevent incidents and liability resulting from employee behavior.

14.7 Summary

Perhaps the most overlooked threat in a security program is the threat posed by employee behavior. As much as 90% of security compromises are the result of actions by an insider. Whether incidents are due to malicious intent or inadvertent employee error, the result is the same: loss of revenue, decreased productivity, and potential liability.

The threats to networks will only continue to grow. This is in part due to the increasing complexity of enterprise systems, which results in a greater possibility of unexpected interactions and software faults. The ability of administrators to keep up with the growing number of threats is decreasing because of increasing demands on their time. The only way to alleviate the burden on IT staff and increase security at the same time is to implement a proactive security program that automates as many functions as possible. Automated content security tools help to effectively and efficiently secure network assets against threats from within an organization.

14.8 References

1. "Information Security: Mechanisms And Techniques," National Institute of Standards and Technology, U.S. Department of Commerce, Gaithersburg, Maryland, January, 2002.

2. Shirley Radack (Ed.), "Selecting Information Technology Security Products," National Institute of Standards and Technology, U.S. Department of Commerce, Gaithersburg, Maryland, 2004.

3. Shirley Radack (Ed.), "Security Considerations In The Information System Development Life Cycle," National Institute of Standards and Technology, U.S. Department of Commerce, Gaithersburg, Maryland, 2004.

4.   John Wack, Ken Cutler and Jamie Pole, "Guidelines on Firewalls and Firewall Policy: Recommendations of the National Institute of Standards and Technology," National Institute of Standards and Technology, U.S. Department of Commerce, Gaithersburg, Maryland, January, 2002.

15

Network Address Translation Deployment

15.1 Chapter objectives

- Enabling Network Address Translations (NATs) and firewalls with the Session Initiation Protocol (SIP)
- Setting up Linux-based firewalls for a small office, home office (SOHO)
- Firewall load-balancing deployment
- Conducting videoconferencing with firewalls
- Deploying a voice proxy firewall

The next big step in Internet usage is going on right now! Real-time person-to-person (P2P) communication, like Internet Protocol (IP) telephony (voice over IP [VoIP]), presence, instant messaging, voice, video, and data collaboration, is all the rage. The Internet standard for such communication is the Session Initiation Protocol (SIP). To be part of this accelerating SIP user community, your network must be prepared for it. To have universal connectivity across the Internet, Network Address Translations (NATs) and firewalls need to be SIP capable, which is currently becoming common.

15.2 Person-to-person communication

The Internet started as a defense, research, and university network. There are two applications that have spread Internet usage to almost all companies and persons in the world: e-mail and web surfing. However, these applications do not direct real-time communication

(RTC) between individuals, a capability that is becoming highly useful as more and more individuals have broadband or a fixed connection to the Internet.

Several forms of P2P communication over the Internet have already been in use for a few years. However, it is just now, when a general standard has been established, that these types of applications have become more available and more widely used. SIP is the Internet standard for such applications and currently has a strongly accelerating growth.

The SIP Center (www.sipcenter.com) is a portal for the commercial development of the SIP. Serving both the SIP community and the wider industry, the SIP Center offers comprehensive technical and market resources, as well as an environment for the testing of SIP implementations.

Note: | URLs are subject to change without notice. |

A powerful driving force for SIP is that Microsoft has announced that all future RTC will be based on the SIP standard. Windows Messenger, which can be downloaded at no charge, already has a SIP mode that provides the user with telephony, voice, video, presence, and instant messaging, and Microsoft recently launched Greenwich, the RTC services for the Windows 2003 server. Greenwich includes a SIP server for safe enterprise usage and a programming application program interface (API), which resulted in numerous SIP applications. With the market impact of Microsoft, there are now tens of millions of SIP users.[1]

15.3 Internet protocol telephony

SIP is also used for ordinary telephony (voice with 3-kHz bandwidth and common number dialing) over IP networks. For this application, the SIP standard is taking over from the earlier H.323 standard, which is a protocol from the standardization organization of the telecom world, the International Telecommunications Union-Telecommunications (ITU-T). H.323 has been used to build islands of VoIP, but most often without interoperability on the IP level between the different operators. Another protocol is Media Gateway Control Protocol (MGCP), or the related H.248/Media Gateway Controller (MEGACO), which sometimes is used to control IP phones on a low level in order for operators to connect these to the old telephone network, the Public Switched Telephone Network (PSTN).

It should be noted that IP telephony (where ordinary telephony is emulated over IP) is only a small part of P2P communication for which SIP was created. Real-time P2P communication is now the next big step in Internet usage, following e-mail and web surfing.[2]

15.4 Routers, firewalls, and NATs

When connecting a PC to the Internet, you do not want it to be accessible to everyone or vulnerable to attacks from hackers. This is especially important if you are constantly connected, for example, via broadband or a fixed line. A firewall protects the PC by only allowing approved traffic and by rejecting attacks and illegal data packets.

On a local area network (LAN), where several PCs or other equipment are connected, it is common to have private IP addresses on the LAN and a single common public IP address to the Internet. That is called NAT and is often an integrated part of the firewall.

Firewalls and NAT routers are designed for data traffic that is initiated from the inside of the private network. If instead the data traffic is initiated from the outside, and even worse, must reach a specific user on the private network, serious problems occur.

This is exactly what is happening with P2P communication via SIP. Therefore, it is highly important that all new firewalls and NAT routers now being installed are designed to support SIP properly and securely.[3]

15.5 Handling SIP

Most firewalls installed today do not handle SIP adequately. The problem occurs for all similar protocols (H.323) where a person on a private LAN is to be contacted. Ordinary firewalls are simply not designed for such data traffic. It is a common misunderstanding that well-known firewalls can be configured to handle SIP traffic, but that is not the case. One problem is that the media streams (voice and video packets) are transferred over dynamically assigned User Datagram Protocol (UDP) ports that are generally closed. Another problem is that the SIP clients inside the firewall cannot be reached by IP addresses because these most often are private and local to the LAN. It simply does not work, unless there is specific SIP support in the firewall.

The same applies to routers that are switching the address space, NATs. NAT routers are used when several users share a common Internet connection with a single IP address. There are also operators only offering private IP addresses to their customers.

15.6 Firewall traversal/SIP NAT

It is, of course, a fundamental problem that P2P communication does not reach the users on the LANs. Various methods and equipment have been suggested to solve this problem in a number of situations, but the most general one is to eliminate the problem where it occurs—in the firewall itself. Firewalls including a SIP server (with a SIP proxy and SIP registrar) that dynamically controls the firewall are available.

A number of firewall vendors have introduced models including a SIP Application Layer Gateway (ALG). These ALGs usually work at a lower level than a proxy, adjusting the data packets on-the-fly: Cisco has introduced such ALGs that also handle incoming calls to multiple users, while other more simple implementations may only support a single SIP user on the LAN. A common limitation of the ALG architecture is that it cannot handle secure SIP signaling via Transport Layer Security (TLS). TLS is strongly recommended by Microsoft to be used with its Greenwich SIP enterprise solution.

SIP-capable firewalls are not more expensive than ordinary firewalls and should be considered for all new installations of firewalls and NATs. If not, there is a high risk that even newly installed firewalls and NATs will have to be exchanged.

Other methods are also proposed for SIP firewall and NAT traversal. For example, Simple Traversal of UDP through NATs (STUN) is a method for getting SIP through existing NATs. It works through keeping holes open in the NAT by dummy traffic and having the SIP clients emulate their looks from the outside of the protected LAN. STUN will not work for all NATs and not for really secure firewalls and may have some scalability and security issues. The SIP client has to implement STUN and integrate it in the SIP stack to make it work.

There are also various tunneling approaches, creating a tunnel through the firewall and then having an ALG in a central place at the SIP operator to cope with the separate address space of the private LANs and their individual users. Special equipment is, therefore, required at the SIP operator, and sometimes special equipment and software are required on the LAN or in the SIP clients. With this approach, the users get locked into a specific SIP operator. This approach typically cannot handle complex configurations, such as interworking between an operator and the Microsoft Greenwich architecture, where a local SIP server on the LAN is used.

For home users (like for SOHOs), Microsoft has suggested an extension to Universal Plug and Play (UPnP) to allow Windows to control the NAT or firewall. Several small inexpensive NATs have implemented these UPnP extensions and thus allow SIP traversal for Windows Messenger (which is SIP based). However, it is not secure to allow every PC on the LAN to open the firewall, so UPnP is not acceptable for a proper firewall that should protect the LAN (in the Greenwich architecture, even Microsoft recommends that UPnP be disabled for high security). Another limitation is, of course, that UPnP control from Windows clients will not help other SIP products (SIP phones) to traverse a NAT or firewall.

Now, with regards to SOHOs, let's take a look at how you should use NAT technology to block access to an internal network demilitarized zone (DMZ). In other words, how would you set up a Linux-based firewall for the SOHO broadband-attached network?

15.7 Employing a Linux-based SOHO firewall solution with NAT technology

With people spending more and more time on the Internet, security is becoming increasingly important. This part of the chapter shows you how to set up a Linux-based personal firewall for the SOHO broadband-attached network. It also takes a look at several SOHO firewalls and assesses whether they can keep your system safe from intruders.

Interest in SOHO firewall technology has soared as more and more people have recognized that the price of the Internet's freedom is eternal vigilance. This part of the chapter also examines the latest in SOHO firewall technology and asks whether existing software is ready or able to keep your PCs private in an increasingly wireless broadband-attached networked world.

The term *SOHO firewall,* as described in this chapter, is one of many appropriated from other industries to fit the needs of technology. Originally, a firewall was a strengthened part of a building's structure designed to keep a fire contained within a specific area. When IT managers and software developers wanted to add security to their networks, the term was used to describe the layers of defense put into a server to protect against unauthorized access.

However, the idea of SOHO firewalls has taken time to develop, with the first products appearing only 4 years ago. Although there has been considerable skepticism about the usefulness of such packages, the market for SOHO firewalls has exploded. With more people spending increasing amounts of time online, there's growing concern among consumers about their system's security. The major software vendors are reacting.

Currently, most standalone PCs do need a SOHO firewall, and quite a bit of protection is now available. Even the most sophisticated SOHO firewall software can't provide complete protection against a determined effort to break in (see FYI 15.1), and, of the SOHO firewalls reviewed in this chapter, none even came close. However, the vast majority of PCs are neither valuable nor interesting enough to be properly attacked.

Although hacking is almost as old as the computer itself (the term was first coined to describe the phenomenon in 1984 in Steven Levy's book *Hackers*), the number of hardcore hackers is limited, and they certainly have other priorities besides SOHO computer systems. Most take pride in not causing damage during intrusion. However, the risk is technically there. With the number of computers spending time attached to the global telecommunications system growing at current rates, SOHO firewall protection is becoming an issue of increasing importance.

There's also a growing amount of options available to the SOHO firewall buyer. This comes from a mix of old and new

FYI 15.1 *SOHO Firewalls Are Not Safe*

It's one thing to rush an application to market without thinking, but it's another to rush a security application to market. That's what's happened with several SOHO firewalls—a product category that was a virtual nonentity 4 years ago, but that is now standard fare for anyone on a broadband connection, including telecommuters and mobile communications.

SOHO firewalls are designed to block suspicious incoming and outgoing traffic on a client or even block an application from using the Internet altogether. It's an important job, because broadband connections are always on and, hence, are easy prey for hacker programs that can sniff out their IP addresses. However, many of these SOHO firewalls have a design that's easy to compromise with just a few lines of code.

Basically, the hack involves known behaviors of these products. Because the SOHO firewalls watch traffic based on port number and application name, all a hacker has to do is rename a virus or Trojan horse to a name that endusers have likely permitted to have access to the Internet.

For example, a hacker could rename a rogue file to *iexplore.exe*, a filename that is not likely to be barred from using the web. If, in fact, the enduser had set his or her firewall to allow that application to access the Internet, the bad file is allowed in.

Everyone is on the SOHO firewall bandwagon, and hardly anyone is doing it right. A Trojan comes along and calls itself a basic application like *netscape.exe,* and they're in. This is not some future problem once the bad guys notice These Trojans exist.

Hopefully, publicizing this kind of hole will tighten those companies up quick. Something this simple is scary. If you have persistent connections popping up everywhere, you don't want that to go unchecked.

There are other problems born out of the rush to get products to market. For example, Sygate's (www.sygate.com/products/) firewall's default settings leave individual programs open to the Internet, until users choose to disable access.

In another example, Symantec (www.symantec.com/index.htm), in an effort to make its product more user friendly, has a list of applications that automatically get permission to access the Internet so users aren't even presented with the choice. Other products such as BlackIce Defender, from Network Ice Corporation (www.digitalriver.com/dr/v2/ec_dynamic.main?SP=1&PN=10&sid=26412), now offer the ability to block outgoing transmissions to the Internet from the client when the client acts as a server.

Both points are valid. These firewalls, however, were rushed to market and were poorly designed, but business is business. Everyone saw a SOHO firewall out there, and they all had to have one.

Although some of the technical vulnerabilities will likely go away in later versions of the products, there is a psychological aspect to the problem. IT managers put an inherent amount of trust in security products, which actually can leave them vulnerable when the products show weaknesses such as these.

There is a tendency because it's security to think, "I can set it and forget it." That's asking for trouble. The number of telecommuters using broadband is increasing. In 2005, unfortunately, most home computers will be very vulnerable to attack, because the security products currently being developed (and that they'll be using), have a lot of security holes in them. Or, worst yet, they will be the dupes that allow a hacker into a SOHO.

companies. Large-scale corporate firewall providers are scaling down their enterprise-level software for SOHO use, and there are new companies that have built their software from scratch.

This part of the chapter approaches these software reviews from an ordinary user's standpoint, looks at how easy a product is to use, and covers the technical facilities of each package. Given that until now SOHO firewall software has been specialist knowledge, you should choose the level of sophistication at which you feel most comfortable.

It's also worth noting that a cut-down version of ZoneAlarm is available for free for download from its web site (www.ezsecure.net/zonealarm.html?OVRAW=ZoneAlarm&OVKEY=zone%20alarm&OVMTC=standard). You should consider trying this first to see whether you like the user interface and the level of functionality that's on offer before investing money in the software.

Note: | URLs can change without notice. |

In this part of the chapter, the feeling from usability testing is that none of these SOHO firewalls is good enough to provide protection from the higher levels of attack. However, it's becoming important for everyone to have at least some level of protection on their computer systems, if only to deter the casual intruder. Ever increasing amounts of high-value information, both business and personal, are being stored on the computer, and smart users will do their best to protect it.

Finally, this part of the chapter provides extensive hands-on examples that provide you with practical experience in the realities of securing SOHO establishments. It will also show you what your options are as far as hardware/software solutions, how to employ a Linux-based SOHO firewall using X products, and how to set up this firewall—focusing on all of the gotchas to watch out for in ensuring that bad guys don't get through.

In any event, a new breed of distributed, centrally manageable SOHO firewalls can help prevent attacks into the enterprise via remote employee PCs. Let's take a look.

15.7.1   Realities of securing SOHOs with firewall protection

In December 2001, a bank in southern California received a call from an online customer asking why one of the bank's computers was trying to hack into his system. It turned out that the machine doing the hacking belonged to the bank's president and had been remotely commandeered by an employee. The president called Conqwest, Inc., an IT security services firm based in Holliston, Massachusetts, which is now rolling out SOHO firewall software across the bank's 136 internal desktop, laptop, and remote computers.

Until recently, companies thought antivirus and virtual private network (VPN) technologies would keep remote worker connections safe, but as more workers have been accessing the Internet through broadband services such as cable modems, exposure to hacking attacks through those machines has increased. In October 2001, for example, a hacker broke into a Microsoft employee's home computer and exploited the VPN connection to penetrate the company's internal network.

At the time of the Microsoft hack, only 17% of 500 security professionals surveyed used any type of firewall to protect remote workers' machines, even though 40% of the reported attacks originated from those machines, according to a report released by Symantec Corporation, a security software vendor. Some managers are tackling this threat by requiring SOHO firewalls on all desktops and laptop computers, both inside and outside the corporate LAN.

You can have a bodyguard at the front door with a bunch of people beating up on him or her, and eventually he or she will get overwhelmed. Or, you can teach everyone karate so they can protect themselves.

However, these firewall products are still evolving, and IT managers face a multitude of feature choices in SOHO firewall software programs and hardware devices. For example, some new products allow for centralized monitoring and policy enforcement for remote desktop firewalls, whereas others may be less sophisticated but easier to use. Still others offer different configuration options depending on an employee's role or whether the remote computer is being used for personal or business use.

Protecting both ends

For example, CyberwallPlus-SV (www.vbxtras.com/products/CyberwallPLUS_error.asp) is an industrial-strength SOHO firewall capable of protecting clustered multiprocessing machines. Cyberwall installs at the kernel level, hardening it against common attacks and, more important, veiling the machine's identity. If hackers can't tell what the machine is, they can't get at it using common exploits associated with those machines, like sendmail if it's a mail server or Internet Explorer if it's a web server. And, CyberwallPlus-SV stands up better to Java and ActiveX mobile code-based attacks than SOHO firewalls.

However, for individual desktops and remotely connected machines, most users want a less-expensive filtering SOHO firewall device that could be centrally managed. CyberwallPlus-SV has no such offering, so some users are choosing ZoneAlarm Pro, which has less-robust features but is cheaper and easier to manage.

If you run ZoneAlarm Pro in a mission-critical environment, it will not hold up under certain applets and hacking tools. The same thing applies to BlackIce and other SOHO firewalls.

Although ZoneAlarm is easy enough to install, it snags on legacy applications and blocks some executable programs from leaving the internal network. ZoneAlarm doesn't work well with unusual applications. But, after some initial network interruptions, the SOHO firewall has proved strong enough to stand up to common exploits launched at individual computers, like port scans that go after vulnerable services and Trojan horses such as Back Orifice.

ZoneAlarm's central management server assimilates reports and alerts from desktop and remote workers' machines, making it easier to separate systematic attacks from simple port probes and false alarms, in addition to its ability to tailor security settings based on a user's role in the company. The security needed by a business person is different than that of network architects.

A matter of discrimination

The ability to discriminate between types of sessions is especially important when dealing with home users' SOHO machines. The employee-owned computer is a big issue for most clients today. It's pretty hard to say, "You have to put this SOHO firewall on your home PC," and your kid starts screaming that he or she can't download Napster or AOL. So, you need some type of tie-in with the VPN client that says the company's SOHO firewall policy only kicks in when connecting for company purposes. Most SOHO firewalls offer some of these distinctions.

On the other hand, CyberArmor SOHO firewall suite, by InfoExpress, Inc. (www.infoexpress.com/), is praised by industry analysts for its ability to discriminate between home use, inbound connectivity to the corporate LAN, and outbound connectivity from inside the LAN to the Internet. That ability is one reason Bell Canada International in Montreal rolled out InfoExpress on 8,000 portable computers and 66,000 installations on internal machines.

The InfoExpress SOHO firewall allows Bell Canada to set different parameters dependent on what mode the user is in. For example, as soon as the user activates his or her VPN client, the software changes from the standard Internet filter set to a predetermined VPN filter set. When the VPN is turned off, the SOHO firewall automatically reverts to Internet mode.

The SOHO firewalls and central management server were easy to install, but one mistake configuring the central management server operating system (such as outdated patches, default passwords, or vulnerable services like FTP) can render the firewall manager ineffective. And the server needs to be fast enough to accommodate an early morning login rush.

Bell Canada looked at 18 SOHO firewalls before settling on CyberArmor because of its easy enduser interface and the fact that the central manager leaves nothing up to the enduser. As a user logs in to the network, CyberArmor quickly scans that machine's security settings and can push out changes to security settings dictated by the administrator. The user never even knows anything is happening.

Some companies are going a step further by requiring a second, stationary filtering hardware device at home and remote offices. In addition, although hardware SOHO firewalls from vendors like Seattle-based WatchGuard Technologies (www.watchguard.com/) aren't portable, some managers say they want extra protection for home PCs. In other words, companies need to absolutely guarantee that nobody can get into their machines and exploit the encrypted tunnel back to their office.

Next are some of the options your project team and vendors should consider to help produce a solid and accurate estimate for hardware and software costs. Let's take a look.

15.7.2 Hardware and software solutions options

As with any infrastructure project, implementing a SOHO firewall solution requires solid research on all hardware and software costs, but estimating the costs of a SOHO firewall involves many that may be overlooked, depending on whether the project is designed to secure Internet connectivity at your corporate headquarters, migrate your existing frame relay network to a VPN solution, or secure servers you might have residing in a colocation facility.

Hardware

Determining the costs of hardware should be a straightforward step for most large deployments, but purchasing a SOHO firewall solution presents a different set of problems, because you need to determine how your vendor sells the components and addon modules. Consider the following example:

- You are deploying a nine-site VPN solution to replace your frame relay.

- You have 800 users at your corporate office.

- The remaining 16 offices each contain between 60 and 80 users.

- You know you will need a robust SOHO firewall at your main site and 16 lower end firewalls at the other locations.

- You will want to allow and secure other Internet traffic to and from these remote locations, so you do not want to use a strict VPN hardware solution.[4]

SEPARATE ENCRYPTION CARD

Will you need to add a separate encryption card at the corporate office to support the traffic of the approximate 460 users coming through the VPN tunnels? You can expect the entry-level costs for this solution to be somewhere between $100,000 and $140,000. This is obviously a rough estimate because estimates vary based on which vendor you select. Here are some other items to consider before requesting pricing from your vendor for your SOHO firewall project:

DIAL-UP INTERNET USERS THAT WILL NEED TO VPN INTO THE SOHO FIREWALL

Each user will be another tunnel that your SOHO firewall will need to terminate, thus requiring more processing. Will the encryption card mentioned previously support these single users, or will the vendor require you to add a separate VPN device to your network to allow the single user VPN access?

REMOTE OFFICES REQUIRE A SEPARATE ENCRYPTION CARD

At the remote offices, you might be required to add a separate encryption card. Will the SOHO firewall you place in these offices be used for general Internet traffic on top of the traffic allowed over the VPN? If so, your vendor might suggest that you offload the encryption to an add-on card here as well, depending on the number of users and the average amount of traffic.

AUTHENTICATE THE INDIVIDUAL VPN USERS

Asking how to authenticate VPN users actually prompts two more questions on the subject: Will you use the user database on your SOHO firewall or use an internal Remote Authentication Dial-In User Service (RADIUS) server to provide authentication? In addition, will you also require two-factor authentication using a product such as RSA's SecurID? What hardware will be involved to do this? You might find that you will need to add a separate server to run the RADIUS functions and individual *token* cards for each remote user to receive his or her generated password.

IMPLEMENTING AN INTRUSION DETECTION SYSTEM

If you are implementing an intrusion detection system within your network, where will you place your sensors, and how many will you have? Does the SOHO firewall vendor provide an intrusion detection product, or will you need to look at a third-party solution?

EXTRA NETWORKING HARDWARE

Will you have a DMZ for external services on your network? If you will be using a fail-over SOHO firewall, will you be separating the heartbeat traffic onto a separate segment? If so, does your existing backbone support the use of virtual LANs (VLANs) for these separate networks, or will you be purchasing new switches during this implementation?

Software

When implementing a SOHO firewall solution, be sure you understand all the software needed to fully install and manage your solution.

FULLY LICENSE A FAIL-OVER FIREWALL

Along with deploying the multisite VPN solution, you also want to add redundancy to your SOHO firewall: You are not concerned about load balancing, and your second SOHO firewall will be in constant hot standby mode.

With that in mind, you should need only one license in your corporate office, right? In some instances, this assumption, albeit logical, is most likely wrong. Check with your vendor to find out whether you have to fully license a fail-over SOHO firewall, as this will significantly increase your costs. You can expect this solution to add $32,000 to $62,000 to your total project costs, or even more depending on the options you choose. Here are a few other questions to consider when estimating the software needed for your implementation.

SOFTWARE COSTS FOR APPLIANCE-BASED SOLUTIONS

You've decided to use an appliance-based SOHO firewall on your network. You like the idea that you will not have to support a separate OS, be it UNIX or Windows NT, because it will simplify support. Be aware that even with an appliance-based solution, you will have software costs. Unlike a true hardware solution, most appliances are simply boxes that allow you to run the SOHO firewall software. You need to purchase the appliance and the software to run on it.

USING ANY EXISTING EQUIPMENT CURRENTLY ON YOUR NETWORK

Suppose you have Cisco routers at each location and would like to add the SOHO firewall feature set to the existing Cisco Internetworking Operating System (IOS). Will your SOHO firewall terminate IP Security (IPSec) tunnels from other vendors? If you are using standard encryption, you might be able to mix vendors, but be careful to fully ensure that your SOHO firewall will be able to terminate VPN tunnels from other vendors. Although using existing equipment will reduce overall costs, don't forget to budget for the additional feature set to expand the VPN capabilities of the existing hardware.

LICENSE THE VPN SOFTWARE FOR EACH USER

Most SOHO firewalls are using a concurrent-server–based licensing model and allow you to freely distribute the VPN client to your users. However, be sure to budget accordingly if there are additional charges for the client software.

MONITOR THE LOGS

Most SOHO firewalls will log all network traffic or allow you to decide which traffic you want to log. The big question is what to do with the copious amount of data that a SOHO firewall generates. Does your SOHO firewall come with the tools to easily view and search the logs? With some SOHO firewalls, you will need a third-party software package to do even the most basic log viewing. Do you also want reports and alerts on traffic? More likely than not, you will need a third-party software package to do so.

MANAGE THIS SOLUTION

Does your SOHO firewall vendor provide the tools to manage these devices from a single location and push security policies to multiple devices, or will you need to purchase add-on software to perform these management functions? In the previous example where you have an 18-site VPN solution, it can become a management headache to remotely connect to each device to add a security policy that is consistent throughout all sites. These days, the predominant method of securing enterprise networks is to set up a firewall, and although some SOHO firewall solutions may be pricey to implement, you can save your company money without sacrificing peace of mind by following a more economical approach.

15.7.3 Employing a Linux-based SOHO firewall solution

This part of the chapter will show and help you build your own SOHO firewall on UNIX clone systems like Linux by using its preinstalled software. Why was Linux chosen? Because Linux is a freely distributed open source system, and you can easily use this system to build a secure software SOHO firewall on a shoestring budget.

Linux preinstalled firewall software

Let's start with the Linux OS and its preinstalled software for building a SOHO firewall. You should use the NAT technology for blocking access to an internal network DMZ. For this example, you should use a Red Hat Linux distribution (www.redhat.com/).

You need to build your kernel distribution with the IP Forwarding, IP Masquerading, IP Firewalling, IP Transparent Proxying, and IP Routing functions. It's assumed here that you're somewhat experienced with the Linux system and its kernel structure, but if you have problems building and compiling your customized kernel, you can refer to a Linux manual. As far as the internal network is concerned (called the *DMZ network*), you'll have to change the network that's being used in this example (10.0.0.0/24, which is a part of private class network 10.0.0.0/8 according to RFC1918) to the one you're using. You can use a network block that you've obtained from your local Internet service provider with public IP addresses. Once you've built and installed your new kernel with the firewall options enabled, you can set up a configuration script, which will start your SOHO firewall. Create (if it does not exist) and edit the file /etc/rc.d/init.d/firewall as shown[5]:

```
# flushing out all rulesets

# this is meaningless on the startup, but a good idea
when restarting the firewall services[5]

ipfwadm -F -f

ipfwadm -I -f

ipfwadm -O -f

# denying all connections, using the default rule

ipfwadm -F -p deny

# allowing all connections from the DMZ network interface

ipfwadm -F -a accept -m -P all -S 10.0.0.0/24

# allowing all incoming connections

ipfwadm -I -p accept
```

Okay, now it's time to take care of the tcpwrappers package that's included in the Red Hat Linux distribution. To begin with, let's enable SecureShell (SSH) connections to your SOHO firewall from the DMZ network to allow you to configure it in case of an emergency. Edit the /etc/hosts.allow file as shown[5]:

```
ALL: 10.0.0.

22: ALL
```

To close all other connections for your DMZ network, you need to edit the /etc/hosts.deny system file[5]:

```
ALL: ALL
```

You've now finished a simple SOHO firewall setup on your Linux system. Of course, the subject of monitoring your SOHO firewall has not been covered. There are many monitoring tools around, such as Big Brother (quest.com/bigbrother/) and Nagios (www.nagios.org/). Some system administrators may want to write their own monitoring tools. This is not a question of SOHO firewall security. You have now reached your objective: You built a SOHO firewall that routes your internal network and denies others access to your network, which might contain classified information.

Finally, does your Linux-based SOHO firewall have a hole in it? New updates fix a potentially disastrous flaw.

15.7.4 Plugging the SOHO firewall leaks

Most software SOHO firewalls adequately protect you from outside hackers who try to access your files or otherwise probe your PC. But what if the danger comes from within? Several personal SOHO firewall vendors have released updates addressing your vulnerability to intruders who get in when you unsuspectingly run a malicious application that masquerades as a friendly one.

Thanks to the Gibson Research web site (http://grc.com/)—best known for ShieldsUp, a test designed to expose a firewall's vulnerability to external attacks—the vulnerability problem has now been solved. One of Gibson's offerings, dubbed *LeakTest* (www.grc.com/lt/leaktest.htm), is a free, easy-to-run download that will tell you whether your SOHO firewall can detect and stop an internal Trojan horse program—innocent-looking software that is spread via e-mail or download. Antivirus software can alert you to known Trojan horses, but if a new one gets through, your SOHO firewall is supposed to provide a second line of defense. Unfortunately, most SOHO firewalls failed LeakTest when it was released initially in December 2000.

Disguised applications

All SOHO firewalls are meant to block unauthorized attempts to access a PC from the outside, but many legitimate applications running on your computer open it to outside access. SOHO firewalls have to let you receive e-mail and web pages, for example.

So how does a SOHO firewall know when an application is legitimate? Most rely on the name of the executable file—for example, netscape.exe—together with the port number assigned to an Internet connection created by a specific application. A malicious Trojan horse could fool the firewall into thinking it was a legitimate application by renaming itself when it ran and using an appropriate port.

Safe attack strategy simulation

LeakTest safely simulates such an attack strategy. After you download the program, it is recommended that you change its name to that of a popular executable Internet application such as Internet Explorer or Eudora. When you run the program, it uses the File Transfer Protocol (FTP) protocol to attempt to connect to one of the Gibson servers. If it succeeds, it confirms your PC's vulnerability (but doesn't send any personal data).

No LeakTest-style Trojan attacks are known to have occurred outside a lab. Still, most major SOHO firewall vendors now have updates that address the problem.

When the test was released, only one major SOHO firewall, Zone Labs' ZoneAlarm, passed. Vendors whose products were fooled by LeakTest include McAfee.com, Network Associates, Sygate, and Symantec. Almost all of them offer free updates now.

These patches change the way the SOHO firewall identifies applications that users have authorized to access the Web. Instead of relying on name and port, the firewalls look at content or code.

Getting this extra protection may inconvenience people. To fully update Norton SOHO Firewall, for example, you may have to run Live Update, its downloadable upgrade service, more than once.

Symantec also turned off Norton's automatic rule creation feature, which results in users being pestered by pop-up authorization request windows.

However, all SOHO firewalls (even ZoneAlarm) rely first on the user's good judgment, and that means not authorizing suspect software.

The bottom line: When it comes to protecting your data, caution is king. It's better to put up with a strict SOHO firewall now than to cry later when some stranger downloads all your personal finance files.

15.8 Summary

In all new installations of firewalls and NAT routers, proper SIP support should be ensured to allow the users on the LANs to use real-time P2P communication, the next big usage of the Internet. Of the various methods proposed for firewall and NAT traversal, the most general and reliable is to solve the problems where they occur, in the firewall or NAT itself. By including a SIP proxy and a SIP registrar for controlling the NAT and firewall, it is possible to handle complex SIP scenarios and to use TLS for secure and private signaling.

Although analysts predict that the market will ultimately consolidate into a single desktop security product or suite that includes intrusion-detection tools, a SOHO firewall, a VPN, and antivirus protection, there's no consensus on just how this will be accomplished. Already, almost every SOHO firewall offers VPN capabilities. Vendors are merging and partnering to bundle mixed products into one integrated product, and some companies, like InfoExpress and Symantec, are taking the suite approach.

In addition, there's the debate over where these Linux-based SOHO firewalls will wind up—as hardware, software, or something more like a network adapter, according to analysts. That's why many IT managers say they'll just wait a while before deploying Linux-based firewalls, in spite of the risks.

Finally, one of the reasons people seem to be fond of SOHO firewalls and other network-based security measures is that they assume they can allow host security to lapse if they secure the perimeter of their network. They are only somewhat correct. Network security is mostly host security. If host administrators assume that the SOHO firewall will protect their hosts from access violations, sooner or later they're in for a nasty surprise. No standalone technology can protect hosts from all access violations, so only the most complex of network and Linux-based security systems, including both SOHO firewalling and monitoring programs, can ensure the safety of your hosts. At the heart of all these technologies is the need for smart planning of the security system as a whole. A bunch of security systems that aren't integrated with one another are no more helpful than the Do Not Enter! sign on an open door.

15.9 References

1. John Wack, Ken Cutler, and Jamie Pole, "Guidelines on Firewalls and Firewall Policy: Recommendations of the National Institute of Standards and Technology," National Institute of Standards and Technology, U.S. Department of Commerce, Gaithersburg, Maryland, January, 2002.

2. "Information Security: Mechanisms And Techniques," National Institute of Standards and Technology, U.S. Department of Commerce, Gaithersburg, Maryland, January, 2002.

3. Shirley Radack (Ed.), "Selecting Information Technology Security Products," National Institute of Standards and Technology, U.S. Department of Commerce, Gaithersburg, Maryland, 2004.

4. "CMS Information Security: Acceptable Risk Safeguards (ARS)," Department Of Health and Human Services, Centers for Medicare and Medicaid Services, Baltimore, Maryland, 2004.

5. Shirley Radack (Ed.), "Security Considerations In The Information System Development Life Cycle," National Institute of Standards and Technology, U.S. Department of Commerce, Gaithersburg, Maryland, 2004.

Section VII

Firewall Remote Access Configuration

16

Privacy and Authentication Technology

16.1 Chapter objectives

- Encrypting with Secure Socket Layer (SSL)
- Deploying strong authentication with one-time passwords
- Using encryption
- Identifying key management
- Using authentication, authorization, and auditing
- Implementing backup, restore, and disaster recovery
- Using load balancing and high availability
- Looking at network and transport database considerations

Very costly breaches continue to occur, even though enterprises worldwide are spending approximately $20 billion per year on IT security.[1] In large part, this is because security efforts have mainly focused on network security rather than privacy and authentication technology.[2] Securing critical data as it is being stored, transmitted, and used within the enterprise is known as *privacy*.

Failure to implement a privacy and authentication solution can have a disastrous effect on an organization. Public disclosure of breaches can be catastrophic to an organization's brand, market capitalization, and consumer trust. Plus, privacy and authentication legislation and the security policies of credit card issuers alike mandate disclosure of breaches, meaning organizations that try to keep a breach secret will be susceptible to civil litigation and steep fines.

The need to augment network security mechanisms with privacy and authentication solutions has never been more vital. Traditional perimeter-oriented technologies are only part of a complete security picture. The following are a few good reasons:

- According to industry analysts, 75% of external-based attacks are tunneling through applications, and so go undetected by a range of traditional security mechanisms.

- Even with a fortified network perimeter, storage systems can be breached via unsecure storage management interfaces and physical storage systems, and data in the databases and applications themselves can be stolen.

- Most estimates cite that now more than 50% of security breaches are perpetrated by internal staff.

- The ongoing battle of patching known exploits is being lost: According to a study by industry analysts, 70% of all security vulnerabilities were simple for attackers to manage, and the number grew 10% over the previous year.[1]

It's no surprise then that in a survey of chief information officers (CIOs) around the world, privacy and authentication rose to the top three on their list of priorities, with security remaining number one. Although the decision to address privacy and authentication is clear-cut, deciding which path to take to achieve it is not.

A comprehensive privacy and authentication solution must address security across the enterprise. Often, organizations deploy security systems to encrypt data in transport between machines but then have the data stored in the clear. Likewise, many enterprises have already purchased multiple highly secure and fault tolerant systems, but security weaknesses can still be present because of the way these systems interface with each other. To achieve privacy and authentication, it is important to think about the security of applications, databases, and the infrastructure that supports them as a whole. Thus, this chapter offers an overview of how to address firewall privacy and authentication in a comprehensive fashion, outlining the key building blocks of firewall privacy and authentication implementation and offering detailed guidance for each of these areas.

16.2 Selecting cryptographic algorithms through encryption

This part of the chapter provides a list of recommendations for choosing among the various cryptographic operations available in implementing a firewall privacy and authentication solution.[3] These cryptographic operations are as follows:

- Data Encryption Standard (DES)
- 3DES
- Advanced Encryption Standard (AES)
- RC4
- Secure Hash Algorithm-1 (SHA-1) and Message Digest-5 (MD5)
- Asymmetric Key Algorithms (RSA)

16.2.1 Data Encryption Standard

Although DES has enjoyed widespread popularity for many years, it is no longer considered secure enough by today's standards. DES should generally not be used in production environments.

16.2.2 3DES

3DES is a more secure alternative to DES and is a widely used symmetric algorithm. If possible, AES should be used rather than 3DES because of the performance advantages offered by AES.

16.2.3 Advanced Encryption Standard

AES is a newer and preferred choice today. It is gaining broad acceptance in the industry because of its performance advantages over 3DES.

16.2.4 RC4

RC4 (a variable key-size stream cipher with byte-oriented operations) should not be used for data protection but for encryption during short-lived sessions. A single key should never be used to encrypt more than one piece of data.

16.2.5 Message Digest and Secure Hash Algorithm

For a number of years, MD5 has been a favorite hashing algorithm, but recent efforts have revealed certain attacks that weaken MD5's protection. In general, SHA-1 should be used over MD5 for hashing data.

16.2.6 Asymmetric Key Algorithms

Asymmetric (public key) algorithms, such as RSA, can be up to an order of magnitude slower than symmetric algorithms. Therefore, if possible, a symmetric algorithm should be chosen.

16.2.7 Additional cryptographic options: modes and initialization vectors

Block encryption algorithms (such as DES and AES) can be used in a number of modes, such as electronic code book (ECB) and cipher block chaining (CBC). In nearly all cases, CBC mode is recommended over ECB mode. ECB mode can be less secure because the same block of plain-text data always results in the same block of cipher text, a property that can be used by an attacker to reveal information about the original data and to tamper with the encrypted data. Many modes, including CBC mode, require an initialization vector (IV), which is a sequence of random bytes used as input to the algorithm along with the plain text. The IV does not need to be secret, but it should be unpredictable.

16.2.8 Options in padding

Symmetric block algorithms, such as DES and AES, have various padding options. Two common padding options are no padding and Public Key Cryptography Standards#5 (PKCS#5). When no padding is used, data to be encrypted must be exactly a multiple of the block size. For example, if AES-128 is used, the data must be a multiple of 16 bytes. No padding can be advantageous in situations in which the size of the data is fixed because the resulting cipher text will be exactly the same size as the plain text (there will be no additional space requirements to store the encrypted data). In situations where the size of the data can vary or is not a multiple of the block size, PKCS#5 padding is recommended. This allows data of arbitrary size to be encrypted with the resulting cipher text at most a block size larger than the plain text. For example, with AES-128 if between 0 and 15 bytes of data need to be encrypted, the resulting cipher text will be 16 bytes. If between 16 and 31 bytes of data need to be encrypted, the resulting cipher text will be 32 bytes.[1]

16.3 Key management

Key management is a fundamental consideration when deploying a privacy and authentication solution. If the keys used to protect sensitive data within an enterprise are not properly secured, attackers may be able to access these data with relative ease. This part of the chapter discusses some of the considerations when managing keys in the context of enterprise firewall privacy and authentication.

16.3.1 Administration and storage centralization

In a highly secure environment, it is important to generate and manage keys in a centralized manner in which strict access privileges are enforced. For example, keys stored across multiple application server and database hard drives are significantly more difficult to manage and protect than keys stored on a centralized platform.

16.3.2 Specialized hardware

A specialized hardware device in which all cryptographic operations are performed securely and in which keys are never visible in the clear is highly recommended. This provides a significantly higher level of security over a pure software solution in which keys are managed and used in the clear. Some highly specialized hardware can provide a level of tamper resistance, so that if an attempt is made to compromise the keys, the hardware will clear all information, including the keys. This type of hardware solution is recommended for enterprises that require an extremely high level of security.

16.3.3 Importing a key

Importing a key into a secure key management system is not recommended because the system has no way of verifying where the key has existed before the import or even if the key has been compromised. If key import is a requirement, the history of the key should be well documented, and all copies of the key should be managed carefully.

16.3.4   Exporting a key

Exporting a key from a secure management system is not recommended because the system will have no means of verifying how the key is used once it leaves the secure environment. If key export is a requirement, exported copies of the key should be managed carefully.

16.3.5   Rotating keys

It is good practice to protect data with newly generated keys periodically. Re-encrypting data with a new key at least once a year is recommended. An important consideration when rotating keys is managing backups and archives. An enterprise must be able to ensure that sensitive data cannot be compromised through the use of old keys and archived data while being able to guarantee access to these data if necessary.[1]

16.4   Auditing, authentication, and authorization

Enterprises need a secure way to identify people and entities that require access to sensitive data. In implementing a solution, administrators need to decide which data will be accessible and who will have access to it. Some methods of access control include passwords, client certificates, biometrics, and tokens.

16.4.1   Authentication

Authentication ensures that an entity is really what or who it says it is. Methods of authentication can be classified as what you know, what you have, or what you are. The traditional what-you-know form of authentication, a username and password, is the least secure. Passwords can be given away, guessed, or stolen. What you have is called a *token*, such as a client certificate or a smart card. What you are can be proven by recording and comparing a voiceprint, fingerprint, retinal scan, or even DNA. In general, the more factors used for authentication, the stronger the authentication is. For example, a system that uses a username and password along with a client certificate provides a higher level of security than one that only uses a username and password.

16.4.2   Authorization

Authorization ensures that only the entities who should have access to resources obtain that access. For authorization to be granted to an entity, it must first be authenticated. Two of the authorization methods available are role-based security and subject/object access control. Role-based security means that authorization is defined based on an entity's responsibilities. For example, an enterprise may choose to create an application role that only has authorization to encrypt credit card numbers and a processing role that only has authorization to decrypt the same information. In a subject/object access control system, every resource (object) has an explicit list of entities (subjects) that are allowed access. The least privilege security principle states that entities should only be granted the absolutely minimal set of privileges necessary to perform their tasks. Additional unnecessary authorization privileges only increase the vulnerability of the system to attack. It is important to be wary of access creep, where employees are granted more and more authorization over time by special request. It is also critical to remember to change an employee's role when he or she changes jobs.

16.4.3   Auditing

Auditing is an extremely important part of a privacy and authentication solution. It allows the enterprise to determine who did what at any given time, including when authentication and authorization were allowed or denied to an entity. A privacy and authentication solution should offer robust logging capabilities and support log signing, to prevent an attacker from tampering with logs. Logs should be analyzed regularly to look for strange behavior that could potentially represent attacks on the enterprise.

16.4.4   Secure the credentials

One of the challenges related to authentication is the ability to properly secure the credentials used to authenticate. Usernames and passwords, if stored on a local machine, should not be kept in the clear. At the very least, some form of encoding or obfuscation should be performed so that this information is not easily humanly readable. Certificates should be stored in a key store that is password protected.

16.4.5 Disaster recovery, backup, and restore

Backup and restore capabilities are critical to ensure that an environment can be recreated in the event of a disaster. It is also important to be able to replicate an existing environment to scale according to the needs of the enterprise. A good solution will allow for a secure mechanism to create backups and perform restores of all keys and relevant configuration information. In some environments, specialized hardware used to protect keys has its own mechanism for backup and restore.[1]

16.5 High availability and load balancing

A load-balanced system is a good way to provide a highly redundant environment and scale performance to meet the needs of the enterprise. A privacy and authentication solution should be able to load balance intelligently across different physical locations and perform monitoring services to determine whether systems are up or down.

In some enterprise environments, it may be desirable to have an active/passive model in which one machine actively services requests while another stands by. In the event that the active system fails, the standby system assumes the IP address of the previously active system and starts to service requests.

16.5.1 Key replication services

Deployments with multiple systems can often be difficult to maintain. Platforms that offer automated configuration and key replication services are more desirable. This simplifies the overall management experience and reduces the chances of errors.[1]

16.6 Transport and network

It is recommended to use SSL at all points in which sensitive data are in transit, both over the Internet and within the enterprise (such as between the application server and the database). A good privacy and authentication solution will allow for secure transmission of sensitive data between all entities across an enterprise.

16.6.1 Firewalls

In general, all administrative ports should be blocked from external networks. Access control lists (ACLs) should be set up to restrict access to certain devices on the network. For example, if a network-based security appliance resides on the network, only those devices that require access for administrative or cryptographic operations should be granted access.[1]

16.7 Encryption of multiple columns: database considerations

If multiple columns of a database table are encrypted, it is strongly recommended to use different encryption keys for each column. That way, even if an attacker manages to compromise a single key, the rest of the encrypted columns will remain secure. The only reason to use a single key to encrypt multiple columns is if the columns all contain values from the same set of data and the encrypted values have to be compared with each other to determine equality (such as when performing a join). The database schema and application logic should be designed to minimize situations where this is necessary.

16.7.1 Creating indexes

Indexes are created to facilitate the search of a particular record or a set of records from a database table. Indexes are created on a specific column or a set of columns. When the database table is selected, and where conditions are provided, the database will typically use the indexes to locate the records, avoiding the need to do a full table scan. In many cases, searching on an encrypted column will require the database to perform a full table scan regardless of whether an index exists. For this reason, encrypting a column that is part of an index is not recommended.

16.7.2 Primary key encryption

Encrypted columns can be a primary key or part of a primary key, because the encryption of a piece of data is stable (it always produces the same result), and no two distinct pieces of data will produce the same cipher text, provided that the key and initialization vector used are consistent. However, when encrypting entire columns of an existing database, depending on the data migration method, database administrators might have to drop existing primary keys and any other associated reference keys, and re-create them after the data are encrypted. For this reason, encrypting a column that is part of a primary key constraint is not recommended. Because primary keys are automatically indexed, there are also performance considerations, as described previously.

16.7.3 Foreign key constraint

A foreign key constraint can be created on an encrypted column. However, special care must be given during migration. To convert an existing table to one that holds encrypted data, all the tables with which it has constraints must first be identified. All referenced tables have to be converted accordingly. In certain cases, the referential constraints have to be temporarily disabled or dropped to allow proper migration of existing data. They can be reenabled or recreated once the data for all the associated tables are encrypted. Because of this complexity, encrypting a column that is part of a foreign key constraint is not recommended. Unlike indexes and primary keys, though, encrypting foreign keys generally does not present a performance impact.

16.7.4 Randomly generated initialization vectors

When using CBC mode of a block encryption algorithm, a randomly generated IV is used and must be stored for future use when the data are decrypted. Because the IV does not need to be kept secret, it can be stored in the database. If the application requires having an IV per column, which can be necessary to allow for searching within that column, the value can be stored in a separate table. For a more secure deployment, but with limited searching capabilities, an additional column can be added to the table and an IV can be generated per row. In the case in which multiple columns are encrypted, but the table has space limitations, the same IV can be reused for each encrypted value in the row, even if the encryption keys for each column are different, provided the encryption algorithm and key size are the same.

16.7.5 Exact match searching

Searching for an exact match of an encrypted value within a column is possible, provided that the same IV is used for the entire column. On the other hand, searching for partial matches on encrypted data within a database can be challenging and can result in full table scans. One approach to performing partial searches, without prohibitive performance constraints and without revealing too much sensitive information, is to apply a Hash Message Authentication Code (HMAC) to part of the sensitive data and store it in another column in the same row. For example, a table that stores encrypted customer e-mail addresses could also store the HMAC of the first four characters of each e-mail address. If a customer service representative wanted to search for all customers whose e-mail addresses began with "john," the system would apply an HMAC on "john" and search through the HMAC column for matches, without having to decrypt every single full e-mail address. This approach can be used to find exact matches on the beginning or end of a field ("john" and "yahoo.com").[1]

One drawback to this approach is that a new column needs to be added for each unique type of search criteria. So if the database needs to allow for searching based on the first four characters and the last five characters, two new columns would need to be added to the table. However, to save space, the HMAC hash values can be truncated to 10 bytes without compromising security to save space. This approach can prove to be a reasonable compromise, especially when combined with nonsensitive search criteria such as zip code, city, etc., and can significantly improve search performance.

16.7.6 Encrypted data encoding

If data are to be managed in binary format, *varbinary* can be used as the data type to store encrypted information. On the other hand, if a binary format is not desirable, the encrypted data can be encoded and stored in a *varchar* field. There are size and performance penalties when using an encoded format, but this may be necessary in environments that do not interface well with binary formats.

16.7.7 Additional space

In environments in which it is unnecessary to encrypt all data within a database, a solution with granular capabilities is ideal. Even if only a small subset of sensitive information needs to be encrypted, additional space will still be required. Make sure that enough space exists to accommodate new fields, metadata, and the temporary space that will be required to perform the data migration.

16.7.8 Backups during pre-migration

Finally, even if sensitive information in production databases is securely protected, it is important to be aware that sensitive data may still exist in the clear in such places as tape backups and database backups. An enterprise must identify all of these locations and replace them with new backups in which the sensitive information is protected.[1]

16.8 Summary

This chapter has offered an overview of how to address firewall privacy and authentication in a comprehensive fashion, outlining the key building blocks of a firewall privacy and authentication implementation and offering detailed guidance for each of these areas. The need to augment network security mechanisms with firewall privacy and authentication solutions has never been more vital. Traditional perimeter-oriented technologies are only part of a complete security picture.

In spite of a range of security technologies being deployed, devastating thefts of sensitive data continue to occur. To address these threats, many organizations are looking to deploy firewall privacy and authentication solutions, which ensure the security of data inside the enterprise. In large part, this is because security efforts have mainly been focused on network security rather than firewall privacy and authentication.[1] Finally, a comprehensive firewall privacy and authentication solution must address security across the whole enterprise. To achieve firewall privacy and authentication, it is important to think about the security of applications, databases, and the infrastructure that supports them as a whole.

16.9 **References**

1. "Data Privacy in The Enterprise: Best Practices for Implementation," Ingrian Networks, Redwood City, California, 2004.

2. Michael Erbschloe and John R. Vacca, *Net Privacy: A Guide to Developing & Implementing an Ironclad ebusiness Privacy Plan,* McGraw-Hill, New York, March, 2001.

3. John R. Vacca, *Satellite Encryption,* Academic Press, Burlington, Massachusetts, September, 1999.

17

Tunneling: Firewall-to-Firewall

17.1 Chapter objectives

- Exploiting virtual private networks (VPNs)
- Exchanging keys between firewalls
- Implementing the IPSec tunnel mode
- Focusing on demilitarized zone (DMZ)
- Keeping the firewall tunneling security rules up to date

The way enterprises and organizations communicate has been changed forever by internetworking. Today, it is easy for a remote worker to access corporate information, for distant sites to constantly exchange data between one firewall and another (called *tunneling*), for partners to receive information in a matter of seconds, and for customers to benefit from instant online services. For private enterprises and the public sector, this leads to huge opportunities, such as the following:

- Improved competitiveness and increased sales: Business-to-business and business-to-consumer electronic commerce sites offer new opportunities to foster loyalty and expand customer or user bases, provide new services, and increase sales.

- Productivity gains and better market responsiveness: By connecting the organization with branch offices, remote and mobile workers, suppliers, business partners, or customers, responsiveness can be increased, research and development accelerated, and strategic partnerships strengthened.

- Substantial communication cost reductions: With easy electronic communication, documentation and transaction costs can be impressively decreased. Moreover, inexpensive network facilities such as the Internet offer low-cost worldwide communication, ahead of private leased lines or remote dial-up access.[1]

17.2 Increasing risk on extranets and intranets

In today's harsh competitive climate, though ultimately important for business, this openness is not risk free, as the following few examples show:

- For European companies, security fears remain the biggest inhibitor to expansion of e-commerce: 69% cite this problem according to industry analysts.

- Eighty percent of European companies are not confident: They are not able to detect a hacking attack according to industry analysts.

- Thirty-three percent of European enterprises have to implement adequate security programs according to industry analysts.

- Seventy-three percent of European enterprises do not know when or how often their security policy is revised according to industry analysts.[2]

Every year, the number of attacks and intrusions grows. Security breaches cost $48 billion yearly according to industry analysts. Hackers, competitors, and malicious or disgruntled employees pick on defenseless systems and system software bugs, weaknesses, or misconfigurations to vandalize corporate web sites; steal, modify, or destroy data; and crash systems or make them unavailable. They lead to a high risk of industrial espionage, fraud, denial of service, and the destruction of precious business information systems.

17.3 Openness with protection of firewall tunneling and Internet security solutions

Enterprises and organizations need strong security to fully benefit from the opportunities offered by intranets, extranets, or the Internet without incurring undue risk. It is a matter of urgency to prevent internal attacks, to safeguard against break-ins, to protect information systems, and to preserve the enterprise's secrets.

Solutions dedicated to protect networks from unwanted intruders, granting specific individuals selective access to information resources and applications, are included under global protection. Control of transactions, filtering of malicious content, protection of confidentiality, and integrity of communications must be ensured. Powerful tools to audit and manage security are also much needed.

Firewalls solutions (especially firewall tunneling) and Internet security are key components of such a security policy. They allow filtering and control of network transactions by protecting the point of interconnection between several networks through firewall tunneling. All traffic passing through the firewall points (web accesses, electronic mail, application transactions) is precisely identified, checked, allowed through or rejected, and eventually encrypted, depending on the rules and regulations defined in the security policy. Interposing security gateways between the outside world and the organization's inner networks or between distinct subnetworks of the same organization meets a fundamental network security need.

Note:
> *Firewall tunneling* refers to the practice of encapsulating a message from one protocol in another, and using the facilities of the second protocol to traverse some number of the network hops. In other words, the data packets are wrapped with another protocol so they can pass through your security (firewalls) and then be unwrapped once they reach the destination.

17.4 Firewall tunneling and Internet security architecture technologies

Internet security and firewall tunneling solutions can be used for both intranet and Internet protection. Let's now look at both solutions.

17.4.1 Protection solutions for the intranet

Intranet protection solutions can be used between internal departments, branch offices, remote sites, or nomadic users, over any kind of private network. With that in mind, firewall tunneling components are used to isolate any critical network segments from the general-purpose enterprise intranet, preventing intrusion from unauthorized internal users and controlling traffic.

Note:

> *Firewall tunneling* also means that you have a way to securely work through your firewalls so you can access network resources as if the firewalls didn't exist.

Although pure intranet networks, internal to the enterprise, are often supposed to be safe, it is wise to ensure specific internal protection for sensitive servers or subnetworks (finance, research and development, sales, manufacturing, etc. [see Figure 17.1]). First, the security requirements of each department may be specific, as enterprises are no longer single trusting entities. They are increasingly becoming a collection of very different suborganizations. Second, attacks frequently come from the inside; statistics show that 53% of attacks are internal, from disgruntled or malicious employees. A third reason to set up protection between internal subnetworks is that the enterprise network is often not truly internal. It frequently consists of leased telecom lines. When very sensitive and business-critical systems are connected, the best guarantee is to install good protection.

Figure 17.1
Internal and external subnetworks.

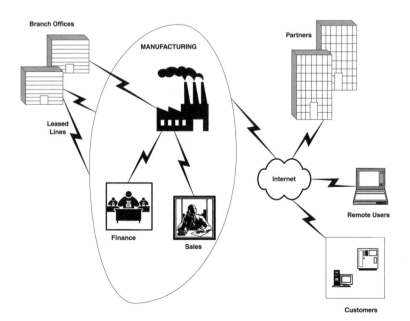

17.4.2 Protection solutions for the extranet and Internet

Extranet and Internet protection solutions can be used between organizations, their branch offices, remote sites, nomadic users, suppliers, partners, or customers, over any public network like the Internet (Figure 17.1). A specific case is that of nomadic users, who need to access the company intranet through remote dial-up access services or through the Internet itself. In both cases, it is, of course, crucial to have good protection.

17.5 Firewall tunneling technologies

There are five main Internet security and firewall tunneling technology approaches to combat intrusion in a Transmission Control Protocol/Internet Protocol (TCP/IP) network:

- Application proxies
- Encryption with VPN
- Management center
- Stateful IP filtering
- Static IP filtering

Note:
> Firewall tunneling technology can be abused. Improper configuration of firewall tunneling software can be a real windfall for would-be hackers. It is important that a firewall tunneling solution be made to work in a very secure fashion.

17.5.1 Application proxies

Application firewalls implement a proxy on the gateway for each TCP/IP application supported. A proxy acts as a relay between the specific applications and their users. Remote users first connect to these proxies and authenticate themselves, as required, before connecting to the target server. All traffic must pass through the proxy, which performs checks and filtering based on the commands specific to the application. For a high level of protection, both types of technique are in fact complementary and must act together to attain the highest level of security.

17.5.2 Encryption with virtual private network

The full development of the web information-sharing potential requires confidence and trust in the ability of network security measurements to safeguard the intellectual capital of the enterprise. VPNs, in ensuring secret business communications, make it possible to conciliate security and telecommunication costs reduction. This represents a powerful complement to access control capabilities of firewalls.

17.5.3 Management center

For large enterprises, the main challenge lies not only in the power of the technology used at each control point, but also in the ability to manage the protection policy centrally and consistently across all enterprise access points, and to change it according to the Internet security context. A company has to be able to close its doors and windows when sunny weather turns to rain.

An enterprise may often use several Internet and intranet firewalls. How does one ensure good protection and apply a genuine security policy without overwhelming security officers with endless configuration tasks or risking security holes caused by misconfigurations? For this, powerful centralized and coherent management capabilities are required.

Numerous suppliers provide protection technology. Only a very few vendors, however, are able to provide such Internet security and firewall tunneling management.

17.5.4 Stateful IP filtering

Advanced firewalls on the market now provide a high security level of IP filtering, called *dynamic* or *stateful filtering*. This filtering provides checking of major Internet protocols (TCP, User Datagram Protocol [UDP], etc.), services (web, mail, FTP, Telnet, etc.), and business applications (remote procedure call [RPC], SQL*Net, etc.) by memorizing and constantly evaluating the state and progress of each connection or transaction.

17.5.5 Static IP filtering

IP firewalls work by filtering IP packets on the network. Each IP packet trying to cross the IP layer is compared with an Access Control List (ACL), using rules concerning the source and destination address, protocol, service, time frame, etc. These rules are used to decide whether the packet is allowed to cross the firewall. Such static filtering devices, like filtering routers, provide a very simplistic filtering, with a low level of protection.

17.6 Demilitarized zone focus

The DMZ is the bridge between the controlled information system and the external world. This is where very important security mechanisms take place.

17.6.1 Isolating the machine

A DMZ separates an external network from directly referencing an internal network. It does this by isolating the machine that is being directly accessed from all other machines. Most of the time, the external network is the Internet, and what is in the DMZ is the web server, but this isn't the only possible configuration. A DMZ can be used to isolate a particular machine within a network from other machines. This might be done for a branch office that needs its own Internet access and access to the corporate network. The frontiers are materialized by the firewalls.

17.6.2 Controlling the flow

Separation is important. Any system should have its important applications separated. This acts as a system of checks and balances to make sure that if any one area goes bad, it cannot corrupt the whole. The DMZ is then in charge of controlling all the flows and redirects some flows to content management systems to check for viruses, for example. To do so, the firewalls must be able to deeply analyze the flows, thanks to IP filtering plus application proxies.

17.6.3 Controlling remote access

The DMZ, as the entrance point to the information technology (IT) system, is the place for controlling remote access. In the DMZ, the integrity and the confidentiality of the data coming from the external world must be checked and ensured. This feature can be provided thanks to encryption. To do so, the firewall tunneling solution must provide VPN capabilities, respecting the IPSec and Internet Key Exchange (IKE) standards, to ensure the interoperability with other firewalls or desktop operating systems.

17.6.4 Authentication mechanisms

To have the safest solution, the DMZ must also provide some authentication mechanism. According to the enterprise organization, this DMZ can have its own user base or can be integrated with the enterprise user base, such as a Lightweight Directory Access Protocol (LDAP) directory, or with the enterprise authentication mechanism, such as Public Key Infrastructure (PKI). Obviously, the front-end equipment must provide this feature: the firewall tunneling solution.

So, because the DMZ is the door to the external world, all the protection features must be managed to avoid any configuration error. Hence, the same console must provide the management of all the DMZ security features. It is the only way to deploy the necessary security mechanism in a cost-effective way.

17.7 Keeping the firewall tunneling security rules up-to-date through enterprise intranets

Large intranets need at least one firewall per site; each firewall needs to know the security rules to apply to each employee. Thus, keeping the firewall tunneling security rules is, of course, the most basic of security operations. Granting employees access to their needed resources requires that each firewall of each site will know how to react when there is a controlled request from any employees.

Finally, LDAP and user profiles can help simplify each firewall tunneling configuration. However, with a large number of firewalls requiring so many configurations each, it becomes critical for security managers to define and deploy rules automatically on each server according to their enterprise security policy from a central point. So, without central administration, one employee can manage up to five firewalls, whereas with secure and consistent central administration, one employee can manage more than 400 firewalls.

17.8 Summary

Although many Internet security and firewall tunneling solutions can be found on today's market, most of them are point security products dedicated to tactical access point protection, but are difficult to manage in large numbers and hard to truly integrate within an enterprise-wide Internet security policy. Good Internet security and firewall tunneling solutions must respect at least four major rules, as follows:

- A high level of trust
- Centralized security management
- Enterprise-class scalability
- High-end protection

17.8.2 A high level of trust

The firewall tunneling solution must be trustworthy, and must be provided by a trustworthy supplier. It must also be certified by renowned independent authorities such as the International Computer Security Association (ICSA) and Information Technology Security Evaluation Criteria (ITSEC).

17.8.3 Centralized security management

A firewall is a key component of any enterprise's security policy. For the best security, lowest cost of ownership, and optimal ease of management, all firewalls installed in an enterprise must be managed centrally from a single console. Security policy officers must not be overwhelmed by repetitive configuration tasks on dozens of firewalls, even remotely or with simple configuration replication capabilities across firewalls. In addition, misconfigurations resulting from human errors represent a real security risk. A good solution must let security officers define a truly business-driven policy, with the proper rules being centrally generated and automatically distributed to all firewall points. Also, and most importantly, the firewall tunneling solution must be able to be managed by global enterprise security management solutions. In other words, you must ensure the following:

- Avoid critical configuration errors.
- Make the recommended multilevel protection possible.
- React fast to isolate infested subnetworks.[1]

17.8.4　Enterprise-class scalability

Enterprises are no longer isolated castles with precise battlements and stoves. Protection is now needed at the border and at the heart of the IT system. In addition, when web access performance is important, the IT nervous system performances are a major concern.

With the Internet being accessible around the world at any time, networks need constant protection. Defenses may be down for just a few minutes, but it only takes seconds to invade an organization's information system! It is thus crucial that a firewall tunneling solution should ensure dependable and high-performance protection with built-in high availability, load sharing, and load-balancing features. The more business-critical the site is to protect, the more numerous the connections to support, and the more essential are the performance and scalability of the firewall tunneling solution. However, even when just one firewall tunneling solution is used on a smaller site, it is important to choose this firewall so it can easily be scaled to grow with the site traffic and the success of the enterprise. In other words, you must choose this firewall tunneling solution because traffic is ever increasing and more and more doors are being opened.

17.8.5　High-end firewall tunneling protection

To ensure good protection, one has to ensure the system is not breakable using backdoors or security weaknesses. This means that security must be ensured at all levels, by both IP checks and application proxies. The solution must provide a complete set of protection facilities, including strong authentication capabilities to ensure that the users are who they claim, and encryption capabilities to keep secret the data exchanged, to grant or deny access in accordance with the security policy, and to prevent information from being disclosed. It must also be able to operate with content security solutions (to filter viruses, malicious Java applets, or ActiveX controls) and to complement firewall tunneling access control protection with strong encryption (to build VPNs) and extended audit and alert facilities.

Finally, it must be able to operate with other security solutions through a set of open interfaces. In other words, it must have an integrated protection for network and applications and fine-grained control.

17.9 References

1. George Bieber, "Information Assurance, Training and Awareness, and Products and Resources," National Institute of Standards and Technology, U.S. Department of Commerce, Gaithersburg, Maryland, January, 2004.

2. John Wack, Ken Cutler, and Jamie Pole, "Guidelines on Firewalls and Firewall Policy: Recommendations of the National Institute of Standards and Technology," National Institute of Standards and Technology, U.S. Department of Commerce, Gaithersburg, Maryland, January, 2002.

Section VIII

Firewall Management

18

Auditing and Logging

18.1 Chapter objectives

- Detecting intruders
- Auditing your firewall setup
- Interpreting log output
- Configuring firewall logging and alert mechanisms
- Logging and monitoring firewalls

You've just finished implementing your new shiny firewall, or perhaps you've just inherited several new firewalls with the company merger. Either way, you're probably curious about whether they are implemented properly. Will your firewalls keep the hackers out there at bay? Do they meet your expectations? This chapter will help you find out. Here you will find recommendations on how to audit your firewall and set up your firewall log activities and your firewall rule base.

18.2 Auditing your firewall

Defining what you expect is your first step in auditing your firewall. What do you want your firewall to do? Most of you should have this already defined in a security policy. Make sure you have an understanding of these before you verify your firewall setup. That way, when you're done with the process, you can compare the results to your expectations. Some of you may be in the situation in which you don't know what to expect. Maybe you are new to the company and need to assess the situation. Or perhaps your company has merged and you have assumed responsibility for several new networks. Regardless, try to define some goals before you start: What would you like to see happen?

18.2.1   **Methodology**

Auditing your firewall setup consists of two parts. First, you want to test the firewall itself, because as a critical system in your security plan, the firewall must be secure. Second, you want to test the rule base, which determines which traffic can pass the firewall. The purpose of the firewall is to control traffic, so you must verify that it is doing its job.

Secured firewall

You need to ensure that your firewall is secure to audit it because any-one from the outside or the inside can access or modify your firewall. First, you want to ensure that it is physically secured with controlled access. Once someone obtains physical access, game over. Next, the operating system (OS) itself should be armored. Review an armoring checklist specifically for your OS. You also need to ensure that the OS fully complies with the armoring checklist. The next step is to scan your firewall, from both your internal network and the Internet (Internet Control Message Protocol [ICMP], UDP, and TCP). You also need to identify which, if any, ports are open on the firewall. On most properly configured firewalls, you should find no open ports, and you should not even be able to ping them.

To start with, a properly armored firewall should have few services. Once the firewall is running, no ports should be exposed unless they absolutely have to be. These ports are for administration, open by default in the control properties. It is highly recommended that you disable them. ICMP is also open by default, so it is highly recommended that you disable this also. If ICMP is open, your network can easily be mapped from the Internet. If you need these ports or services to administer your firewall, then set up a rule that limits which source IP addresses can connect to them. The idea in securing your firewall is to deny access whenever possible. Every rule base should have a lock-down rule at the beginning that denies any traffic to the firewall; that way, your firewall is sealed from the world. If you need access to the firewall, have the rule go before the lock-down rule. All other rules should go after the lock-down rule. Many people consider this a ghosting rule, thinking that it hides the firewall, but it doesn't. What it does do is protect your firewall, ensuring that whatever other rules you put in later, your firewall will still be protected. The lock-down rule, when placed first, protects against that. The whole purpose of scanning your firewall is to ensure that you have not accidentally exposed it to unauthorized users.

Rule base

You need to audit your rule base once you have audited your firewall. The goal is to ensure that the firewall is enforcing what you expect it to. You can do this by scanning every network segment from every other network segment. You want to validate that the firewall is accepting only the traffic that you allow. Many firewalls have several network segments, such as demilitarized zones (DMZs). Make sure you validate the rule base by scanning from every one of these segments. It is highly recommended that you place a system on your DMZ and attempt to penetrate the internal network, because your DMZ is highly vulnerable. This simulates if one of your DMZ systems is compromised (such as a DNS or web server) and ensures that your internal network is still protected by the firewall. Remember, your firewall rule base should deny everything, allowing only that which is specifically allowed. The fewer services you accept and the fewer rules you have, the more secure your environment. If during your audit you are not sure whether a service should be blocked, block it. If no one complains, then it was not needed.

Encryption/authentication

There are several other features you need to test, specifically authentication and encryption. Often, firewalls are expected to authenticate users to access a resource. For example, if you expect users to be authenticated before they access your web site, confirm this for yourself. You should try accessing the web site without authenticating and see what happens. It is extremely easy to make a mistake when you implement a rule base. What you thought was password protected may be wide open to the world. You should apply the same test for encryption. If you have resources that should only be accessed while encrypted, test it out. Also, you should try accessing the resources without encryption, and see whether it can get you there. In addition, run a sniffer such as snoop or tcpdump during the test. Make sure your data are actually being encrypted. You need to verify your expectations. So, are your resources protected in the manner you expected?

Additional services

For additional services, firewalls today can work with a third software, like virus scanning in e-mail or content filtering. If you are using any of these third-party services with your firewall, you need to test them. For example, for virus scanning, send an e-mail through the firewall to ensure your virus scanning is working. If it isn't, you will need to review your configuration and resolve the problem. Be sure to retest the configuration to ensure the fix works.

Deeper digging

Once you have identified available resources, you can begin to dig deeper. You've determined what the firewall allows through, but now what threat does that pose? This is where things become fuzzy, where auditing your firewall setup can become auditing your network. You are no longer auditing your firewall, but auditing the resources behind the firewall. However, because this information will be important to you, let's now look at the basics. The goal is to determine what potential vulnerabilities exist for the accessible resources. You should review each accessible resource and identify vulnerabilities. For example, if you determine that the firewall allows HTTP access to several IIS web servers, you then have to determine what threats that poses (hint: there are a lot!). Or if you identify a system running wu-ftpd 2.4.2 VR17, you should consider upgrading to the latest version. If a vulnerability exists, you either have to fix the vulnerability or decide whether the risk is worth the service. Various tools can help you identify vulnerabilities. You should also find several tools you feel the most comfortable with and use them.

Now, let's look at firewall logging. In particular, this part of the chapter covers the configuration of firewall logging, alert mechanisms, and monitoring.

18.3 Logging

After you have verified your firewall and rule base, review the logs. Did the firewall detect all of your scans, and did it set off the expected alerts? What traffic did it log, and how? If your firewall did not detect most of this activity, something is wrong, and you need to be able to see this information. Also, by reviewing the rule base, you will have a better understanding of what to look for when auditing your logs. If you are going to log the rule, log it long so you get all the information.

18.3.1 Configuration of firewall logging

You want your firewall systems to log activities pertinent to firewall operation and the rules the firewall will enforce. For significant firewall events, you want your firewall system to alert you in real time that these events have occurred. There are two types of logging that you need to specify for your firewall systems: logging associated with the packets arriving and departing the firewall (packet denied, packet forwarded) and logging associated with the operation of the firewall software and the system on which it runs (no more disk space, no more memory, firewall logs are full).

There are logging options associated with each packet-filtering rule for most firewall software. Every packet processed by such a rule has these options applied to it for the purposes of logging. An example is to log packets denied by the firewall software. Logging options can also be used to specify the level of logging, which commonly includes real-time alert mechanisms such as paging, electronic mail, or executing an arbitrary program.

Reasons for logging

Ensuring the continued operation of the firewall system is the most important reason for logging. Logged events related to the operational status of the firewall are critical to preventing and recovering from failures. They are also an important auditing tool to ensure that the proper security configurations (packet filters, proxies) are installed on the firewall system. Logs of this sort are generally small and can have long-term value for various purposes.

Concerns about security are completely apart from firewall operational concerns. Logs can be useful for you to determine how an intrusion might have occurred for the purpose of improving the quality of the firewall implementation. Logs for this purpose have value only during the time when intrusions can be reasonably resolved—usually no more than 4 to 5 weeks.

Logs might also be used in intrusion detection. Intrusion detection is the process of detecting attempted, failed, and successful attacks against your network. Logs for this purpose may have historical value.

You should use alert mechanisms to notify you of any significant event. Because log files are typically voluminous and difficult for humans to process, it is generally impractical to depend on manual analysis of logs to detect significant events.

Design the logging environment: how to do it

To design the logging environment, you need to know how to do it first. You need to determine the following:

- How log files are to be backed up and recovered
- The location of firewall log files
  - On the firewall system itself
  - On a remote logging host accessed via a network
- The expected size of log files
- The rate at which data are logged to the log files
- Who needs access to the log files and the level of access
- Whether logging is to be encrypted[1]

Therefore, with the preceding in mind, the following general heuristics are recommended to guide your design:

- Do not allow disk space requirements to be a constraining factor for logging. Disks are inexpensive, so make sure you have enough disk space on both the firewall host and the central log host for local logging.
- If you log to a host other than the firewall host, make sure your packet filter logging is configured not to create log entries for log packets. Otherwise, this will create an infinite logging loop.
- Log to both local log files on the firewall host and a central log host. Log as much information as you can locally and keep it for as long as disk space permits. Log to the central log host only information that you need or will use.
- Use a separate logging-only network to log to the central logging host. This prevents logging from affecting normal traffic. You can

use this logging-only network to log intrusion-detection traffic as well.[2]

PACKET FILTER RULES: SELECT LOGGING OPTIONS

On each packet filter rule, design the logging options. You need to decide what purpose is served by logging packets affected by the rule. Generally, logging for its own sake is not a wise use of resources. Logging options for each rule may include the following:

- Packets that are denied upon arrival at the firewall system
- Packets that arrive or depart within a specified time or date interval
- Packets that are denied upon departure from the firewall system[3]

You might be able to configure other aspects of logging that relate to packets being filtered, in addition to logging options for each rule. For example, your firewall software may support summarization of individual filter logs. These can be useful for seeing trends and, in general, are more valuable to keep for an extended period than the individual log entries.

It is occasionally interesting to track a particular kind of traffic, although it is not a typical practice to log packets that are permitted by filter rules. For this purpose, you might consider adding a redundant filter rule (one that either permits or denies packets that are already permitted or denied by another rule) just so you can specify different logging options for that rule. If you do this, make sure to document that the rule is redundant and is not essential to the implementation of your security policy.

If you are replacing an existing firewall system, thoroughly examine the logging options specified by your existing system. Consider retaining those logging options for rules in the new configuration that are consistent with your security policy.

ALERT MECHANISM CONFIGURATION DESIGN

To ensure that important event notifications are delivered to the appropriate people as quickly as possible with a minimum number of false notifications, you should design the real-time alert function of your firewall system. These may include notification of the following:

- Changes to certain files on the firewall system
- Operational events (logs full, memory or disk shortages, system reboots)
- Packet filters being modified or disabled on the firewall system
- Successful logins to the firewall system
- Unsuccessful user and host login attempts[3]

It is further recommended that you establish a central alert mechanism that also operates on the central log host if you followed the recommendation in the preceding to establish a central log host. It may be that if you choose this approach, the firewall alert mechanism can be disabled and all alerts can be handled by one system.

Thoroughly examine the alert options specified by your existing system if you are replacing an existing firewall system. Consider retaining those parts of the alert mechanism configuration that remain consistent with your current security policy and your firewall system operation policy.

POLICY CONSIDERATIONS: SUPPORTING TOOLS ACQUISITION OR DEVELOPMENT

Acquire or develop tools that monitor your log files and summarize the content of your log files beyond those provided by the vendor. These will provide you with the capability to review only those events of interest.

Unless your design includes enough disk capacity to retain log records until they are discarded, you will need to develop log file archive mechanisms. It is recommended that you use Write Once, Read Many (WORM) devices for all archiving. Your organization's networked systems security policy should also do the following:

- Require notification to designated administrators of suspicious behavior that can be detected by the firewall system. This would include events related to the firewall.

- Require your firewall system to record all significant activity (such as administrative changes and attempts to breach filter rules) by doing thorough auditing and logging.

- Specify guidelines for
  - Handling archived log information
  - How long information should be retained and discarding log information

- Specify that configuring logging and alert mechanisms for your firewall system is performed in an environment isolated from your operational networks.

- Specify system logs that record failed login attempts and requests to disable filter rules.[3]

18.3.2 Firewall monitoring

Significant events on firewalls fall into three broad categories: critical system issues (hardware failures and the like), significant authorized administrative events (rule changes, administrator account changes), and network connection logs. In particular, let's briefly look at how to capture the following events:

- Adds/deletes/changes of administrative accounts

- Changes to firewall policy

- Changes to network interfaces: Need to test whether the default OS logging captures this information or whether the firewall software records it somewhere (any invocation of UNIX ifconfig or the equivalent?)

- Host OS log messages: For the purposes of this chapter, you should capture these data at the minimum severity (maximum verbosity) required to record system reboots, which will record other time-critical OS issues, too.

- Network connection logs, which include dropped and rejected connections, time/protocol/IP addresses/usernames for allowed connections, maybe amount of data transferred[3]

The preceding list contains more than just network connection information. An observant firewall administrator will notice that. Thus, most firewall logging tools focus on network connection records, because protecting network connections is the most obvious task performed by the firewall, and because they're typically in a predictable format. At least, logging formats are relatively stable on any given platform, OS, and firewall application.

However, a vital component of system and security administration is tracking administrative changes on your firewalls, and records of administrative changes are often hard to track down.

Network connection logs

When most system administrators think about network connection logs, they think about firewall logs. Because firewalls are gateways between networks of varying trust levels, they provide an obvious place to record information about network traffic.

Finally, dropped connection logs are not particularly interesting without some additional work once a firewall is installed and configured with the appropriate rule set. Dropped packets are events that didn't happen after all, so they're attacks that didn't succeed or connection attempts that violated your policy and weren't allowed through. Extracting information like numbers of port scans or top-ten sources of dropped packets usually requires writing a script, although more firewall developers are including those sorts of summary reports in their default installations.

18.4 Summary

A firewall is only as good as its implementation. With today's dynamic Internet access, it is easy to make mistakes during the implementation process. By auditing your firewall setup, you can ensure that the firewall is enforcing what you expect it to in a secure manner.

This chapter helps you in one of two situations. First, you have certain expectations of what your firewall can or cannot do, and you want to meet those expectations. Second, you do not know what to expect, so you need to audit your firewall to learn more. Either way, this chapter has hopefully helped you out.

On the other hand, several areas are beyond the scope of this chapter. For example, this chapter does not cover how to specifically audit or hack a network—that is a different subject. Also, this chapter does not discuss which firewall is better than others. Each firewall has its own advantages and disadvantages. What is going to make or break you is not choosing the best firewall, but implementing it correctly. In other words, that was the purpose of this chapter: to make sure your firewall was implemented correctly and behaves as you would expect it to.

18.5 References

1.   George Bieber, "Information Assurance, Training and Awareness, and Products and Resources," National Institute of Standards and Technology, U.S. Department of Commerce, Gaithersburg, Maryland, January, 2004.

2.   John Wack, Ken Cutler, and Jamie Pole, "Guidelines on Firewalls and Firewall Policy: Recommendations of the National Institute of Standards and Technology," National Institute of Standards and Technology, U.S. Department of Commerce, Gaithersburg, Maryland, January, 2002.

3.   "How to Develop a Network Security Policy: An Overview of Internetworking Site Security," Sun Microsystems, Santa Clara, California, 2004.

19

Firewall Administration

19.1 Chapter objectives

- Managing your firewall remotely
- Providing high availability
- Protecting standalone machines
- Maintaining your firewall
- Managing firewall security

In today's technological society, the administration and management of firewall technology is crucial. The protection of today's consumer on the Internet is key to the success of e-business companies and should take precedence over other duties. The cost of firewall technologies should never be shortchanged and should be included in the administration costs. Obtaining highly qualified, trained, and quality system administrators is often a difficult task. It is proven that system administrators often do not identify, protect against, or prevent firewall intrusions. It is important that system administrators upgrade their systems with patches and bug fixes as soon as problems occur. If a firewall or other safeguard is not properly maintained, it might become unsecure and permit break-ins while providing the illusion that the site is still secure. To assure customers that your site is safe, your company should incorporate the importance of firewall administration in their security policy. Management should also demonstrate its commitment to the importance of the administration of safeguards and firewalls by employing a full-time staff dedicated to this and ensure proper funding for procurement and maintenance of such technologies.

312 19.3 Managing your firewall remotely

19.2 System administration

Continued system administration should be the rule, not the exception. It is recommended that sites do the following:

- Standardize operating system versions and software, making installation of patches and security fixes more manageable.

- Institute a program for efficient site-wide installation of patches and new software.

- Use services to assist in centralizing system administration if it will result in better administration and better security.

- Perform periodic scans and checks of server systems to detect common vulnerabilities and errors in configuration, and to ensure that a communication pathway exists between system administrators and firewall/site security administrators to alert the site about new security problems.

- Finally, ask yourself: What kind of firewall does my company need? A firewall or safeguard technology may be well suited for one company but not another.[1]

19.3 Managing your firewall remotely

Firewall monitoring to achieve five nines (99.999%), as it is better known to the IT world, is not as unrealistic as 100% would be and much more critical to success than only four nines. These numbers aren't just buried metrics in some broader, more strategic financial formula. In fact, they are the relentlessly sought-after magic numbers that all IT people are now striving to achieve from their very first day on the job. The percentage relates to something that is absolutely mission critical for almost all organizations and something that is easily tied to revenues and profits: the uptime of their IT infrastructure. It's very simple, really. Downtime of these firewalls results in downtime to the web site or applications that organizations' customers use to make purchases and drive revenue.

For the IT world, the quest for the five nines is a constant uphill battle. Dozens, even hundreds, of IT professionals can be employed while the organization still doesn't achieve the target number or any other exceptionally high percentage. Just how difficult is it to achieve such high uptime? The five nines equate to less than 5 minutes of downtime during the 525,600 minutes in an entire calendar year. Given the complexity of enterprise web infrastructures, that's a very difficult ambition and level of monitoring to achieve.

Most companies realize the necessity of monitoring their firewalls internally to be able to achieve the highest possible uptime. It's not rocket science; they need to know about firewall problems as quickly as possible to prevent it from coming down. On the other hand, despite the significant investments in people and technology that most companies make on internal monitoring of firewalls, the highest possible uptime never comes, and their return on investment (ROI) is significantly smaller than it could be.

19.3.1 Achieving high uptime

High uptime isn't an uncommon achievement. Proactive monitoring and alerting helps ensure threats don't become full-fledged reactionary problems that leave the IT team with tunnel vision for resolving that one problem and neglecting everything else. That's the crucial juncture where uptime is in serious jeopardy.

The key to achieving high uptime is actually much more than optimal efficiency in monitoring configuration and alerts and an experienced IT team. One of the biggest parts of the equation is the often overlooked aspect of what goes on outside the firewall. Some might think what happens outside the firewall is typically outside of their control. This may be true to the extent that they cannot generally influence performance and availability problems at the Internet backbones (ISPs) themselves. However, there are numerous benefits to understanding and resolving availability problems from outside the firewall that have a very real direct impact on the availability of firewalls and applications.

One scenario

For example, imagine that a company is successfully monitoring the availability of systems and web infrastructure from behind its firewall. The company has invested in monitoring solutions and is using these solutions to successfully ensure its systems are up 24/7 and its web site is always available to users. The company has accomplished this by proactively deploying alerts on potential threats to availability, eliminating false alarms, and providing an unmatched breadth and depth of monitor types that ensure every system, network resource, and application that is critical to the business is running. IT is finally on track to becoming a proactive, service-driven organization, except that the company is not meeting its service-level agreements.

Disaster strikes one day. Angry users are phoning in complaints that the company's web site is down, and they can't get the information they need or finish the purchase they were planning to make.

All the green lights on the monitoring screens show that the DNS servers, web servers, databases, and other systems, services, and applications are up and running. So where is the problem originating?

When their HTTP traffic was routed through a particular backbone, only a hosted monitoring service would notify an IT group that the users who called in experienced difficulties. Availability was just fine for everyone inside the company and maybe even for all users except those in, say, Hong Kong.

Therein lies one of the fundamental benefits of understanding availability impacts inside and outside the firewall. Monitoring externally helps provide a normalization of monitoring that, quite simply, cannot be achieved with only an internal solution. Monitoring behind the firewall can be largely affected by your internal network traffic. Increases or decreases in traffic on the network can provide a false sense of response time because internal users are much closer to the source than those outside the firewall, who must connect over the public backbones.

To provide validation about the performance of a company's network, monitoring from multiple locations outside the firewall can also help. Using both an external monitoring service and internal monitoring products can enable companies to compare the availability measurements of Internet-affected traffic with the traffic that connects directly through its network rather than the Internet at large. These can be distinctly different numbers that can offer a new perspective on just how available the company's infrastructure really is.

Ideal external monitoring will provide monitoring of mission-critical network services, URLs, and even URL sequences (often referred to as *transactions*), from numerous locations around the world. A company might choose these locations based on which ones are most strategic to its business or nearest to its customers. Either way, the more locations and ISPs that it monitors, the better a company's understanding of true availability from different geographies and peering points and the closer it will be to achieving optimal availability.

A company can take the preceding benefits a step further by isolating availability problems to specific peering points or ISPs along the outside path to its infrastructure by monitoring from multiple locations. Although it generally can't influence any changes at the ISPs themselves, this can give you a solid understanding of what geographies have the most performance problems and where the company might want to consider creating or making changes to a mirror of its web site or application to better service local users. If a company only monitors behind the firewall or from only one location outside, it is missing half the picture and is left to continue monitoring with only a subset of users in consideration. This information is useful in determining whether to mirror a web site for a specific geography, escalating problems with ISPs, and responding to customer complaints. Because customers view the company as responsible for the entire experience, it is important to respond to customer concerns regarding performance and availability, even if it is outside the company's direct control.

Worse scenario

Here's another even worse scenario. Perhaps your users weren't complaining about slow response times, but they were complaining that the company's systems and applications were not responding at all.

The IT group doesn't see how this could be the case when it is reporting very high uptime and response time measurements, especially after checking an internal monitoring product's console and reports. An external monitoring service would have enabled this company to discover a misconfiguration in, perhaps, its firewall. The misconfiguration was allowing internal traffic to go through but was preventing anybody outside the company from being able to access its web systems. In such a draconian situation, the company was running the risk of every single user outside its walls being unable to get to its web site or applications, while the entire IT team rejoiced in the high availability its internal monitoring technologies were showing. Nevertheless, they were completely oblivious to what users were really experiencing. As devastating as such a situation sounds, it is not uncommon for companies that do not monitor from outside the firewall.

19.3.2 External and internal solution monitors

If it's more relevant to end users, why not buy a hosted service? Monitoring systems and applications from inside the infrastructure is as crucial to a company's overall IT strategy as monitoring from the outside, and having only one or the other provides only a partial picture.

For example, because internal monitors are much closer to the source of potential problems within a company's network and not the path to it, factors such as backbone/ISP failures are kept from obscuring measurements and problems that are specific to the infrastructure. Covering both internal and external monitoring can provide a much more accurate view on availability and where the problems are actually rooted.

Also crucial is the proximity of internal monitors to a company's infrastructure. Because they are physically located within and are monitoring inside the infrastructure, a finer granularity of measurements is possible. This will help cultivate a more precise problem diagnosis that can only be achieved with an internal monitoring solution, at least when it comes to availability problems that have their root inside the company's infrastructure. People at the site can generally correct problems detected by such a solution, because they control the machines and the networks.

For purposes of automatically taking corrective action, another benefit is that internal monitors have direct privileged access to the firewalls. Although security options can be set to grant access rights to an external monitor's server, that is typically not the way infrastructures are configured.

Internal monitoring is critical, but it's not enough. Companies also need to be able to monitor their mission-critical systems from outside the firewall, from numerous locations around the world. This combination will bring a company much closer to 100% availability.

With the preceding in mind, the amount of money you invest into safeguards is directly related to the level of security you implement. Maintaining your firewall will extend its life, certify it is working, optimize its services, ensure that it is still producing a secure environment, allow you to perform upgrades, and ensure that the components of the firewall are still functioning and interacting with each other.

19.4 Maintenance of a firewall

In choosing a firewall or any other safeguard technology, you must ensure they have a management/monitoring module. Monitoring your system includes protecting the confidentiality of your customers but also involves monitoring the sensitivity of your devices and the security of your network. Most firewalls should have inspection mechanisms, but others also include authentication and encryption technologies. While maintaining your firewall, you should incorporate logs of services such as the number of e-mail messages, average size of e-mail messages, average time between web accesses, average size of FTP objects retrieved, number of Telnet sessions, etc. Good habits, steps, and procedures you should follow to keep your firewall working properly include the following:

- Back up all firewall components (hosts and routers).

- Be careful when adding management accounts on a firewall, including adding accounts, removing old accounts, and constant changing of passwords, especially after a user has been removed.

- Closely monitor the log reports of traffic passing through the firewall.

- Constantly monitor the entire system, and make sure the firewall has an auditing system; if it doesn't, install one.

- Be alert for abnormal conditions of your firewall.

- Create security-checking reports that will aid in identifying security holes.

- Create a procedure to ensure risks are identified (audit logs, activity reports, configuration, and security checklists).

- Appropriately assign responsibilities, including proper resource allocation.

- Develop a file access policy, and designate restricted areas on the disk farm.

- Develop a strong, reliable contingency plan.

- Develop an authorization and authentication procedure for new users and services.[2]

19.4.1   Performing firewall maintenance

As previously explained, a firewall is designed to protect network resources. Through a firewall, information can be securely shared among servers and workstations. They are a common form of security for any organization that has data to protect from mainly external sources. Firewalls are designed to block incoming traffic by preventing access through open ports. After installing a firewall, however, it is not necessarily safe to say that the organization is now protected against denial-of-service (DoS) attacks. How can the network administrator know if the firewall is doing its job?

First, the system that supports the firewall must be properly maintained. The network administrator should create a list of all field-replaceable components for this system. Once this list is compiled, the components should be located in a safe storage area so in the event of a system failure the components can be readily available. An ideal situation is to have a totally redundant firewall system so that security would not be compromised in the event of a primary system failure.

Second, whenever a change is made to the firewall configuration, perform a backup immediately to reflect that change. For example, there may be rules set up to perform specific functions. Whenever an update to any rule is made, the network administrator should perform an immediate backup of the configuration.

Third, have the firewall vendor test both the firewall software and the system hardware periodically for leaks. The testing procedure should include scanning the firewall system to determine the presence of known vulnerabilities and, if any are found, the immediate application of patches or fixes. Alternatively, the network administrator should have third-party certified vendors perform the same tests to ensure that the firewall's vendor does not have a bias. The tests should be performed when there is the least network traffic, because test scripts can possibly overload a network. The person conducting the tests should be supervised by either the CIO or the network administrator, so questions can be asked about the testing procedure and results presented by the tests.

Fourth, the results of the tests should be stored in a secure location to prevent unauthorized persons from accessing them.

Fifth, as part of the testing phase, the firewall alarms and thresholds should also be tested. Delays in receiving alarms via e-mail or pager should be addressed.

Sixth, some vendors may require remote access to the firewall to perform testing procedures whenever there is a problem. This should be avoided unless there is written assurance from the vendor and approval by the client company's legal advisor.

But how do you know if your firewall is healthy? Does it need a physical?

Firewall physical

In cyberspace, your firewalls need routine checkups if they're to remain healthy. Like the human body, computer equipment ages with time and wear and tear. It's not enough to know that you correctly installed your firewall. You have to run it through a firewall physical to ensure it stays in tiptop shape. Here are six things to examine:

- Configuration files
- Disk damage
- CPU load
- Daemons
- Systems files
- Log anomalies[3]

CONFIGURATION FILES

No matter how tight you lock down your firewall during installation, all bets are off once it goes live. Your firewall security policy should dictate configuration parameters in high-level, nonspecific terms. You should develop and monitor firewall-specific policies with configuration details, such as what traffic is allowed or what services use proxies.

The policy should specify the steps for modifying a firewall's configuration, including what authorization is needed to make changes, who is permitted to make changes and when, how to document the changes, etc. The policy should also dictate a separation of duties, where one person does the work, another documents the changes, and a third tests and reviews the new setup.

DISK USAGE

Disk usage is important if you store logs on the firewall, but even more so if you don't. In the first case, an abnormal increase in the rate of disk usage could indicate a problem in the log cleanup procedures. In the latter case, it could mean someone has installed a rootkit. In any case, you must develop a baseline of what constitutes normal firewall disk usage. Most problems (security or otherwise) take a system out of its normal state.

CPU LOAD

Similar to disk usage, the CPU load is an indicator of system health. Again, you must know what normal is. A low CPU load doesn't necessarily mean all is well, but an abnormally high one almost always means something is wrong. It could be anything from a DoS attack to the loss of your outside network connection.

DAEMONS

Each firewall has a normal set of daemons that must be running to operate correctly, such as a name server, system logging program, network dispatcher, or authentication server. Are all those that should be running doing so? If not, why not? What else is running that shouldn't be?

SYSTEM FILES

A critical system file changes for three reasons: An administrator purposefully changed it, perhaps as part of a scheduled upgrade; an administrator accidentally changed it; or an attacker changed it. Again, your policy for firewall configuration changes must cover how to correctly document system file changes.

LOG ANOMALIES

Firewall logs, of course, are a great source of health information, documenting all traffic that is permitted and denied. Because of the amount of data, checking for log anomalies should be an automated process. Naturally, what constitutes an anomaly will change over time, but only if you document it.

Continued health prescription

No checkup uncovers all problems, so it's important to verify your firewall's health continuously. Run a packet scanner to ensure it has the correct configuration. If you want to be a bit more aggressive, run a vulnerability scanner.

Security is all about paranoia, and a daily firewall checkup may be just what the doctor ordered. By checking the preceding six indicators daily, you'll keep your firewall alive and kicking.

Now, let's look at how to report and manage incidents for firewalls. This chapter also looks at the keys to unlocking your firewall's secrets.

19.5 Managing firewall security

As previously explained, the firewall is a gateway between two networks. Typically, this gateway is implemented between a trusted network (your corporate network) and the Internet. The firewall's job is to ensure that all traffic moving from one network to the other conforms to your organization's security policies. In other words, the firewall inspects all incoming and outgoing communications and decides whether to allow the data to pass through or whether to reject or log the information. The existence of Virtual Private Networking (VPN) technology enhances the decision to include a decision to encrypt the communication. For the purposes of this part of the chapter, the focus is on the firewall and firewall management technologies. VPN management is primarily an extension of firewall technology to include the encryption/decryption of particular traffic at the firewall.

19.5.1 Firewall products common functionality

The firewall itself comes with capabilities for building the rules of allowable communications between networks. Basic functionality includes the following:

- Application layer filters analyze data streams for or from a specific application. This mechanism is used to protect against known exploits such as unsafe SMTP commands or attacks against internal Domain Naming System (DNS) servers.

- Log file viewer is a simple application for viewing events in the log file. The more advanced log viewers are color-coded to designate severity.

- Advanced firewalls can log events to a remote location, providing some level of consolidation of firewall events.

- Out-of-the-box support for common protocols such as Hypertext Transfer Protocol (HTTP), File Transport Protocol (FTP), Internet Relay Chat (IRC), H.323, and Transparent HTTP. The firewall can also be configured to support additional protocols by designating the protocol type and port to be used.

- *Packet filtering:* IP packet filters are static, and communication through a specific port is always either allowed or blocked. *Allow filters* allows all traffic through at the specified port. *Block filters* always prevents the packets from passing through.

- *Policy or configuration editors:* building and enforcing policies regarding communication types, destinations, and sources. For example, a firewall can be configured to prevent traffic from a specific source.[4]

The point of this functionality is to allow you to define the rules of engagement between your network and the outside world. The firewall is the omnipotent Internet gatekeeper for your organization. It knows all and could control all (at least as far as Internet traffic is concerned). However, IT organizations rarely extract the true value of their firewalls. For various reasons, the potential for enhancing the security of the enterprise goes unrealized. The truth is that most firewalls are actually misconfigured.

Note:

> According to industry analysts, 76% of sites with certified commercial firewalls are still vulnerable to attacks because of misconfiguration or improper deployment.

Good firewall administrators know that their firewall is keeping valuable secrets. More importantly, they know how to discover those secrets and use that information to better protect their enterprise.

Next, this chapter details two complementary technologies (firewall activity reporting and analysis) that help these administrators maximize the organization's return on its firewall investment.

19.5.2 Analysis and activity reporting of firewalls

Firewall log files represent a rarely mined IT gem. These logs contain information on how effectively the firewall is performing, as well as a record of all incoming and outgoing activity. This valuable information can help companies optimize their networks, prevent security breaches, and manage employee Internet usage policies.

More specifically, firewall reporting products add value to your firewall by allowing administrators to mine critically important security data on a daily basis. The reports generated by the products help IT groups do the following:

- Take control of bandwidth usage by analyzing and reporting on user and department consumption.

- Track and automatically categorize inappropriate Internet usage to address potential legal exposure.

- Identify timing of bandwidth spikes to understand peak traffic loads and possible bandwidth drivers.

- Identify bandwidth hogs—users or applications that are taking up bandwidth.

- Summarize, organize, and analyze firewall errors.

- Break down protocol usage.

- Effectively manage limited budget dollars.

- Accurately predict and justify bandwidth needs through trend analysis.[4]

19.5.3 Enterprise firewalls: automated event response and real-time monitoring

Although it's important to be able to analyze historical firewall activity, reporting alone cannot help you stop a security breach in progress.

However, real-time detection of suspicious activity along with automated response actions can stop a hacker in his or her tracks.

So, what should you do if your firewall is attacked? First of all, you should assess the situation. It will be important to ask questions such as the following:

1. Did the hacker succeed in breaking into the site?

2. Is the intruder still acting in your system?

3. What is the best solution in controlling the situation?

4. Is this attack an inside threat?[4]

Second, you should cut off the link. It will be important to ask the following questions:

1. Do you need to shut down the server, and if so, can you?

2. Do you care about tracking down the hacker, and if so, what connections do you need to shut down so you don't lose him or her?

3. Are other clients affected, and if so, how?

4. If you shut down the server, what information can you afford to lose?[4]

Third, you should analyze the problem. You must add up all of the problems and come up with the results. You need to put a logical plan together and make sure to think carefully about the actions you are about to take. Once you put your plan together, bounce it off of someone who is not directly related to the problem. This will help in choosing the optimal solution.

Fourth, you should take action. You now need to implement your emergency response plan. You need to make sure that management, users, and service providers are aware of the problem, and you owe them a reasonable time frame for the restoration of the system. With the preceding in mind, the following list details the most important benefits of firewall incident management:

1.   Firewall log file information consolidation

2.   Misconfiguration detection

3.   Configuration settings backup

4.   External attacks identification

5.   Single point of monitoring

6.   Automated responses[4]

Firewall log file information consolidation

In large organizations, there is a need to consolidate and protect all log information. This is done through a single data store to meet company- and industry-mandated audit requirements.

Misconfiguration detection

Misconfiguration of your firewall can result in your network being vulnerable to attack. With the vast number of configuration settings, errors can easily creep into your system. Configuration errors can become even more prevalent when multiple administrators make changes to the firewall settings. This helps to ensure that the firewall configuration policy is maintained. If the firewall is out of compliance, you receive an alert so you can fix the problem.

Configuration settings back up

If your management server and firewall computers ever go down, it is important to be able to restore them as quickly as possible. Having a routine backup process ensures that you always have an up-to-date backup available to restore your system to its original state.

External attacks identification

One way to protect your network from external attacks is to watch for malformed packets or unusual port scanning activity. If you receive a large number of port scans from the same host, it is likely that a malicious user is targeting your network. You can configure an automated notification to be sent to the members of a specific notification group to respond to the attack.

Single point of monitoring

In today's large network environments, using multiple applications to monitor network activity can slow down the IT team and prolong problem resolution. Speedy identification of firewall issues can ensure that perimeter security is maintained. This allows you to avoid sifting through numerous event logs to identify when attacks are underway or when configurations are out-of-date. Additionally, to help maintain the integrity of this information, it is stored in a secure central repository.

Automated responses

Finally, some rules contain automated scripts to run in response to identified external attacks. For example, if the firewall cannot start up properly because of network problems, an e-mail notification can be sent or an administrator can be paged to take care of the problem.

19.6 Summary

With their mass migration to the Internet to conduct business with their customers, companies are increasingly more vulnerable to security breaches than ever before. It is crucial that companies take an active role in safeguard and firewall technology and commit the needed time, money, and resources to administrating, controlling, and monitoring their systems. Privacy has become more important in consumer livelihood. Companies need to be responsible with and for their actions. This includes protecting their sites and preventing possible break-ins. At the very least, you must remember three basic web site security requirements: confidentiality, integrity, and availability. Excellence in these areas will be achieved by regulating the flow of users, services, and activity of your site through a predetermined set of rules called the *network security policy*.

This chapter focused on why monitoring from outside the firewall is so crucial. It also provided several examples of situations in which availability is jeopardized because internal monitoring solutions are not able to analyze half the problem.

The chapter also provided an understanding of how to maximize the effectiveness of enterprise firewalls. The chapter covered what a firewall is and its role in securing e-commerce infrastructures. The chapter then reviewed the capabilities commonly found within most software firewalls. Critical functionality was explored in terms of its value and benefits. Specifically, the practical use of firewall reporting was detailed, along with the importance of real-time monitoring, event notification, and automated response to close the loop on suspicious firewall activity. The combination of these technologies ensures comprehensive firewall effectiveness.

19.7 References

1. George Bieber, "Information Assurance, Training and Awareness, and Products and Resources," National Institute of Standards and Technology, U.S. Department of Commerce, Gaithersburg, Maryland, January, 2004.

2. John Wack, Ken Cutler, and Jamie Pole, "Guidelines on Firewalls and Firewall Policy: Recommendations of the National Institute of Standards and Technology," National Institute of Standards and Technology, U.S. Department of Commerce, Gaithersburg, Maryland, January, 2002.

3. "How to Develop a Network Security Policy: An Overview of Internetworking Site Security," Sun Microsystems, Santa Clara, California, 2004.

4. Jack McCullough, "Beyond the Firewall: Using a Layered Security Strategy to Address Internal Security Threats," SurfControl, Scotts Valley, California, 2003.

20

Summary, Conclusions, and Recommendations

20.1 Chapter objectives

- Designing and implementing future firewalls
- Thwarting future firewall attacks
- Recommending future firewall technology
- Evaluating firewall intrusion-prevention systems

Today, protecting internetworked applications from malicious code is of utmost importance to IT security professionals, particularly when applications are available across the Internet. But even business-to-business connections using encrypted Internet channels and private leased lines or internal connections between organizational departments introduce risks to applications on the protected side of the security perimeter. The business problems associated with being hit and then cleaning up after a malicious software event or after an attacker gets a foothold on the internal network are already well known. Therefore, risk reduction and prevention of such attacks are the focus.[1]

Over the last 3 years, great confusion has set in around the role of the firewall in this prevention effort. A common reaction to the increased volume and damage of high-profile attacks happening today is that you have a firewall, but these attacks are still getting inside your network. You thought your firewall was supposed to protect your network and applications!

So today two basic types of Firewall Intrusion Prevention Systems (FIPSs) are prominent in the market: host based (application-specific software plug-ins) and inline (gateways on the network). This book has dealt exclusively with firewall security, but categorizing the wide variety of firewall security solutions available under one term, *firewall,* has created much confusion.

20.2 Summary

This book has discussed the nature of known threats (already identified and understood), unknown threats (first-time day-zero), and how dealing cost effectively and efficiently with *both* is the ultimate goal for IT security. Given this daunting task, it is self-evident that no single technical security mechanism can deliver a total umbrella of protection. A multilayered defense–in-depth strategy of protection is called for. This strategy, however, introduces serious IT challenges.

Today, a growing number of new security products are flooding the security market, precisely because application-specific threats are circumventing widely deployed, high-speed screening firewalls. These new products are competing for the time and attention of an already overburdened IT community.

Embracing a multilayered defense–in-depth strategy of protection means more systems to buy, deploy, learn, manage, update, and depend on for perimeter security services. This situation is not tenable. Perimeter firewall security deployments that aren't manageable with staff already in place introduce new points of failure and additional performance bottlenecks. Fewer systems are desired, not more. Central policy management and reduced systems cost and administration is called for.

This book has provided commonsense clarity about perimeter firewall security and was written for busy IT professionals. The book also included simple ways for any organization to evaluate new emerging application firewall technologies.

The demand for connecting people, applications, and networks increases as reliance on the Internet increases in importance in the world of electronic business. Successful businesses are aggressively expanding connectivity, and connected organizations are more and more at risk due to the increased volume, sophistication, and distribution speed of Internet-transported attacks. Over time, network attacks have evolved into application-level attacks and blended attacks. Recently, an entirely new class of application-specific threats have arisen, thereby circumventing widely deployed firewalls. In addition, most experts in the industry have made numerous analyses related to the imperative need for application security solutions.

20.3 Conclusions

Recently, industry analysts agreed that one of the most pressing issues facing firewalls today and in the future is finding ways to address growing complexity in networks and applications. Firewalls have changed roles many times since their inception because of a number of factors: ease of manageability, growing concerns about connectivity with the Internet, and now the threats that arise from application-layer security breaches.

In the past, firewalls filled roles as device-level filters and were used to centralize the movement of traffic in and out of the network. Later, they were used to segment the network. Now they are beginning to go back to their roots, appearing in routers and switches and even in network interface cards (NICs).

Part of the reason for this historical shift is that firewalls were never a perfect solution. Organizations are better with them than without them, but they are just one of many tools in the toolbox.

With firewalls migrating into diverse parts of the network, management has become a significant problem. Vendors need to create centralized means of writing rules for distributed firewalls.

Another problem with firewalls is that they are largely black boxes. One cannot analyze the rules in the firewall and ascertain whether new rules will cause conflicts. For example, most people don't even know whether their firewall examines non-IP packets.

Vendors are coming at these problems from many angles. Some companies have combined multiple features in their firewalls, including the ability to load balance and the application of multiple policies. It is easier to apply multiple policies to a packet once it is broken open rather than to repeat that process multiple times with many boxes.

However, conducting so many functions in a single box must limit either the speed or the functionality of the device. Here, scaling with multiple boxes to facilitate faster throughput is recommended.

Other vendors are putting firewall capability in routers and even in NICs, which creates a management headache. Security professionals need to create policies for firewalls in hundreds, if not thousands, of devices, which will require better centralized management capabilities.

So, because of growing security vulnerabilities in everything from applications and operating systems to content, the role of the firewall is likely to increase rather than decrease. There are no standards or even agreed-upon approaches to how the firewall will evolve. Right now, it is the IT manager's job to make sense of the mess and determine which approach works best for him or her.[2]

20.4 Recommendations

The challenge of simply understanding the basic role of the numerous firewall products available today and the claimed technology advances from the market leaders is difficult enough for security professionals, but the challenge goes well beyond that. The bigger challenge is understanding what the products really do and don't do and what they can and cannot protect against with a high degree of assurance.

For example, hybrid firewalls offer a solid architecture for multi-layered, defense–in-depth firewall security, delivering the ability to protect against known and unknown attacks. This is true not only because of the security technology they bring to bear on the problem, but also for additional and equally important reasons, which include the following: central management of multiple security functions and the ability to perform on today's high-speed networks—individually, in active/active high-availability pairs, in clusters of appliances managed as one, or in widely distributed deployments.

Hybrid firewalls supporting a superset of security filtering technologies, including next-generation application proxies, offer a natural security platform for maturing intrusion detection system (IDS) technology to find its true long-term partner. Security appliances with hybrid firewall and antivirus capabilities, in concert with IDS/Firewall Intrusion Detection Systems (FIDSs) features, would do the most complete high-performance job of protecting against both known and unknown attacks. The emphasis here is on completeness of coverage and high performance.

The major issue in IT security today is protecting networked applications, and the biggest buzzword related to that goal is *FIPS,* a strategy that focuses on dealing with known application-specific threats with inline appliances. Today's FIPS vendors are primarily developing firewall-like security appliances targeted at filtering single applications in real time like port 80 HTTP web traffic, e-mail, or possibly voice over IP. These systems, however, look at only single protocols (albeit important ones), out of many thousands of protocols traversing the Internet. Therefore, any security technology that deals with only one major protocol and then focuses its full attention on identifying and preventing anomalies and known attacks within that one protocol is obviously limited in utility. In addition, any product that claims to be a general-purpose firewall without deep application awareness and application proxy controls is also limited in attack protection. In short, both approaches are far from a mature, multiprotocol hybrid firewall.

Most FIPS companies are attempting to plug the now well-known hole in the leading commodity firewalls that do little or no application-level security work on port 80 (or really any port for that matter) when in stateful inspection mode. These timely vendors see what the hacker community has realized for some time: that the surest way to find an open pathway through today's best-known firewalls is to use port 80. Today's most damaging high-profile threats like Code Red, NIMDA, SQL slammer, MS/Blaster, and Sasser are application-specific attacks that tunnel right through leading firewalls' stateful inspection mechanisms by introducing elements of the attack in the application layer.[3]

Today, computer security is evolutionary by its very nature. It follows a well-known threat–countermeasure cycle. As new threats arise, new countermeasures are built. This phenomenon points out that react-and-patch security is not enough. Everyone in the industry has seen the billions of dollars in damage that the latest attack du jour (virus attack of the day) viruses and worms have caused against Microsoft and other well-known software systems like Sendmail and Bind. The recommended solution to these attacks (the countermeasure) is almost always to download, test, and apply a patch as fast as you possibly can. Updating your antivirus attack-signature database is also recommended. Keeping every application and operating system that you use on your network patched to the latest level, however, is not a realistic solution to staying secure in real time. Keeping your networked applications patched to the latest level is extremely labor intensive and leaves systems open to problems for too long a period to be considered an effective proactive strategy. Patching systems also means downtime because it normally requires downloading the patch, testing, installing, and then rebooting systems. Furthermore, some patches actually make things worse by introducing new bugs that disrupt previously working systems.

A transition must be made from this react-and-patch strategy to something more proactive. Currently, no single product provides the full level of defense needed to accommodate a complete defense strategy for applications focused on preventing known and unknown attacks. Therefore, the segmented market revolves around several types of security products and tools, grouped around different fundamental security problems. The product segments include, but are not limited to, the following:

- Antispam
- Antivirus
- Clientless SSL VPN (new)
- Firewall
- IPSec VPN
- Identity management
- Intrusion detection (IDS)
- Mail security for both inbound and outbound use of e-mail
- Outbound web access content filtering
- Patch management
- Signature-based firewalls (FIPS) with deep packet inspection (*new*)
- User authentication
- Web SSO and URL resource authorization[4]

Today, the separate product offerings in their respective segments reenforce the wisdom that defense–in-depth, multilayered security provides the best model approach to defending networks and applications. However, there are too many separate products and too many tasks to address the problem cohesively.

So, the question you really don't want to ask, but should, is: Do you have to purchase, learn, configure, and maintain all of that? No, but most larger organizations get pretty close to it or are actually working on doing just exactly that.

20.4.1 Purchasing, learning, configuring, and maintaining

Unfortunately, most of the preceding tool segments lack the integration to cover the entire risk profile. Managing this best-of-breed, multilayered menagerie of systems is a huge challenge! And understanding the enormity of that challenge brings clearly into focus another key threat to staying secure today: wrongly configured or inadvertently misconfigured security software. This is a major problem rooted in the following:

- Not enough people
- Not enough money
- Not enough time
- Too many systems to deal with at one time[5]

A comprehensive defense strategy, unlike an inline FIPS, focuses on prevention of both known and unknown threats by combining an IDS solution with a hybrid application firewall, application proxies, antivirus filtering, SSL termination, IPSec termination, and more under a single construct. As previously described, traditionally, security has been implemented through the deployment of several separate pieces of technology, each one addressing a different type of threat. More recently, the types of threats have escalated in type and number to such a degree that the number of security tools has also reached such an all-time high, creating confusion and an approach that is no longer practical.

The growth of e-commerce, regulatory requirements, and demand for more remote access to a network points to the fact that security can no longer be an afterthought, and it can't be an unrelated hodge-podge of software, appliances, and other devices, each with its own interface. The management and administration of a collection of security systems capable of addressing each and every one of these areas requires more and more overhead, staffing, and expertise. Very few companies have the people-power to dedicate to such a monumental task. Such a diverse collection of systems is also very inefficient and full of redundant operations.

The solution is clearly more functions in fewer appliances and tighter integration with the existing mission-distinct security products that are necessary to achieve comprehensive attack protection, especially with the many security technologies that have become necessary to deal with the rising threat. The time has come in the evolution of security technology for multifunction all-in-one security appliances. The challenges are scaling performance and high availability.

As you know, it takes a secret to keep a secret. Career security professionals who are tasked with protecting the world's most important networks rely on a set of bedrock principles that form the foundation of their approach to security. Knowing these simple principles and using them to evaluate alternative solutions can be helpful.

20.4.2 Effective firewall security: baseline design principles

As previously stated, it takes a secret to keep a secret: All computer security lives under this baseline principle. In other words, all computer security is protected by secrets: the location of a room, the IP address of a server, the software version of an application, the names of the superuser computer operators, a password, a cryptographic key, and a sequence of steps. For example, no matter how clever and sophisticated and hard to break a cryptographic algorithm may be, if you have the secret key, you have the data. That is why banks go to such extreme care to store and protect access to the master ATM keys. This is why keeping proprietary information about protected networks and applications secret is so very fundamental to good security. A related principal is security through obscurity.

So, if it takes a secret to keep a secret, then it will come as no surprise that the first computer security solution, after physically locking the world's very first computers in a room, was the use of passwords.

Today, an ID password prompt is the only truly ubiquitous computer security solution in the world. Password prompts are a supported feature in nearly every system and application on the market today.

Therefore, all access should be denied unless explicitly allowed. Firewalls in particular should be based on this principle. Firewalls should be capable of stopping everything out of the box. Many companies that have failed to remember this have been burned. A major firewall vendor, for example, shipped with SNMP services running in the default configuration for some time until a vulnerability exploiting the service became public.

Stateful inspection firewalls became wildly popular in great part because they are fast and easy; you can get just about anything through a stateful inspection firewall without waiting for application-aware filters to protect the open connection. Many people don't understand this principle. They often report that their firewall is fast and doesn't cause any problems for their users. The reason this may be true is that many unsuspecting users of stateful inspection firewalls allow all access unless explicitly denied by creating a high-level rule. Hard to believe? Industry field technicians have seen this all too often in competing firewalls when reviewing their access control list (ACL) rules. This is, of course, the very opposite of the fundamental "deny all access unless explicitly allowed" security principle.

This principle is closely associated with the "least privilege" principle. The principle of least privilege is close to deny all access. It follows directly from the "deny all" principle in the following way: Once an administrator decides to allow access to or through any security product, the next principle of good security is to give the user the least amount of privilege using that access rule as possible. The more one can restrictively control the use of a connection through a firewall, the more the exposure to malicious code or attacks of any kind is reduced.

Firewalls must be able to demonstrate in-depth application awareness and granular application control to live up to this principle. Examples of such limitations include access to the use of only a few specific commands, limitations to a specific server, specific times and days of the week, specific file types and maximum sizes, and so on. If one does not follow the principle of least privilege, the exposure of the network and associated applications is equivalent to leaving one's house open and unlocked for people to come and go as they please. This is definitely not the desired level of security that's called for.

So, does this mean that you are looking at a threat countermeasure? Well, a classic truism in the security business (whether you're building vaults for banks, fences for nuclear power plants, or software for computer systems) is that you cannot avoid the ever-escalating threat–countermeasure cycle of protection. For example, you build the world's strongest bank vault, and you are absolutely convinced that the vault is impossible to break into. It defeats every known attack. Of course, as it turns out, it is not impossible to break into. Someone eventually finds a vulnerability that your design never anticipated, and a new security threat to your bank vault design emerges. In response, you modify the design in whatever way seems prudent to eliminate the discovered vulnerability. Such responses represent what is called a *countermeasure*. This classic security cycle is termed the *threat– countermeasure cycle*.

Now, if your enemy is after you, would you prefer being able to run fast, hide well, have something with which to defend yourself, or all of the above? The answer is, of course, all of the above. This baseline principle of computer security design seems obvious when you put it in such personal terms. However, the leading firewalls for almost a decade offered only one simple defense mechanism (outside of VPNs and authentication). This single mechanism is *stateful inspection*.

However, one line of defense is not enough, which is why many security professionals who are chartered with protecting the world's most important networks believe in tiered firewall security. They put high-speed screening firewalls (Check Point, NetScreen, or others) at the Internet boundary and then back them up with high-assurance application firewalls.

Finally, a heat up is expected for the high-speed screening firewall market. The future is now. Let's take a look.

20.4.3 Final recommendation: purchase a high-speed firewall

Thanks to more corporate deployments in both primary and branch offices, 2004 was a big year for firewalls, but a new report by industry analysts suggests the market for basic firewalls is about to heat up even further.

According to industry analysts, firewall shipments grew by 34% in 2004 to a total of 795,000 units. However, as more businesses deploy multifunction security appliances, the market will speed up considerably.

Network security, a growing concern for businesses since 2002, is changing. A business must not only secure its perimeter, but it should also prepare for infected devices connecting directly to the LAN.

In many cases, mobile workers may pick up viruses outside the company's network and then bring their infected PCs back into the office and connect to the LAN, infecting the network. Businesses need to protect themselves not only from threats from the outside, but also from threats on the inside.

Finally, industry analysts project that the firewall market will grow to 2.9 million units in 2009. That figure has increased from previous projections, in part because vendors are not folding as much security into other network devices like routers and switches as was once forecasted. For now, businesses will continue to buy all their firewalls as separate pieces of equipment. They will not necessarily be part of a router or a switch, as was previously predicted.

Thus, the market for standalone firewalls will continue for the foreseeable future. Enterprises will always want a certain number of firewalls that they can manage independently of other devices.

As security features are rolled into more networking gear, it may be hard for businesses to know exactly how much they are spending on security. But one thing is certain: Firewall prices will continue to drop. Our final recommendation is to buy one now!

20.5 References

1. "How to Develop a Network Security Policy: An Overview of Internetworking Site Security," Sun Microsystems, Santa Clara, California, 2004.

2. Jack McCullough, "Beyond the Firewall Using a Layered Security Strategy to Address Internal Security Threats," SurfControl, Scotts Valley, California, 2003.

3. Eric Hall, "Internet Firewall Essentials, Network Design Manual," CMP Media, London, 2004.

4. George Bieber, "Information Assurance, Training and Awareness, and Products and Resources," National Institute

of Standards and Technology, U.S. Department of Commerce, Gaithersburg, Maryland, January, 2004.

5.   John Wack, Ken Cutler, and Jamie Pole, "Guidelines on Firewalls and Firewall Policy: Recommendations of the National Institute of Standards and Technology," National Institute of Standards and Technology, U.S. Department of Commerce, Gaithersburg, Maryland, January, 2002.

Section IX

Appendixes

Contributors of Firewall Software

Advanced Technology & Free—Sygate Personal Firewall (http:// soho.sygate.com): Advanced user-friendly software that protects your personal computer from malicious hackers and other intruders.

Advanced Virus Firewall (http://www.virusmd.com): Uses a Trojan firewall.

Agnitum Ltd. (http://www.agnitum.com): Tauscan is a Trojan horse detection and removal program. Simple to install and use, it detects more Trojan horse programs than any other application of its kind and safely removes them from your system's registry. Tauscan is updated weekly and is compatible with all security/antivirus software. A 30-day trial is available.

Anti Spy Software (http://www.spy-software-solutions.com): Anti Spy software will scan your system for spyware, Trojans, and viruses, allowing you to delete them in seconds. Also provides a firewall and port scanner for ultimate protection.

Anti Spyware SpySweeper Download at SafestWare (http://www. safestware.com): Anti Spyware, key logger, and spy software removal; hackers prevention; and Trojan remover tools. SafestWare protects you and your business from the new digital pests, thiefware, spyware, adware, Trojans, hacker tools, and many other malicious software.

Armor2net Personal Firewall (http://www.amor2net.com): Personal firewall software that stops hackers and data thieves and protects your PC from Internet-borne threats. Only one Armor2net can meet your requirements in multiple fields of Internet security and Internet privacy, such as intrusion detection, monitoring net state, granting and denying access on a per-application basis, blocking the dangerous sites, and net lock. Stops pop-up ads. Removes spywares.

Astaro (http://www.astaro.com): Fully integrated software appliance including firewall, VPN, virus protection, content filtering, QoS, load balancing, and high availability. Delivered on a single CD with hardened Linux operating system.

AuditBox (http://www.auditbox.net): Tools, tips, and information for security audit of firewalls, LANs, networks, and small systems.

Basilisk-Secureworx (http://www.secureworx.com): Low-cost firewall appliance, simple to install and maintain, and perfect for the SME environment.

BizGuardian VPN/Firewall (http://www.bizguardian.co.uk): Protects you and your network from destructive intruders, while allowing you to browse the Internet safely.

BullGuard (http://www.bullguard.com): Protects your PC from hackers and viruses. With full antivirus, firewall, and backup protection, BullGuard secures your PC from the menaces of the web. BullGuard features full e-mail protection, no matter what e-mail client you use. The antivirus database is maintained and updated around the clock. Powerful scan engines ensure detection and removal of all the newest viruses. Also, all peer-to-peer applications such as Kazaa and ICQ.

Ciseware Professional Firewall (http://www.ciseware.com): A rapid rule-based chaining firewall for securing both individual machines and network-perimeters.

Computer Monitoring Software (http://www.computer-monitoring. com): Offers computer and Internet monitoring software for secretly recording all PC activities.

CryptoHeaven (http://www.cryptoheaven.com): Secure e-mail, secure online file storage and sharing, secure instant messaging.

CryptoTunnel VPN2GO (http://www.cryptotunnel.com): The first product in the CryptoTunnel family being launched and uses the latest encryption technology available.

DriveCrypt: 1344 Bit Military Strength hard disk encryption (http://www.securstar.com): A cryptographic program, bringing 1,344-bit military strength encryption to your computer and protecting your data transparently.

ElectricHighway Security Solutions (http://security.electrichighway. co.uk): Provides security solutions to protect your data.

Employee Monitoring Solutions (http://www.employee-monitoring. com): Offers network monitoring software for secretly recording e-mails, chats, web sites, keystrokes, applications, and much more for each PC in your network. Remotely monitoring and control each PC from one centralized location.

EnterNet FireWall (http://www.enternet.net): A Swedish-made firewall.

Firewall Builder (http://www.fwbuilder.org): A multiplatform object-oriented firewall configuration and management tool. It consists of a graphical user interface (GUI) and set of policy compilers for IP tables, IP filter, pf, and Cisco PIX.

Firewall Servers (http://www.firewal-servers.co): Manufacturer of software and appliances for network security, Internet firewalls, content filtering, and VPNs.

Firewall security and Internet sharing software (SolidShare) (http://www.solidshare.net): SolidShare provides firewall security and Internet connection sharing/proxy server/modem sharing on your LAN. SolidShare supports most applications and protocols like DNS, HTTP/HTTPS, Telnet, SMTP, POP3, NNTP, ping, traceroute, MSN Game Zone, Battle.net, Westwood online, FTP, RealPlayer, QuickTime, ICQ, Napster, and IRC. SolidShare also performs dial on demand and automatically hangs up when the idle time reaches the maximum value.

Firewall.Net—Guide to personal firewalls (http://www.firewall-net.com): Guide to install and configure your own personal firewall.

GFI LANguard Network Security Scanner (http://www.gfi.com): LANguard Network Security Scanner (LNSS) is a freeware tool to audit network security and proactively secure it. LNSS scans entire networks from a hacker's perspective and analyzes machines for open ports, shares, security alerts/vulnerabilities, service pack level, installed hotfixes and other NETBIOS information such as hostname, logged on username, users, etc. It does OS detection and password strength testing and detects registry issues.

High security remote access Internet (http://www.ncp.de): High-security remote access through the Internet (VPN and PKI).

Home PC Firewall Guide (http://www.firewallguide.com): Learn how to protect home and small-office computers and networks from hackers by using personal firewall, antivirus, antiTrojan, and privacy software plus low-cost hardware routers with firewall features.

ID-Synch User Provisioning Software (http://idsynch.com): Creates, updates, and deletes login IDs based on input from an authorization workflow engine, central user administration console, or rules-based provisioning system.

IF-2002 (http://www.internetfilter.com): Uses filtering technology. The filtering products IF-NOT and IF-ONLY work with client, proxy server, and ISP server for Windows 2000, NT, and XP, and all Linux systems, as well as NetBSD and Mac OS-X.

ISS—Internet Security Scanner (http://www.iss.net): ISS allows you to audit the security on your network.

InJoy Dial-up Networking Firewall (http://www.fx.dk/injoy): Adds unprecedented flexibility, intelligent automation, and intuitive control to traditional modem- and ISDN-based dial-up networking. In addition to a wealth of mission-critical connectivity options, the InJoy Dialer provides modern Internet collaboration features, such as next-generation firewall security, seamless IPSec VPN integration, superior Internet gateway capability, intuitive management, and complete access control.

InJoy Firewall (http://www.fx.dk/injoy): Provides unique multiplatform next-generation technology for enterprise servers, including powerful seamless IPSec VPN integration. The intrusion prevention solution combines static signatures with behavioral rules technology, providing the safest possible, most cost-effective, and complete security solution for customers in any industry.

Internet Reporting tool for firewalls (http://www.softex.net): Soft-ex manufactures communications management software. It has a product for analyzing the log files produced by most firewalls, ISA server, Checkpoint, Cyberguard, etc.

Internet sharing and firewall—SolidShare (http://www.solidshare.net): SolidShare provides firewall security and Internet sharing on your LAN, allowing you to connect anyone on the network to the Internet with only one ISP account and one modem. After installing SolidShare, anyone on the local network will be able to transparently and securely access the Internet. The built-in firewall can prevent resource exposure and defend from an attack.

LANguard Security Event Log Monitor (http://www.gfi.com): This is an update to a current listing LANguard S.E.L.M. Performs intrusion detection by network-wide monitoring of the security event logs of all Windows NT/2000 servers and workstations. Its extensive reporting features identify machines being targeted and local users trying to hack internally.

LANguard patrolling firewall (http://www.gfi.com): Guards against Internet and network misuse. Monitors and protects against external threats (hackers), internal threats (unauthorized access), and unproductive use of the Internet.

Look 'n' Stop personal firewall (http://www.looknstop.com): Provides permanent and highly secured protection against Internet hacker attacks.

Mail Essentials (Free 5-User version) (http://www.gfi.com): E-mail server security software. Server-based PGP encryption solution that allows users to send and receive automatically encoded/decoded messages—encompasses various important security and management features.

Mail Security for Exchange/SMTP (http://www.gfi.com): Provides e-mail content checking, exploit detection, and antivirus for Exchange/SMTP. Can be deployed at the gateway level or at the information store level (based on the Exchange 2000 VS API). Key features include multiple virus engines (don't depend on one only), e-mail content and attachment checking (quarantine dangerous e-mails), exploit shield (e-mail intrusion detection and defense), and e-mail threats engine (analyzes and defuses HTML scripts, .exe files, and more).

Mail essentials for Exchange/SMTP (http://www.gfi.com): Protects your users from current and future e-mail attacks and viruses! Mail essentials for Exchange/SMTP is an e-mail content checking and antivirus gateway that removes all types of e-mail–borne threats before they can affect your e-mail users. Viruses, spam, dangerous attachments, and content (such as Word macros, HTML scripts) can be removed/reviewed before they reach your mail server. Successfully prevented viruses such as the "Love Letter" and AnnaKournikova.jog.vbs from infecting users!

pcInternet Patrol (http://www.pcinternetpatrol.com): A new type of security software designed to solidify personal firewalls and antivirus by introducing real-time positive identification for applications and their components.

ProjectSCIM encrypted messaging (http://www.projectscim.com): Extremely secure encrypted messaging that allows client-server or peer-to-peer communications.

B

Worldwide Survey of Firewall Products

There are lots of firewalls on the market, and choosing the right one for a customer is much harder than most people think, because it's a balancing act between requirements, convenience, and cost. Usually the latter is the overwhelming concern for companies, even at the expense of the other two considerations. So, to give you an idea of the firewall products on the market and their strengths and weaknesses, here's a rundown of those products. Keep in mind this is not a rigorous survey!

Probably the most popular firewall among UNIX users is Check Point Software's Firewall-1, a version of which is distributed by SunSoft for its workstations and servers. Firewall-1 uses a different approach to firewalls developed by Check Point (http://www.checkpoint.com) that provides a very high level of protection for machines inside the network. All packets entering the firewall are inspected and screened. The system can learn about new protocols and application packets once installed, which makes Firewall-1 flexible for the future. As a full-featured firewall, Firewall-1 is a superb product with almost no impact on the host server. Because the firewall software is part of the operating system kernel, it is nearly impossible to hack, and the system is fast. Administration requires practice, and the software is not cheap, but Firewall-1 has got to be the dominant firewall because of its strengths, not a savvy marketing campaign.

CyberGuard's CyberGuard (http://www.cyberguard.com) remains a favorite because of its ease of installation, light load on a UNIX or a Windows NT server, and maintenance simplicity. Because CyberGuard can be loaded from a CD-ROM onto any supported machine, it is simple to add to existing networks without requiring more hardware or hardware upgrades. CyberGuard is priced competitively and although other firewalls equal it in many aspects (such as Firewall-1), there is no reason to switch yet.

For Windows NT users, a leading firewall product is NetGuard's Guardian (http://www.ntguard.com). Guardian is recommended by Microsoft as a firewall for NT systems. One of the strengths of Guardian is the ease with which it can be installed and configured. Routine maintenance is trivial, too, leading to a low profile on the network and less work for the administrator. Although Guardian is a fairly straightforward firewall product, the management aspect is what sells most people. Reports and real-time status windows are attractive, customizable, and useful.

Milkyway's SecurIT is for those who want a traditional UNIX firewall. SecurIT is based on a rebuilt and security-oriented UNIX kernel from BSD. SecurIT has been tested by the Communications Security Establishment and was found secure. Milkyway is an Ottawa-based company (http://www.milkyway.com) whose approach to a firewall is that not only must the firewall protect the network, but it must also protect itself, so SecurIT is very difficult to hack.

CYCON's Labyrinth (http://www.cycon.com) is an interesting firewall product because it provides bi-directional network address translation with a connection tracking method that offers both firewall and network management capabilities. The true strengths of Labyrinth are difficult to appreciate if you are not a UNIX guru or heavily into network management, so suffice it to say this is an impressive product. There's a demo version available for free from the web site, along with lots of descriptions of the product. As with the other firewalls mentioned, Labyrinth isn't cheap, but it offers lots of protection for the money.

Raptor System's Eagle suite of firewall software (http:/www.raptor.com) is an application-level firewall. A complete family of products, the Eagle products, allows you to choose which components of a firewall are to be installed and used and can be expanded to handle remote and mobile computing easily. The Eagle Firewall is the main product in the family, providing traditional firewall capabilities. Add-ons provide other features, such as remote site and workgroup security.

Advanced Network and Services, Inc. (ANS), offers InterLock, a firewall produced by a not-for-profit consortium of U.S. universities and industry partners like IBM, MCI, and Nortel Networks. ANS was purchased by AOL in 1995 and now protects AOL's huge membership network. Although designed for customization to meet each network's requirements, InterLock is available as a standalone solution. More information is available from its web site (http://www.ans.net).

Want simplicity? How about Global Technology's GNAT Box. The software can even be shipped on a floppy, to show how small and trim it is. GNAT Box (http://www.gnatbox.com) is designed to be a simple, fast, unobtrusive firewall that eliminates lots of the features of other firewalls that users don't necessarily need (like the ability to Telnet into the firewall or use it as a mail server). Surprisingly, GNAT Box is effective, inexpensive, easy to work with, and worth looking into.

There are a lot more firewall products on the market (many dozen more, in fact), but these are the ones that have stood out for their features and abilities. Before choosing a firewall for a customer or making a recommendation, scan some of the online network management magazines for reviews and product announcements. They tend to be up-to-date and offer the latest in network security testing. Every network that is attached to the Internet should have a firewall, regardless of its size. The size, cost, and manageability of that firewall are the choices you and your customers need to make.

Firewall Companies

1. ASL Security Ltd. (http://asl-security.com)

2. Actane Controller (http://www.actane.com)

3. Alloyant Technologies (http://www.alloyant.com)

4. Anti Spy (http://www.computer-monitoring.com)

5. Ashley Laurent (http://www.ashleylaurent.com)

6. Atipa Corporation (http://www.atipa.com)

7. BizGuardian VPN Firewall (http://www.bizguardian.com)

8. Border Manager (http://www.novell.com)

9. Borderware Technologies (http://www.borderware.com)

10. CONNECT:Firewall (http://www.sterlingcommerce.com)

11. CSM Proxy Plus (http://www.csm-usa.com)

12. Cequrux Technologies (http://www.cequrux.com)

13. Clavister firewall (http://www.clavister.com)

14. ComSocks (http://www.linkbyte.com)

15. Compresoft (http://www.compresoft.com)

16. Conclave (http://www.interdyn.com)

17. Coolfire (http://www.symbolic.com)

18. Cyberguard (http://www.cyberguardcorp.com)

19. DigitalSentinel Network Appliance (http://www.digital-sentinel.com)

20. EGG NSA (http://www.eggfirewall.com)

21. EMS-global Managed Security Solution (http://www.ems-global.com)

22. Eland Systems (http://www.elandsys.com)

23. Enterworks (http://www.enterworks.com)

24. ExFilter (http://www.exnet.com)

25. FINSYSTEM (http://www.finsystem.net)

26. FirePlug Edge Project Home Page (http://www.belcarra.com)

27. FireWall and VPN Solutions for the Enterprise (http://www.firewallz.com)

28. Firewall & VPN Product (http://netsentron.com)

29. Firewall-1 (http://www.checkpoint.com)

30. Freegate (http://www.seeq.com)

31. Gauntlet (http://www.tis.com)

32. Global Information Security, Inc. (http://www.infotecs.biz)

33. Greencomputer.com (http://www.greencomputer.com)

34. HotBrick Security Solutions (http://www.hotbrick.com)

35. IBM Firewall for AIX (http://www.ibm.com)

36. InJoy Firewall (http://www.fx.dk)

37. Industrial Defender: Security for Mission-Critical Control Systems (http://www.verano.com)

38. Ingate Firewall (http://www.ingate.com)

39. Ingate Systems AB (http://www.ingate.com)

40. InnerTek Software (http://www.innertek.com)

41. Interspace Computers (http://www.interspacecomputers.com)

42. Intranode - ActiveSentry (http://www.intranode.com)

43. KarlBridge/KarlRouter (http://www.karlnet.com)

44. LiveFire Labs (http://www.livefirelabs.com)

45. Lucent Managed Firewall (http://www.lucent.com)

46. Merilus Technologies, Inc. (http://www.merilus.com)

47. NATuralWall (http://www.naturalip.com)

48.   NEGOTIATOR by Futures Inc. (http://www.futures-inc.com)

49.   Net SecurityMaster (http://www.solsoft.com)

50.   NetScreen 100 (http://www.juniper.net)

51.   NetWolves Technologies, Inc. (http://www.netwolves.com)

Commercial Products or Consultants Who Sell or Service Firewalls

1. A Complete Solution (http://www.omniroute.com): Network engineering, Internet design and services, Internet security, web design.

2. ActivSupport Networking, Security, Development, San Francisco (http://www.activsupport.com): ActivSupport is a consulting firm that delivers end-to-end information technology solutions to growing businesses. Powered by ActivSupport, companies and organizations are able to leverage the use of technology to realize their goals. Its professional network services include design, implementation, support, and security.

3. AdvancedNet Communications, Inc. FIREWALL MASONS (http://www.advnetcom.net): Carlsbad, California–based firewall experts. "Expert SnapGear installers." Firewall test links are at http://www.advnetcom.net/fts.htm.

4. BEL Network Integration & Support, LLC. (http://www.belnis. com): BEL Network Integration & Support provides network and information security consulting services to protect your local and wide network configurations. It also provides data and information protection assessments and solutions. These services include vulnerability assessments, penetration tests, security architecture, and firewall security technology integration.

5. CREDO NET (http://www.credo.net): Raptor and Security Consulting, 22941 Triton Way, Suite 241, Laguna Hills, CA; 888-88-CREDO.

6. Cadre Computer Associates (http://www.ccr.com): Firewall-1, Secured ISP, Internet development. 3000 Chemed Center, 255 East Fifth Street, Cincinnati, OH 45202-4726; 513-762-7350.

7. Cambridge Network Security (http://www.camnetsec.com): Cambridge Network Security is a network security consulting firm with primary operations in Boston, Massachusetts, and Berlin, Germany. It helps its clients mitigate the risk of an information security breach through continual risk assessment and the application of appropriate software, hardware, and policy solutions. Its services are aimed at protecting the confidentiality, integrity, and availability of the clients' information assets.

8. CerbTech (http://www.cerberustechnologies.net): CerbTech delivers enterprisewide application security applications in timely manner with understanding of company security policies and product security requirements.

9. Cole Design and Development (http://www.coledd.com): Linux servers, network security.

10. Computer PS (http://www.computerps.com): Specializes in Internet security firewall systems for business and organizations.

11. Conjungi (http://www.conjungi.com): Gauntlet, Seattle, Washington.

12. Counterpane Systems (http://www.counterpane.com).

13. Data network security consulting firm, Houston, Texas (http://www.netunlim.com): Firewall-Solutions provides consulting on security of B2B, B2C, other e-commerce and general network firewall operations, upgrades, and installations. It is focusing on the Houston business area but works nationwide.

14. Testmasters, Inc. (http://www.testmastersinc.com): Provides a wide spectrum of information security services, including Security Test and Evaluation, Vulnerability Assessments, and Information Security Workshops.

15. EMJ America (http://www.wdlsystems.com): AFS 2000, BorderWare and others. 1434 Farrington Road, Apex, NC 27502; 800-548-2319.

16. Enterprise System Solutions (http://www.essi.com): Borderware.

17. Epi Security Industries (Episec, Inc.): Unix system and network security (http://www.episec.com): Internal and external host security, network auditing, firewall design and implementation, security education, ongoing support contracts, and a whopping guarantee to boot. Internet security for the paranoid.

18. Ernst & Young (http://www.ey.com).

19. FishNet Consulting Services (http://www.kcfishnet.com): Firewall-1 and Security consulting, 7007 College Blvd., Suite 450, Overland Park, KS 66211-2424; 913-498-0711

20. Garrison Technologies (http://www.garrison.com): Security consulting, firewalls, audits, etc. 100 Congress Ave., Suite 2100, Austin, TX 78701; 512-302-0882.

21. IBM Business Recovery Services (http://www.ibm.com).

22. Information security and networking portal (http://www.networksgroup.com): Comprehensive cross-referenced site relating to information security and networking solutions from NetWorks Group and leading manufacturers.

23. Infotech Canada, Inc. (http://www.infotechcanada.com): NT security/firewall implementation and testing.

24. Intelligix, Inc. (http://www.intelligix.com): Expert firewall and other security consulting services. Cisco PIX, NetScreen, Raptor/Velociraptor, SonicWall, Checkpoint, and ISA server. Design, architecture, implementation, C&A, penetration testing, auditing, risk management, policies, and guidance.

25. Internet Security Blanket Corporation (http://www.isblanket.com): Internet Security Blanket Corporation was founded in 2001 and is a provider of security solutions, including assessments, vendor implementations (IDS, firewalls, VPNs, SSL-based VPNs), and managed services. Its customers range from small companies with fewer than 50 people to enterprise Fortune 500 customers with 100,000+ employees and clients in the financial, insurance, government, manufacturing, and education sectors.

26. KVA Communications, Ltd. (http://www.kva.com): KVA Communications has a proven track record of securing corporate and government networks using state-of-the-art security tools.

27. LURHQ Corporation (http://www.lurhq.com): Security consulting, firewalls, web server security. P.O. Box 2861, Conway, SC 29526; 843-347-1075.

28. Mergent International (http://www.mergent.com): Gauntlet Security consulting.

29. Midwest Data Recovery, Inc. (http://www.midwestdatarecovery. com): Free evaluations. No data/no charge policy. Provides data recovery for hard drives, tapes, RAID systems, digital camera disks, and all magnetic and optical media except VHS.

30. Naked Ape Consulting (http://nakedape.cc): Naked Ape Consulting provides network, server, security, and software design and support services to businesses in the Portland, Oregon, area or onsite anywhere in the world.

31. NetComm2000 (http://www.netcomm2000.net): Design, implement, and maintain network technology. It handles all aspects of network technology, from introduction and design to back-end security. Certified MCSE, CNE, CCNA.

32. Netrex (http://www.netrex.com): Secure Internet Solutions Firewall-1. 3000 Town Center, Suite 1100, Southfield, MI 48075; 800-3-NETREX.

33. Netsphere, Inc. (http://www.netsphereinc.com): Linux IPCHAINS IPTABLES, Cisco PIX, installs.

34. Network & Security Consultant (http://mohanmk.tripod. com): BS7799 Lead Auditor, Checkpoint, Watchguard, Citrix, Cisco, Novell, Nortel Networks, and Microsoft-Certified IT Network Security Consultant.

35. Network Associates (http://us.mcafee.com): Gauntlet and many security products. 3965 Freedom Circle, Santa Clara, CA 95054; 408-988-3832.

36. Network Presence, LLC (http://www.networkpresence.com): Professional services firm specializing in designing and securing enterprise computer networks.

37. Network Security (http://www.nsec.net): Firewall-1, NetScreen, and others. 369 River Road, North Tonawanda, NY 14120; 716-692-8183.

38. Network Thinking Solutions (http://www.networkthinking. com): Raptor/Velociraptor Setup and Maintenance. SonicWall setup and maintenance.

39.   Omniroute (http://www.omniroute.com): Network engineering, Internet design and services, Internet security, web design.

40.   Orbis Internet (http://www.pixiuscorp.com): Sidewinder and Security consulting. 475 Cleveland Avenue North, Suite 222, St. Paul, MN 55104; 612-603-9030.

E

Establishing Your Organization's Security

With worldwide connections, someone can get into your system in the middle of the night when your building is locked up. The Internet allows the electronic equivalent of an intruder who looks for open windows and doors. Now, a person can check for hundreds of vulnerabilities in just a few hours.

Most network-based computer security crimes go unreported, yet the statistics are alarming: According to industry analysts, most breeches of Internet and data security are kept quiet. The most amazing stories are never printed, so you never hear about them from anyone.

Companies are experiencing different types of losses. Examples include service interruption, whereby attackers effectively shut down the network gateway to the outside world or someone wantonly removes a central password file; theft of online corporate assets or interception of sensitive e-mail or data as they are transmitted; and fraudulent misrepresentation of either data or someone as a user. Many companies unknowingly increase the vulnerability to their computer network, all in the name of improving productivity:

- By adding a remote access e-mail gateway so employees can access e-mail while away from the office, companies may unwittingly provide a "side door" into their computer network, especially if strong authentication measures are not implemented.

- By adding a World Wide Web site and FTP server so their customers can instantly retrieve product information and software fixes from anywhere in the world at any time of the day or night, companies may be unaware that they are providing an "electronic tunnel" to other nonpublic corporate data.

- By embracing Electronic Data Interchange (EDI) as a state-of-the-art vendor order and payment system, a company could be allowing criminals access to both inventory and checkbook.

Yet too much security can be as counterproductive as too little security. As companies come to rely on internetworking to lower the costs of doing business—e-mail for communications, web sites for information publishing, FTP for software update distribution, and EDI for supplier–vendor transactions—the productivity gains become too compelling to ignore.

A firewall security policy is required to establish an enterprise-wide program of how both internal and external users interact with a company's computer network, how the corporate computer architecture topology will be implemented, and where computer assets will be located. The policy weighs possible threats against the value of personal productivity and corporate assets that need different levels of protection.

E.I   Firewalls

As previously discussed in the book, a firewall is the point at which your private company network and a public network, such as the Internet, connect. A firewall system is a hardware/software configuration that sits at this perimeter, controlling access into and out of your company's network. Although in theory firewalls allow only authorized communications between the internal and external networks, new ways are constantly being developed to compromise these systems. However, properly implemented, they are very effective at keeping out unauthorized users and stopping unwanted activities on an internal network. Firewall systems protect and facilitate your network at a number of levels:

- They allow e-mail and other applications, such as FTP and remote login as desired, to take place while otherwise limiting access to the internal network.

- They provide an authorization mechanism that provides a level of assurance that only specified users or applications can gain access through the firewall.

- They typically provide a logging and alerting feature, which tracks designated usage and signals at specified events.

- They offer address translation, which masks the actual name and address of any machine communicating through the firewall. For example, all messages for anyone in the technical support department would have their address translated to techsupp@company.com, effectively hiding the name of an actual user and network address.

- They are adding new functionality, such as encryption and virtual private networking capabilities. Encryption is the coding, or scrambling, of data and keeps unintended users from reading the information. Virtual private networks employ encryption to provide secure transmissions over public networks such as the Internet.

Firewall systems can also be deployed within an enterprise network to compartmentalize different servers and networks, in effect controlling access within the network. For example, an enterprise may want to separate the accounting and payroll server from the rest of the network and allow only certain individuals to access the information.

Finally, you should consider that all firewall systems have some performance degradation. As a system is busy checking or rerouting data communications packets, the packets do not flow through the system as efficiently as they would if the system were not in place.

F

Network Interconnections: A Major Point of Vulnerability

Conducting a thorough firewall network security audit has never been more critical. Almost every organization is connected to the Internet in some way, the number of network interconnections between organizations is growing, and the ranks of telecommuters are increasing. Of course, for an audit to be effective, you need to know where and how to look for the major point of vulnerability.

Before starting a firewall network security audit, you should create a project plan that describes what you are preparing to do and the purpose of each step. A full audit should be comprehensive and include the following items:

- Desktop software vulnerabilities and policies
- External and internal firewall network vulnerabilities (including partner relationships)
- Host vulnerabilities (Windows, UNIX, Mac, etc.)
- Internal firewall network vulnerabilities
- Organizational procedures
- Password procedures
- Remote user procedures

As you can see from the preceding list, much more than technology needs to be addressed to complete a successful firewall network security audit. A good audit will involve management and will evaluate the policies (or lack thereof) that an organization has in place regarding installed software, passwords, and so on. A formal firewall network security audit consists of four phases:

- Assessment—During this phase, information is gathered and problems are identified and analyzed.

- Critical fixes—Problems that are extremely serious or that require only simple quick fixes are addressed during this phase.

- Update other fixes—During this phase, fixes with low to intermediate priority are addressed.

- Continuing work—This phase never ends. The information from the prior three phases is used to continually maintain the environment and keep it secure. Of course, this process should be undertaken on a regular basis to keep things secure.

Perhaps the most humbling aspect of assessing your systems is seeing just how vulnerable your interconnection environment is. Who knew that your predecessor had secreted holes in the firewall so he could remotely control the servers with Virtual Network Computing without having to go through the hassle of logging in to the virtual private network? That's the kind of thing you are likely to find.

In addition, as organizations grow, so do their networks and services. But the way that everything interacts is not always carefully investigated. I'm sure that every reader can sympathize with the administrator who gets handed a task when his or her plate is already overflowing and completes it as quickly as possible with every good intention of going back and fixing potential holes after the fact.

If you are setting up the assessment for your organization and you played a role in developing its infrastructure, do your best to remove yourself from the situation. It will be hard to honestly assess the interconnection environment if you have to defend decisions you made in the past. If you do find yourself heading up the assessment efforts, you can take some basic steps to begin to investigate.

Talk to your IT department peers and create detailed, accurate firewall network diagrams. This type of information gathering serves two purposes. First, it helps you to quickly identify where there may be major weaknesses in a firewall network. Second, it gives you infrastructure documentation. By carefully diagramming the firewall network as it exists (not from your memory), you may discover, for example, that there is a firewall network interconnection from the switch in front of your firewall to a switch behind it.

A number of other areas should be addressed during this phase of your firewall network security audit. For one thing, you need to determine exactly what is open to the outside world. Don't just rely on the firewall; test it for vulnerabilities.

G

Deterring Masqueraders and Ensuring Authenticity

Access control technologies ensure that only authorized users or systems can access and use computers, networks, and the information stored on these systems, and these technologies help protect sensitive data and systems. Access control simplifies network security by reducing the number of paths that attackers or masqueraders might use to penetrate system or network defenses. Access control includes three control types: boundary protection, authentication, and authorization.

Boundary protection technologies demark a logical or physical boundary between protected information and systems and unknown users. Boundary protection technologies can be used to protect a network (e.g., firewalls) or a single computer (e.g., personal firewalls). Generally, these technologies prevent access to the network or computer by external unauthorized users. Another type of boundary protection technology, content management, can also be used to restrict the ability of authorized system or network users to access systems or networks beyond the system or network boundary.

Authentication technologies associate a user with a particular identity. People are authenticated by three basic means: by something they know, something they have, or something they are. People and systems regularly use these means to identify people in everyday life. For example, members of a community routinely recognize one another by how they look or how their voices sound—by something they are. Automated teller machines recognize customers because they present a bank card—something they have—and they enter a personal identification number (PIN)—something they know. Using a key to enter a locked building is another example of using something you have. More-secure systems may combine two or more of these approaches.

Although the use of passwords is an example of authentication based on something users know, several technologies are based on something users have. Security tokens can be used to authenticate a user. User information can be coded onto a token using magnetic media (e.g., bank cards) or optical media (e.g., compact disk–like media). Several smart token technologies are also available that contain an integrated circuit chip that can store and process data. Biometric technologies automate the identification of people using one or more of their distinct physical or behavioral characteristics—authentication based on something that users are. The use of security tokens or biometrics requires the installation of the appropriate readers at network and computer access points.

Once a user is authenticated, authorization technologies are used to allow or prevent actions by that user according to predefined rules. Users can be granted access to data on the system or to perform certain actions on the system. Authorization technologies support the principles of legitimate use, least privilege, and separation of duties. Access control could be based on user identity, role, group membership, or other information known to the system.

Most operating systems (OSs) and some applications provide some authentication and authorization functionality. For example, user identification (ID) codes and passwords are the most commonly used authentication technology. System administrators can assign users rights and privileges to applications and data files based on user IDs. Some OSs let you group users to simplify the administration of groups of users who require the same levels of access to files and applications.

G.I   Boundary protection: firewalls

As explained throughout the book, firewalls are network devices or systems running special software that controls the flow of network traffic between networks or between a host and a network. A firewall is set up as the single point through which communications must pass. This enables the firewall to act as a protective barrier between the protected network and any external networks. Any information leaving the internal network can be forced to pass through a firewall as it leaves the network or host. Incoming data can enter only through the firewall.

Firewalls are typically deployed where a corporate network connects to the Internet. However, firewalls can also be used internally, to guard areas of an organization against unauthorized internal access. For example, many corporate networks use firewalls to restrict access to internal networks that perform sensitive functions, such as accounting or personnel.

Personal computers can also have firewalls, called *personal firewalls*, to protect them from unauthorized access over a network. Such personal firewalls are relatively inexpensive software programs that can be installed on personal computers to filter all network traffic and allow only authorized communications. Essentially, a firewall can be likened to a protective fence that keeps unwanted external data out and sensitive internal data in.

Typically, a firewall is a network device or host with two or more network interfaces: one connected to the protected internal network and the other connected to unprotected networks, such as the Internet. The firewall runs software that examines the network packets arriving at its network interfaces and takes appropriate action based on a set of rules. The idea is to define these rules so they allow only authorized network traffic to flow between the two interfaces. Configuring the firewall involves setting up the rules properly. One configuration strategy is to reject all network traffic and then enable only a limited set of network packets to go through the firewall. The authorized network traffic would include the connections necessary to perform functions like visiting web sites and receiving electronic mail.

There are eight kinds of firewalls: packet filter firewalls, stateful inspection firewalls, application proxy gateway firewalls, dedicated proxy firewalls, hybrid firewall technologies, network address translation, host-based firewalls, and personal firewalls/personal firewall appliances. Packet filter firewalls are routing devices that include access control functionality for system addresses and communication sessions. The access control functionality of a packet filter firewall is governed by a set of rules that allows or blocks network packets based on a number of their characteristics, including the source and destination addresses, the network protocol, and the source and destination port numbers. Packet filter firewalls are usually placed at the outermost boundary with an untrusted network, and they form the first line of defense. An example of a packet filter firewall is a network router that employs filter rules to screen network traffic.

Stateful inspection firewalls keep track of network connections that are used by network applications to reliably transfer data. When an application uses a network connection to create a session with a remote host system, a port is also opened on the originating system. This port receives network traffic from the destination system. For successful connections, packet filter firewalls must permit inbound packets from the destination system. Opening many ports to incoming traffic creates a risk of intrusion by unauthorized users who may employ various techniques to abuse the expected conventions of network protocols such as Transmission Control Protocol (TCP). Stateful inspection firewalls solve this problem by creating a directory of outbound network connections, along with each session's corresponding client port. This "state table" is then used to validate any inbound traffic. The stateful inspection solution is more secure than a packet filter because it tracks client ports individually rather than opening all inbound ports for external access.

Application proxy gateway firewalls provide additional protection by inserting the firewall as an intermediary between internal applications that attempt to communicate with external servers such as a web server. For example, a web proxy receives requests for external web pages from inside the firewall and relays them to the exterior web server as though the firewall were the requesting web client. The external web server responds to the firewall and the firewall forwards the response to the inside client as though the firewall were the web server. No direct network connection is ever made from the inside client host to the external web server.

Dedicated proxy servers are typically deployed behind traditional firewall platforms. In typical use, a main firewall might accept inbound network traffic, determine which application is being targeted, and then hand off the traffic to the appropriate proxy server (e.g., an e-mail proxy server). The proxy server typically would perform filtering or logging operations on the traffic and then forward it to internal systems. A proxy server could also accept outbound traffic directly from internal systems, filter or log the traffic, and then pass it to the firewall for outbound delivery. Many organizations enable the caching of frequently used web pages on the proxy server, thereby reducing firewall traffic. In addition to possessing authentication and logging functionality, dedicated proxy servers are useful for web and electronic mail content scanning.

Hybrid firewall technologies are firewall products that incorporate functionality from several types of firewall platforms. For example, many vendors of packet filter firewalls or stateful inspection packet filter firewalls have implemented basic application proxy functionality to offset some of the weaknesses associated with their firewall platforms. In most cases, these vendors implement application proxies to provide improved logging of network traffic and stronger user authentication. Nearly all major firewall vendors have introduced multiple firewall functions into their products in some manner; therefore, it is not always a simple matter to decide which specific firewall product is the most suitable for a given application or enterprise infrastructure. Selection of a hybrid firewall product should be based on the supported feature sets that an enterprise needs.

Network Address Translation (NAT) technology is an effective tool for "hiding" the network addresses of an internal network behind a firewall environment. In essence, NAT allows an organization to deploy a network addressing plan of its choosing behind a firewall while still maintaining the ability to connect to external systems through the firewall. NAT is accomplished by one of three methods: static, hiding, and port. In static NAT, each internal system on the private network has a corresponding external routable Internet Protocol (IP) address associated with it. This particular technique is seldom used because unique IP addresses are in short supply. With hiding NAT, all systems behind a firewall share the same external routable IP address while the internal systems use private IP addresses. Thus, with a hiding NAT system, a number of systems behind a firewall will appear to be a single system. With port address translation, it is possible to place hosts behind a firewall system and still make them selectively accessible to external users.

Host-based firewalls are firewall software components that are available in some OSs or as add-ons. Because a network-based firewall cannot fully protect internal servers, host-based firewalls can be used to secure individual hosts.

Personal firewalls and personal firewall appliances are used to secure PCs at home or remote locations. These firewalls are important because many personnel telecommute or work at home and access sensitive data. Home users dialing an Internet service provider (ISP) may potentially have limited firewall protection available to them because the ISP has to accommodate many different security policies. Therefore, personal firewalls have been developed to provide protection for remote systems and to perform many of the same functions as larger firewalls. These products are typically implemented in one of two configurations. The first configuration is a personal firewall, which is installed on the system it is meant to protect; personal firewalls usually do not offer protection to other systems or resources. Likewise, personal firewalls do not typically provide controls over network traffic that is traversing a computer network; they protect only the computer system on which they are installed. The second configuration is a personal firewall appliance. In most cases, personal firewall appliances are designed to protect small networks such as networks that might be found in home offices. These appliances usually run on specialized hardware and integrate some other form of network infrastructure components into the firewall itself, including the following: cable or digital subscriber line broadband modem with network routing, network hub, network switch, Dynamic Host Configuration Protocol (DHCP) server, Simple Network Management Protocol (SNMP) agent, and application proxy agents. In terms of deployment strategies, personal firewalls and personal firewall appliances normally address connectivity concerns that are associated with telecommuters or branch offices. However, some organizations employ these devices on their organizational intranets, practicing a layered defense strategy.

Centrally managed distributed firewalls are centrally controlled but locally enforced. A security administrator—not the end users—defines and maintains security policies. This places the responsibility and capability of defining security policies in the hands of a security professional who can properly lock down the target systems. A centrally managed system is scalable because it is unnecessary to administer each system separately. A properly executed distributed firewall system includes exception logging. More advanced systems include the capability to enforce the appropriate policy, which is enforced depending on the location of the firewall. Centrally managed distributed firewalls can be software- or hardware-based firewalls. Centrally managed distributed software firewalls are similar in function and features to host-based or personal firewalls, but their security policies are centrally defined and managed. Centrally managed distributed hardware firewalls combine the filtering capability of a firewall with the connectivity capability of a traditional connection.

G.I.I **Effectiveness of the technology**

When properly configured, all firewalls can protect a network or a PC from unauthorized access through the network. Although firewalls afford protection of certain resources within an organization, there are some threats that firewalls cannot protect against: connections that bypass the firewall, new threats that have not yet been identified, and viruses that have been injected into the internal network. It is important to consider these shortcomings in addition to the firewall itself to counter these additional threats and provide a comprehensive security solution. Each type of firewall platform has its own strengths and weaknesses.

Packet filter firewalls have two main strengths: speed and flexibility. Packet filter firewalls can be used to secure nearly any type of network communication or protocol. This versatility allows packet filter firewalls to be deployed into nearly any enterprise network infrastructure. Packet filter firewalls have several weaknesses: They cannot prevent attacks that exploit application-specific vulnerabilities or functions; they can log only a minimal amount of information, such as source address, destination address, and traffic type; they do not support user authentication; and they are vulnerable to attacks and exploits that take advantage of flaws within the TCP/IP protocol, such as IP address spoofing.

Stateful inspection firewalls share the strengths and weaknesses of packet filter firewalls, but because of the state table implementation, they are generally considered to be more secure than packet filter firewalls. Stateful inspection firewalls can accommodate other network protocols in the same manner as packet filters, but stateful inspection technology is relevant only to TCP/IP.

Application proxy gateway firewalls have numerous advantages over packet filter firewalls and stateful inspection firewalls. First, application proxy gateway firewalls are able to examine the entire network packet rather than only the network addresses and ports. This enables these firewalls to provide more extensive logging capabilities than packet filters or stateful inspection firewalls. Another advantage is that application proxy gateway firewalls can authenticate users directly, whereas packet filter firewalls and stateful inspection firewalls normally authenticate users based on the network address of their system (source, destination, and type). Given that network addresses can be easily spoofed, the authentication capabilities inherent in application proxy gateway architecture are superior to those found in packet filter or stateful inspection firewalls. The advanced functionality of application proxy gateway firewalls also results in several disadvantages when compared with the functionality of packet filter or stateful inspection firewalls. First, because of the "full packet awareness" found in application proxy gateways, the firewall is forced to spend a significant time reading and interpreting each packet. Therefore, application proxy gateway firewalls are generally not well suited to high-bandwidth or real-time applications. To reduce the load on the firewall, a dedicated proxy server can be used to secure less time-sensitive services, such as e-mail and most web traffic. Another disadvantage is that application proxy gateway firewalls are often limited in terms of support for new network applications and protocols. An individual application-specific proxy agent is required for each type of network traffic that needs to go through the firewall. Most vendors of application proxy gateways provide generic proxy agents to support undefined network protocols or applications. However, those generic agents tend to negate many of the strengths of the application proxy gateway architecture, and they simply allow traffic to "tunnel" through the firewall.

Dedicated proxy servers allow an organization to enforce user authentication requirements and other filtering and logging of any traffic that goes through the proxy server. This means that an organization can restrict outbound traffic to certain locations, examine all outbound e-mail for viruses, or restrict internal users from writing to the organization's web server. Because most security problems originate from an organization, proxy servers can assist in foiling internally based attacks or malicious behavior.

In terms of strengths and weaknesses, each type of NAT—static, hiding, or port—is applicable in certain situations; the variable is the amount of design flexibility offered by each type. Static NAT offers the most flexibility, but it is not always practical because of the shortage of IP addresses. Hiding NAT technology is seldom used because port address translation offers additional features. Port address translation is often the most convenient and secure solution.

Host-based firewall packages typically provide access control capability for restricting traffic to and from servers that run on the host, and logging is usually available. A disadvantage of host-based firewalls is that they must be administered separately, and maintaining security becomes more difficult as the number of configured devices increases.

Centrally managed distributed software firewalls have the benefit of unified corporate oversight of firewall implementation on individual machines. However, they remain vulnerable to attacks on the host OS from the networks, as well as to intentional or unintentional tampering by users logging in to the system that is being protected. Centrally managed distributed hardware firewalls filter the data on the firewall hardware rather than on the host system. This can make the distributed hardware firewall system less vulnerable than software-based distributed firewalls. Hardware distributed firewalls can be designed to be unaffected by local or network attacks via the host OSs. Performance and throughput of a hardware firewall system are generally better than they are for software systems.

Preventing Eavesdropping to Protect Your Privacy

An amazing amount of personal information is readily available on the Internet. For example, if you've forgotten the date of a friend's birthday, just check http://anybirthday.com. That brings up another disquieting thought. Just how many companies or web sites use a birth date to verify identification? Once you know the birthday, it's simple to send a free, digital greeting card, but when you e-mail that card to a friend, have you also given it to marketers looking for new customers? In fact, have you compromised your friend's privacy or passwords?

It is not only individuals who worry about privacy. So do companies, although businesses may call the problem one of confidentiality. You all know company information is readily available on the Internet. As the greatest competitive intelligence gold mine of modern times, the Internet is now rife with cyber-prospectors and claim-jumpers. Many information professionals are familiar with the dichotomy of searching the Internet for as much information on the competition as possible, while trying to help prevent your own companies and your fellow employees from posting too much.

In fact, you must be careful not to disclose too much. As information professionals, sometimes the very questions you ask can be too revealing—even without identifying information attached. Searchers could seriously compromise companies' interests if certain patent or trademark questions became known. Also, given the rapid improvements in database mining techniques, it's possible that merely an increased number of questions concerning a particular company or technology could tip off investors to impending business activities.

While the marketing arms race rages on the new web frontier, information professionals must carefully balance privacy concerns against convenience, efficiency, and cost issues. It's another information dimension to take into account, along with more familiar themes of information ownership/rights, fair use, verifiability, currency, etc. But missteps along the virtual privacy dimension of information could have disastrous consequences for clients and information professionals alike.

Privacy is a hot topic this election year because of the Patriot Act, with discussions in government legislatures, court decisions, and lots of articles in both the popular and the professional press. Much of this media coverage has focused on consumer and individual privacy. Although some of these issues overlap, the privacy concerns of information professionals can differ significantly from consumer and individual concerns in several areas:

1. The definition of "sensitive" information: For consumers, sensitive "identifying" information includes name, address, credit-card numbers, SSNs, etc. Information professionals have broader concerns along this axis of information privacy:

   - A company is often more easily identified than an individual, and the identifying information is less well protected. For example, many web sites capture surfers' IP addresses, which can be traced back to specific companies.
   - Key information may be revealed solely through the substance of the questions asked, without any identifying information attached.
   - The definition of what might identify individuals or companies is changing because of improvements in database and data-mining software.

2. Motive: Consumers seek privacy primarily to avoid information harvesting for marketing purposes, while searchers seek to guard their clients from competitive intelligence gathering as well.

3. Roles played: Consumers act primarily for themselves and their families, whereas information professionals usually serve as information intermediaries, acting for their clients and companies. Info pros may also have information privacy responsibilities extending beyond their own direct actions and decisions. They may play a leadership role in educating their companies, clients, and coworkers about information issues and provide input for information policy formulation.

Some privacy solutions may apply equally well to both info pros and consumers. For example, consumers are advised to designate only one credit card for Internet purchases and to scrutinize bills carefully in an attempt to minimize any losses through security lapses. Of course, info pros should follow the same practice with company credit cards. Some of the advice relating to "sensitive questions" could apply to both consumers and information professionals, although the application of that advice may apply to different subjects (medical conditions versus potential acquisition targets).

Some privacy concerns regarding online research may primarily interest information professionals. However, it's interesting to note how many topics, previously of interest solely to info pros, have migrated into broader arenas of discussion. Many Internet-related topics, such as search engine technology, electronic copyright issues, and, of course, privacy concerns, frequently discussed across the length and breadth of the Internet, were introduced in the information science literature.

If the substance of certain queries became known, particularly queries concerning intellectual property and legal subjects, it might cause significant problems for clients. For example, a trademark must be maintained and "in use" to remain valid. If a competitor were alerted that someone was inquiring about his or her trademark, he or she could quickly "dust it off" and put it back in use. Additionally, if the company holding the trademark became aware of external interest in the trademark, the company's executives would be much better prepared for negotiating a higher price for licensing the trademark.

Another example might be a search for a domain name. As the market price paid for catchy domain names soars, you might wonder about the privacy of the "Is this domain name available?" search itself. Could a domain name search site watch for specific interesting queries, then grab the idea and register it quickly before you have a chance? Could the same site regularly notify paying clients when inquiries appear close to their licensed domain names? Or might someone use a network sniffer to track inquires on a specific site?

In patent searching, one could really find out quite a lot about a proposed invention by examining the search strategy, particularly within the sciences and in technical fields. The information thus revealed might even give the idea away completely or at least allow others to start developments along the same path.

Asking certain questions might trigger other kinds of privacy attacks. For example, inquiries into particularly sensitive areas might alert a company to someone's interest; the company could then try to get a subpoena and force the ISP or search site to reveal who was asking. Particular inquiries might alert a government department or organization that might have an even easier time finding out who was asking.

And, of course, in matters involving litigation, it becomes crucial to find out who knew what and when they knew it. Knowing what one party's researchers searched for in very specific subjects could give a good deal of circumstantial evidence to the opposing side. It certainly might give more force to a company or opposing party's arguments for subpoenas or discovery motions.

Finally, it's important to start a quest for online privacy by securing your computer from intrusion. Various products can assist you, including access control software and hardware, encryption software, security testing sites and software suites, firewalls (especially important for high-speed "always on" connections), and physical security systems. There are special solutions for laptop security while traveling, including cables, theft alarms, and even some ways to restrict the angles of view on your laptop to prevent your airline seatmate from seeing your work.

Thwarting Counterfeiters and Forgers to Retain Integrity Through a Reverse Firewall

Firewalls protect networks from incoming packets. In contrast, the reverse firewall protects the outside network from packet flooding distributed denial-of-service (DDoS) attacks that originate on the inside. The reverse firewall drastically reduces the impact of DDoS attacks mounted from inside the network. DDoS attacks are usually conducted through "zombies" (i.e., computers that have come under the control of the attacker). The reverse firewall chokes off packet flooding attacks before they exit the network where they originate. This appendix describes the reverse firewall, how it works, and its benefits as a DDoS defense to the infrastructure owner and to the Internet.

DoS and DDoS packet flooding attacks are an increasing problem. A recent study by industry analysts estimates more than 5000 attacks a week. Many sites of commercial importance have become targets, including CNN, eBay, Yahoo, and Microsoft. Establishing DDoS attacks is a serious threat to e-commerce and e-business. The Computer Emergency Response Team (CERT), the Internet security watchdog, was itself targeted in successful DDoS attacks in March 2001. CERT warns repeatedly that there is currently no technology to deal with this problem and recommends general vigilance and administrative measures to minimize the potentially devastating impact of a DDoS attack.

The Internet infrastructure has vulnerabilities that make it very difficult to defend against packet flooding attacks. As stated previously, most DDoS attacks are carried out via "slaves" or "zombies." Using these machines, the attacker can launch a coordinated but well-disguised attack on a victim and avoid detection. With near universal availability of permanent and faster connections to the Internet, and with the attendant decrease of network security expertise per individual computer, there is no scarcity of potential zombies. All ISPs, universities, and owners of infrastructure must be concerned about their computers being used in this fashion.

There is no deployed technology that has successfully defended against DDoS attacks. Most of the approaches focus, perhaps understandably, on protection of customer sites against incoming attacks. This turns out to be very difficult to do with today's Internet architecture and protocols. Several startups are working on developing DDoS defense technology based on smart filtering of incoming packets at ISPs and upstream routers.

There are two current forms of defense that have at least some utility in preventing attacks that originate from a local network. They are both universally recommended and hardly ever actually used in practice! These are prevention of zombie infestation and ingress filtering.

Computer owners are encouraged to keep up-to-date on software patches to prevent the exploitation of widely known vulnerabilities. Intrusion-detection systems (IDSs) can sometimes alert network administrators to the fact that their systems are in imminent danger or have been compromised. Several scanning tools can search for known "malware" such as attack scripts and viruses.

ISPs should refuse to forward packets with clearly invalid IP source addresses. This has been widely recommended for years but still seems rare.

They both have substantial benefits apart from preventing flooding attacks from originating within a network. Unfortunately, although they do help, they do not actually solve this problem. The first is similar to virus scanning. There are always new vulnerabilities. All an administrator can do is try to defend against the ones that have been recognized and patched. This can also absorb as much effort as the administrator is willing to expend, so even the best protection is a trade-off between cost and benefit. Furthermore, this approach is possible only to the extent that the owner of the local network actually controls the hosts inside. This works well for a corporate network, less so for an academic network, and not at all in the case of an ISP.

The second approach happens to be very useful against the most prevalent packet flooding attacks currently in use, because these tend to randomize the source addresses of the attack packets, making it harder for the victim to find the origin of the attack packets.

However, source address filtering does not prevent the attack. If more providers start filtering impossible source addresses, then the attacks will simply stop relying on this vulnerability.

A traditional firewall protects a network from incoming packets. What makes the reverse firewall a unique divide is that it protects the outside from packet flooding attacks that emanate from within the network. This is particularly useful for all owners of Internet infrastructure providing Internet connectivity. Such entities include the following:

- *Corporate networks*: provide Internet connectivity to workstations that are used by employees. Corporations generally have a great deal of control over the machines on their networks.

- ISPs: offer high-speed Internet access to customers via dedicated network connections such as DSL and cable.

- *Universities*: provide computers for use within the campus community, along with high-speed Internet connectivity for those computers. Often, members of the community may be allowed to connect their own computers to the high-speed campus network.

The reverse firewall works by filtering the outgoing packets from a network. The difference between a legitimate application that uses high bandwidth and a packet flooding attack is that in the former case the machine at the other end of the conversation is participating in a two-way conversation, whereas the attack is one sided. Unlike other network infrastructure, a firewall is in a position to distinguish these two cases, because all of the traffic between the local network and the outside (the Internet) passes through it.

What is called a *reverse firewall* is, therefore, simply one part of the functionality that could and should be provided by firewalls. All it does is limit the rate at which it forwards packets that are not, in some sense, replies to other packets that were forwarded in the other direction. Of course, it must be possible to send some packets that are not replies, for instance, to start a new conversation. However, such packets need not be transmitted at a high rate.

The machines of greatest value to attackers are those with fast Internet access, because it is from these machines that they can send packet floods at very high rates. The reverse firewall reduces the value of these machines for such an attack to that of a slow dial-up connection, or even less. Attackers try to amass collections of hundreds or thousands of zombies from which to attack simultaneously. The reverse firewall, however, reduces the effectiveness of a zombie by a similar factor!

Most infrastructure owners trust their users not to mount packet flooding attacks, but this does not eliminate the problem. As described earlier, it is much more likely that some hosts inside a local network will be taken over by remote hackers for use as zombies in coordinated DDoS attacks.

Although DDoS attacks are mainly targeted at a victim outside the infrastructure provider's local network, they are, in fact, also attacking the legitimate users of the local network infrastructure. In particular, the attacker is using as much of the outgoing bandwidth as the zombie machines can consume. This is bandwidth that is, therefore, no longer available to other legitimate users of the network. Furthermore, if upstream providers charge for network usage (rather than a flat rate), the attacker is actually directly increasing the costs to the network owner. By using the reverse firewall appropriately, the infrastructure owner gains the tangible benefit that attacks from one network segment cannot disrupt customers from other segments.

As DDoS attacks increase in frequency and impact, perceptions about the responsibilities and liabilities of being an infrastructure owner are shifting. There is understandable pressure on infrastructure owners to be more diligent and proactive in ensuring that they are not unwitting hosts of lethal DDoS attacks. The reverse firewall is a tool with which the infrastructure owner can accomplish that goal.

The Cs3 Reverse Firewall approach (rate limiting of unexpected packets and the use of fair scheduling by places) is inherently superior to existing solutions that scan for known attack script signatures on potential zombie computers because it requires no updates as attackers change their methods and level of sophistication.

Most commercial entities are understandably interested in protecting their own infrastructure from becoming the targets of DDoS attacks. Interestingly, the reverse firewall functionality is completely symmetric with respect to incoming and outgoing traffic. In other words, it does protect the local network from the outside the same way it protects the outside from the local network.

Unfortunately, this is not adequate to defend the local network from the outside.

This is related to the fact that the outside is normally much bigger than the inside. It is true that large numbers of attack packets from the outside will be stopped at the network's firewall, but this is too late to protect the communication between the inside and the outside. The problem is that during a packet flooding attack, most of the packets that legitimate customers send to the victim will be lost long before they reach the victim's firewall. As a result, a comprehensive DDoS defense will require more major infrastructure changes. In fact, the larger the network owned by infrastructure providers, the more beneficial it will be for them to incorporate these additional features within their network infrastructure to protect themselves and the outside.

How many reverse firewalls does an infrastructure owner need? This is a cost/benefit trade-off. One firewall can handle the traffic from a large number of machines. However, it can stop only the attack traffic that flows through it. To prevent one internal machine from denying service to another, the two have to be separated by a firewall. In fact, the same reverse firewall can be used to protect different internal network segments from one another by connecting each network segment to a different network interface card in that firewall. Such a firewall would not only protect the inside network from the outside network and vice versa, but it would also protect the different internal segments from one another.

As an example, it is reasonable that for a university network, one might install a separate reverse firewall (or separate network interface card as discussed previously) for each dormitory or department. Then a zombie in the physics department, for example, would affect only the physics department and not the rest of the campus. If it is important to prevent an attack originating in one part of the physics department from affecting another part, then those two parts must be separated and given different firewalls. Such reasoning is applicable for ISPs, universities, and all other infrastructure owners who have limited control of the hosts on their network.

Avoiding Disruption of Service to Maintain Availability

A denial-of-service (DoS) attack is one that is intended to compromise the availability of a computing resource. Common DoS attacks include ping floods and mail bombs—both intended to consume disproportionate amounts of resources, starving legitimate processes. Other attacks are targeted at bugs in software and are intended to crash the system. The infamous "ping of death" and "teardrop" attacks are examples of these.

DoS attacks can be leveraged to subvert systems (thus compromising more than availability) and disable them. When discussing the relevance of DoS attacks to a security system, the question of whether the system is "fail-open" arises. A fail-open system ceases to provide protection when it is disabled by a DoS attack. A fail-closed system, on the other hand, leaves the network protected when it is forcibly disabled.

The terms *fail-open* and *fail-closed* are most often heard within the context of firewalls, which are access-control devices for networks, as previously explained in this book. A fail-open firewall stops controlling access to the network when it crashes but leaves the network available. An attacker that can crash a fail-open firewall can bypass it entirely. Good firewalls are designed to "fail-close," leaving the network completely inaccessible (and thus protected) if it crashes.

Network ID systems (IDSs) are passive; they do not control the network or maintain its connectivity in any way. As such, a network IDS is inherently fail-open. If an attacker can crash the IDS or starve it of resources, she or he can attack the rest of the network as if the IDS wasn't even there. Because of the obvious susceptibility to DoS attacks that network IDSs have, it's important that they be fortified against them.

Unfortunately, DoS attacks are extremely difficult to defend against. The resource starvation problem is not easily solvable, and there are many points at which the resources of an IDS can be consumed. Attacks that crash the IDS itself are easily fixed, but finding all such vulnerabilities is not easily done.

Developing Your Firewall Security Policy

A firewall security policy is a document that describes requirements for an organization's firewalls. In fact, multiple documents may be required in larger operations. It's not unthinkable to have separate enterprise-wide, site-specific, branch office, home office, and traveling employee firewall documents, instead of a single monolithic firewall document covering all potential boundary scenarios through which individual systems or internal networks connect to the Internet.

The contents of such a document must include numerous headings and address numerous topics, as shown in Table K.1. The order is not significant; however, these are the activities for which the researcher would want to provide a detailed description of procedures, review, and assessment for ease of use and admissibility. A number of these systems have been mentioned in passing throughout the book.

Table K.1 *Firewall Security Policy Checklist Form*

Firewall And Security Policies
Firewall and Security Policy Checklist Form
Date: _____

Whether your organization has firewalls and a security policy or not, it's prudent to regularly evaluate your security approach. Review and make sure that the following activities are adhered to before implementing any further firewall technology and/or security policy additions or changes (check all tasks completed):

Identify which resources must absolutely be secure and in which order of priority:

_____ 1. Mission critical
_____ 2. Redundant backup system(s)
_____ 3. Secondary
_____ 4. Base systems

Table K.1   *Firewall Security Policy Checklist Form (Continued)*

Identify minimum security needs for the following wide area network (WAN) connections:
_____ 5. Employee remote dial-up
_____ 6. Office-to-office virtual private network (VPN)
_____ 7. Employee and vendor broadband (DSL, cable modem, etc.)
_____ 8. Vendor access
_____ 9. Business-to-business access

Security team access to network documentation:
_____ 10. Network diagrams
_____ 11. Trending data
_____ 12. Protocol utilization
_____ 13. Data points
_____ 14. Access points
_____ 15. Major vendors' point of contact information (ISP, telco, firewall vendor)

Security team knowledge of the order in which systems must be restored:
_____ 16. The security response team must have a full understanding of which systems need to be restored to full operation and in what order.
_____ 17. Does this order meet your business objectives and priorities?

The information disclosure policy should address the following in relationship to a security issue:
_____ 18. What information is shared with others?
_____ 19. Is information shared internally, departmentally, externally, etc.?
_____ 20. Under which circumstances?
_____ 21. Mission critical information.
_____ 22. Secondary intrusion information.
_____ 23. Who has the authority to initiate information disclosure (Chief Security Officer, legal, human resources [HR])?

Provide a way of documenting, distributing, and following up on security violation reports. For example:
_____ 24. Denied access messages
_____ 25. Failed passwords/login attempts
_____ 26. Attempts to access back doors

Provide for alternative communication methods for intruder attacks/penetrations. Consider using:
_____ 27. Cell phones
_____ 28. Numeric pager codes
_____ 29. Fax machines

Establish your cycle of updates and mock drills:
_____ 30. Are policies and procedures updated regularly (quarterly, biannually, annually)?
_____ 31. Do you involve multiple departments (IT, HR, legal, upper management)?
_____ 32. Do you run periodic drills to test your systems and your procedures?

Review the legality of your security policy and procedures. Working with your HR department and legal counsel, consider the following:
_____ 33. Are your policies enforceable?
_____ 34. Do your polices and practices conform to local, state, and federal laws?
_____ 35. Are you providing due diligence to protect confidential information?
_____ 36. Is there a clear-cut procedure for a chain of custody for documentation from an intrusion?
_____ 37. Are the team and the company legitimately protected in case of a severe intrusion?

Table K.1   *Firewall Security Policy Checklist Form (Continued)*

_____ 38. What would be your company's risks if an attacker were to penetrate the systems of another company that uses your systems?

_____ 39. Do your policies and procedures provide for proper care of customer information?

_____ 40. What are your liabilities if confidential data (corporate, vendor, customer) is taken and used by an intruder?

Reviewed lessons learned:

_____ 41. Does your firewall intruder-alert detection system work?

_____ 42. Do your response procedures work?

_____ 43. Do your processes provide for the correct steps to neutralize any additional threats?

_____ 44. What did not work?

_____ 45. What can be changed to bolster your procedures?

The firewall security policy document itself:

_____ 46. A statement of purpose that indicates the document is intended to set standards and state rules and guidelines for firewalls, and state the role(s) firewalls are intended to play within the organization.

_____ 47. The roles or types of individuals who may be authorized to install and manage firewalls should be identified, including terms like employees, vendors, contractors, agents, business partners, and so forth.

_____ 48. The types of computers or dedicated systems that may be used should also be specified to indicate whether only computers that belong to the organization may be used for such purposes or whether personally owned or third-party machines may also be used.

_____ 49. Specify the types or kinds of firewalls to be used. This may require enumerating specific security appliances or firewall devices, or types of hardware configurations allowed, and what kind of software should be installed on them.

_____ 50. Use of auxiliary or add-on components, such as content filters, proxies, VPN server software, or other items should also be addressed.

_____ 51. A general section that states the user's obligation to honor other security policy requirements, meet legal obligations, adhere to information protection and confidentiality requirements, and so forth. This is where numerous other documents in the library will typically be invoked, including acceptable use policies, encryption policy, VPN policy, and so forth.

_____ 52. A statement of requirements that must be met before a firewall can be deployed in a production environment, including access controls, baseline configurations, rules or filters for specific TCP and/or UDP ports, IP services and content restrictions where applicable, security and authentication details, and so forth. The idea is to create a minimum set of standards to ensure that firewalls impose the right kinds of barriers between the inside and outside worlds.

_____ 53. It's also important to address issues related to requests from users to bypass firewall security (sometimes called punching through the firewall) for specific protocols or services when outright filtering, blocks, or proxy support would otherwise prevent their use.

_____ 54. Enforcement provisions, usually in the form of warnings about consequences for failing to adhere to policy, with specific penalties described for specific offenses.

_____ 55. Many such documents also include a glossary of all technical terms that appear in the text, to make it absolutely clear to users what's intended by the language used.

Other elements common to security policy documents of all kinds include various sign-offs, revision dates, identification of responsible parties, feedback solicitation, and so forth. Make these points a part of your overall policy document design, too.

Glossary

Abuse of privilege: When a user performs an action that he or she should not have, according to organizational policy or law.

Access control: A mechanism for limiting use of some resource (system) to authorized users.

Access control list (ACL): A list associated with a resource (system) that specifies the authorized users.

Access Control Lists: Rules for packet filters (typically routers) that define which packets to pass and which to block.

Access router: A router that connects your network to the external Internet. Typically, this is your first line of defense against attackers from the outside Internet. By enabling ACLs on this router, you'll be able to provide a level of protection for all of the hosts "behind" that router, effectively making that network a demilitarized zone (DMZ) instead of an unprotected external LAN.

Application-level firewall: A firewall system in which service is provided by processes that maintain complete TCP connection state and sequencing. Application-level firewalls often re-address traffic so that outgoing traffic appears to have originated from the firewall, rather than the internal host.

Asymmetric cryptosystem: An information system using an algorithm or series of algorithms that provide a cryptographic key pair consisting of a private key and a corresponding public key. The keys of the pair have the properties that (1) the public key can verify a digital signature that the private key creates, and (2) it is computationally not feasible to discover or derive the private key from the public key. The public key can, therefore, be disclosed without significantly risking disclosure of the private key. This can be used for confidentiality and for authentication.

Authentication: The process of determining the identity of a user who is attempting to access a system.

Authentication token: A portable device used for authenticating a user. Authentication tokens operate by challenge/response, time-based code sequences, or other techniques. This may include paper-based lists of one-time passwords.

Authorization: The process of determining which types of activities are permitted. Usually, authorization is in the context of authentication: Once you have authenticated a user, he or she may be authorized for different types of access or activity.

Backdoor: A security hole in a compromised system that allows continued access to the system by an intruder even if the original attack is discovered.

Bastion host: A system that has been hardened to resist attack and which is installed on a network in such a way that it is expected to potentially come under attack. Bastion hosts are often components of firewalls or may be "outside" web servers or public access systems. Generally, a bastion host is running some form of general-purpose operating system (OS) (Unix, VMS, NT, etc.) rather than a ROM-based or firmware OS.

CA: Certification authority.

CERT: Computer Emergency Response Team.

Certificate: A set of information that at least identifies the certification authority issuing the certificate; unambiguously names or identifies its owner; contains the owner's public key; and is digitally signed by the certification authority issuing it.

Certification: Means independently verifying certain information about transactions in the electronic environment.

Certification authority (CA): A CA provides to users a digital certificate that links the public key with some assertion about the user, such as identity, credit payment card number, etc. CAs may offer other services such as time-stamping, key management services, and certificate revocation services. An independent trusted source that attests to some factual element of information for the purposes of certifying that information in the electronic environment.

Certification practices statement (CPS): A statement of the CA's practices with respect to a wide range of technical, business, and legal issues that may be used as a basis for the CA's contract with the entity to whom the certificate was issued.

Challenge/response: An authentication technique whereby a server sends an unpredictable challenge to the user, who computes a response using some form of authentication token.

Chroot: A technique under Unix whereby a process is permanently restricted to an isolated subset of the file system.

Cipher text: a message that is encrypted.

Circuit-level gateway: A specialized function that relays TCP connections without performing any additional packet processing or filtering.

Clear text: A message that is not encrypted.

Closed network/closed user group: Systems that generally represent those in which certificates are used within a bounded context such as within a payment system. A contract or series of contracts identifies and defines the rights and responsibilities of all parties to a particular transaction.

Confidentiality: The property that data or information is not made available or disclosed to unauthorized individuals, entities or processes.

CPS: Certification Practices Statement.

Cross-certification: Practice of mutual recognition of another CA's certificates to an agreed level of confidence. Usually evidenced in contract.

Cryptographic checksum: A one-way function applied to a file to produce a unique "fingerprint" of the file for later reference. Checksum systems are a primary means of detecting file system tampering on Unix.

Cryptographic key: A parameter used with a cryptographic algorithm to transform, validate, authenticate, encrypt, or decrypt data.

Cryptography: The discipline that embodies principles, means, and methods for the transformation of data to hide its information content, establish its authenticity, prevent its undetected modification, prevent its repudiation, and/or prevent its unauthorized use.

Data-driven attack: A form of attack in which the attack is encoded in innocuous-seeming data that is executed by a user or other software to implement an attack. In the case of firewalls, a data-driven attack is a concern because it may get through the firewall in data form and launch an attack against a system behind the firewall.

Decrypt: To undo the encryption process.

Defense in depth: The security approach whereby each system on the network is secured to the greatest possible degree. May be used with firewalls.

Digital signature: Data appended to a message that allows a recipient of the message to prove the source and integrity of the message.

Directory service: A service provided on a computer network that allows one to look up addresses (and perhaps other information such as public key certificates) based on usernames.

DNS: Domain Name Service.

DNS spoofing: Assuming the DNS name of another system by either corrupting the name service cache of a victim system or compromising a domain name server for a valid domain.

Dual-homed gateway: A system that has two or more network interfaces, each of which is connected to a different network. In firewall configurations, a dual-homed gateway usually acts to block or filter some or all of the traffic trying to pass between the networks.

EDI: Electronic data interchange.

Electronic commerce: A broad concept that covers any trade or commercial transaction that is effected via electronic means; this would include such means as facsimile, telex, electronic data interchange (EDI), Internet, and the telephone. For the purpose of this report the term is limited to those commercial transactions involving computer to computer communications whether using an open or a closed network.

Electronic data interchange (EDI): A system allowing for intercorporate commerce by the automated electronic exchange of structured business information.

Electronic signature: Any symbol or method executed or adopted by a party with present intention to be bound by or to authenticate a record accomplished by electronic means.

Encrypt: To scramble information so that only someone knowing the appropriate secret can obtain the original information (through decryption).

Encryption: The transformation of data by the use of cryptography to produce unintelligible data (encrypted data) to ensure its confidentiality.

Encrypting router: See "Tunneling Router" and "Virtual Network Perimeter."

FAQ: Frequently asked questions.

Firewall: A system or combination of systems that enforces a boundary between two or more networks.

FTP: File Transport Protocol.

Hash function/hashing: A hash function is a mathematical process based on an algorithm that creates a digital representation or compressed form of the message, often referred to as the message digest in the form of a "hash value" or "hash result" of a standard length that is usually much smaller than the message but nevertheless substantially unique to it.

Host-based security: The technique of securing an individual system from attack. Host-based security is OS and version dependent.

ICMP: Internet Control Message Protocol.

Insider attack: An attack originating from inside a protected network.

Integrity: The property that data or information has not been modified or altered in an unauthorized manner.

Internet firewall: A system or group of systems that enforces an access control policy between an organization's network and the Internet.

Intrusion detection: Detection of break-ins or break-in attempts either manually or via software expert systems that operate on logs or other information available on the network.

IP spoofing: An attack whereby a system attempts to illicitly impersonate another system by using its IP network address.

IP splicing/hijacking: An attack whereby an active established session is intercepted and co-opted by the attacker. IP splicing attacks may occur after an authentication has been made, permitting the attacker to assume the role of an already authorized user. Primary protections against IP splicing rely on encryption at the session or network layer.

ISO: International Standards Organization.

ISP: Internet service provider.

ISS: Internet security scanner.

Key: A quantity (number) used in cryptography to encrypt or decrypt information.

Least privilege: Designing operational aspects of a system to operate with a minimum amount of system privilege. This reduces the authorization level at which various actions are performed and decreases the chance that a process or user with high privileges may be caused to perform unauthorized activity resulting in a security breach.

Logging: The process of storing information about events that occurred on the firewall or network.

Log retention: How long audit logs are retained and maintained.

Log processing: How audit logs are processed, searched for key events, or summarized.

NAT: Network Address Translation.

NCCUSL: National Conference of Commissioners on Uniform State Law.

Network-level firewall: A firewall in which traffic is examined at the network protocol packet level.

Non-repudiation: A property achieved through cryptographic methods that prevents an individual or entity from denying having performed a particular action related to data (such as mechanisms for non-rejection or authority [origin]; for proof of obligation, intent, or commitment; or for proof of ownership).

NPKI: National Public Key Infrastructure.

Open network/system: One in which, at the extremes, unknown parties, possibly in different state or national jurisdictions, will exchange/trade data. To do this will require an overarching framework that will engender trust and certainty. A user of online services might go through a single authentication process with a trusted third party, receive certification of their public key, and then be able to enter into electronic transactions/data exchanges with merchants, governments, banks, etc., using the certificate so provided for multiple purposes.

Packet filtering: A feature that allows a router to make a permit/deny decision for each packet based on the packet header information that is made available to the IP forwarding process.

PARRA: Policy and Root Registration Authority.

PCMCIA: Personal Computer Memory Card International Association.

Perimeter-based security: The technique of securing a network by controlling access to all entry and exit points of the network.

PKAF: Public Key Authentication Framework.

PKI: Public key infrastructure.

Policy: Organization-level rules governing acceptable use of computing resources, security practices, and operational procedures.

PPP: Point-to-Point Protocol.

Private key: The private or secret key of a key pair, which must be kept confidential, and is used to decrypt messages encrypted with the public key or to digitally sign messages that can then be validated with the public key.

Proxy: A software agent that acts on behalf of a user. Typical proxies accept a connection from a user, make a decision about whether the user or client IP address is permitted to use the proxy, perhaps does additional authentication, and then completes a connection on behalf of the user to a remote destination.

Proxy service: Special-purpose, application-level code installed on an Internet firewall gateway. The proxy service allows the network administrator to permit or deny specific applications or specific features of an application.

Public key: A key whose value can be published widely without compromising encryption or digital signature processes. Typically, a public key can be used to encrypt but not decrypt, or to validate a signature but not to sign.

Public key cryptography: An asymmetric cryptosystem in which the encrypting and decrypting keys are different and it is computationally not feasible to calculate one from the other, given the encrypting algorithm. In public key cryptography, the encrypting key is made public, but the decrypting key is kept secret.

Public Key Infrastructure (PKI): Supporting infrastructure, including nontechnical aspects, for the management of public keys.

Relying third party: The entity, such as a merchant, offering goods or services online that will receive a certificate as part of a process of completing transactions with the user.

Repudiation: Denying that you did something or sent some message.

RFC: Request for Comment.

SATAN: Security Analysis Tool for Auditing Networks.

Screened host: A host on a network behind a screening router. The degree to which a screened host may be accessed depends on the screening rules in the router.

Screened subnet: A subnet behind a screening router. The degree to which the subnet may be accessed depends on the screening rules in the router.

Screening router: A router configured to permit or deny traffic based on a set of permission rules installed by the administrator.

Secret key cryptography: A cryptographic system in which encryption and decryption are performed using the same key.

Session stealing: See "IP Splicing."

Sign a message: To use your private key to generate a digital signature as a means of certifying, or proving you generated, some message.

Signature (digital): A quantity (number) associated with a message that only someone with knowledge of your private key could have generated, but that can be verified through knowledge of your public key.

Signature dynamics: A form of electronic signatures that involves the biometric recording of the pen dynamics used in signing the document.

SLIP: Serial Line Internet Protocol.

SMTP: Simple Mail Transfer Protocol.

Social engineering: An attack based on deceiving users or administrators at the target site. Social engineering attacks are typically carried out by telephoning users or operators who are pretending to be an authorized user, to attempt to gain illicit access to systems.

TCP: Transmission Control Protocol.

Time stamping: An electronic equivalent of mail franking.

Trading partner agreement: A contractual arrangement that specifies the legal terms and conditions under which parties operate when conducting transactions by the use of EDI. It may cover such things as validity and formation of contract admissibility in evidence of EDI messages processing and acknowledgment of receipt of EDI messages security confidentiality and protection of personal data recording and storage of EDI messages operational requirements for EDI—message standards, codes, transaction, and operations logs technical specifications and requirements liability, including use of intermediaries and third-party service providers dispute resolution applicable law.

Trojan horse: A software entity that appears to do something normal, but that contains a trapdoor or attack program.

Trusted third party: An entity trusted by other entities with respect to security-related services and activities, such as a CA.

Tunneling router: A router or system capable of routing traffic by encrypting it and encapsulating it for transmission across an untrusted network, for eventual deencapsulation and decryption.

UDP: User Datagram Protocol.

UNCITRAL: United Nations Commission on International Trade Law.

UNIDROIT: International Institute for the Unification of Private Law.

UN/EDIFACT: United Nations Electronic Data Interchange for Administration, Commerce and Transport.

User/subscriber: An individual procuring goods or services online who obtains a certificate from a CA. Because both consumers and merchants may have digital certificates, which are used to conclude a transaction, they may both be subscribers in certain circumstances. This person may also be referred to as the *signer of a digital signature* or the *sender of data message signed with a digital signature*.

Verify: To determine accurately that (1) the digital signature was created by the private key corresponding to the public key and (2) the message has not been altered because its digital signature was created.

Verify a signature: Perform a cryptographic calculation—using a message, a signature for the message, and a public key—to determine whether the signature was generated by someone knowing the corresponding private key.

Virtual network perimeter: A network that appears to be a single protected network behind firewalls, which actually encompasses encrypted virtual links over untrusted networks.

Virus: A replicating code segment that attaches itself to a program or data file. Viruses might contain attack programs or trapdoors.

Unfortunately, many have taken to calling any malicious code a "virus." If you mean "Trojan horse" or "worm," say "Trojan horse" or "worm."

Worm: A standalone program that when run copies itself from one host to another and then runs itself on each newly infected host.

X.509: A standard that is part of the X.500 specifications, which defines the format of a public key certificate.

Index